The Moral Philosophers

The Moral Philosophers

An Introduction to Ethics

Second Edition

Richard Norman

OXFORD UNIVERSITY PRESS

1998

OXFORD

UNIVERSITY PRESS

Great Clarendon Street, Oxford OX2 6DP

Oxford University Press is a department of the University of Oxford.
It furthers the University's objective of excellence in research, scholarship,
and education by publishing worldwide in

Oxford New York

Auckland Bangkok Buenos Aires Cape Town Chennai
Dar es Salaam Delhi Hong Kong Istanbul Karachi Kolkata
Kuala Lumpur Madrid Melbourne Mexico City Mumbai Nairobi
São Paulo Shanghai Taipei Tokyo Toronto

Oxford is a registered trade mark of Oxford University Press
in the UK and in certain other countries

Published in the United States
by Oxford University Press Inc., New York

British Library Cataloguing in Publication Data

Data available

Library of Congress Cataloging in Publication Data
Norman, Richard (Richard J.)
The moral philosophers : an introduction to ethics / Richard
Norman.—2nd ed.
Includes bibliographical references and index.
1. Ethics—History. 2. Ethics. I. Title.
BJ71.N73 1997 170—dc21 97–27130

ISBN 0–19–875217–2
ISBN 0–19–875216–4 (Pbk.)

10 9 8

Typeset by Best-set Typesetter Ltd., Hong Kong
Printed in Great Britain
on acid-free paper by
Biddles Ltd, King's Lynn, Norfolk

Preface to the First Edition

A book such as this, aiming to cover a large area of philosophy, is bound to involve many intellectual debts. To those who taught me moral philosophy, those with whom I have taught moral philosophy, and those to whom I have taught moral philosophy, I am most grateful for all that I have learned from them and all the stimulation I have gained from them.

More specifically I should like to thank Chris Cherry, Bruce Landesman, Sean Sayers, and Tony Skillen for reading all or part of the first draft and making valuable comments, Karen Jones for all her help with the process of revision, and Sue Macdonald, Eileen Barker, Pat Evans, Yvonne Latham, and Jane Neame for their help with the typing.

When a previous book of mine on ethics was published, my landlady, to whom I gave a copy, commented 'It must be very good—I can't understand a word of it.' My hope is that, in this respect at least, the present book is less good.

January 1983

Preface to the Second Edition

In this new edition the first eight chapters remain largely unchanged, with only some small additions and deletions and some minor rewording here and there. Chapters 9 to 11 of the first edition have, however, been replaced by the new Chapters 9 to 12. Two of the replaced chapters are those which dealt with the implications of Marxism and of psychoanalysis for moral philosophy. I have omitted them with some regret. I remain committed to the claims I made there about the importance of Marxist and psychoanalytic ideas, particularly because of the ways in which they call into question the very idea of 'morality' as traditionally conceived. The chapters as they stood, however, fitted uneasily into a book which is intended to be read alongside some of the standard texts of moral philosophy. Marx and Freud were not primarily moral philosophers and, important though their influence is, none of their writings can reasonably be given the status of a classic work of moral philosophy. In this edition the idea of a 'critique of morality' has been explored in a new chapter on Nietzsche. The renewed interest in Nietzsche's work in recent years seemed in any case to make such a chapter a good idea, and Nietzsche's *On The Genealogy of Morals* is a good text to add to the list of those which my chapters are intended to accompany. A much-abbreviated version of my discussion of Marx and Freud is now incorporated into the Nietzsche chapter.

Chapter 11 of the first edition dealt briefly with some themes in twentieth-century ethics. That material is considerably expanded in the new Chapters 10 to 12. Those chapters still make no claim to provide anything like a comprehensive survey of twentieth-century work in moral philosophy, but they may, at any rate , help the reader to identify some main tendencies in a large and complex body of work, and indicate ways in which themes from the classic tradition have been continued by contemporary writers.

In revising the book I have again benefited greatly from other people's advice. I should like to thank Eve Garrard, David McNaughton, Hugh LaFollette, James Rachels, Karen Jones, and Sean Sayers for their very helpful comments on the text, and Tim Barton of Oxford University Press for suggesting that I prepare a new edition, and for his valuable guidance at all stages of the process.

February 1997

Contents

1

Introduction
Ethics and its History

The area of philosophy traditionally known as 'ethics' or 'moral philosophy' is the attempt to arrive at an understanding of the nature of human values, of how we ought to live, and of what constitutes right conduct. The present book is intended as an introduction to ethics. I shall present some of the main positions in ethics which have been advocated by different philosophers, and convey some idea of the variety of these and the disagreements between them. I shall not, however, be neutral. In part this is inevitable; one cannot escape judgements about which positions are important enough to be taken seriously and to be worth discussing, and about how much attention they merit. My non-neutrality will not end there, however. I shall attempt a critical assessment of the different positions, and thereby work towards some conclusions about what a correct ethical theory would look like.

'Ethics' or 'moral philosophy' (I use the terms interchangeably) is not concerned solely with the elucidation and justification of 'morality' in the narrow sense. What precisely that narrow sense is, we shall have to consider in due course. However, it is clear that to assess people's conduct as immoral or as morally admirable is to consider it from only one point of view, and not the only possible one. In the study of moral philosophy we are concerned more generally with questions about how one ought to live, about what could count as good reasons for acting in one way rather than another, and about what constitutes a good life for human beings, meaning thereby not necessarily 'morally good', but treating as an open question, where would be the proper place for morality in the good life, and whether indeed it has any place there at all.

Many contemporary philosophers distinguish between 'substantive ethics' or 'normative ethics' on the one hand, and what they call 'meta-ethics' on the other. Substantive ethics, they say, is concerned with the question, 'What kinds of action are good or right?', whereas meta-ethics is concerned with the question, 'What is it to say of an action that it is good or right?' One way of understanding this second question is as a question about the correct analysis of the *language* used in the first question. Thus one important aim of meta-ethics is to discover not what is good, or what is right, but what we *mean* when we say of something that it is 'good' or 'right'. Another way of putting it is to say that meta-ethics is concerned with the examination of *concepts*—with analysing concepts such as 'good' and 'right', rather than with actually using the concepts to talk about human conduct. Or again, meta-ethics is concerned with examining the *logic* of ethical discourse—with questions such as, 'How do we *know* that one course of action is better than another?', 'Can we ever really be said to *know* such a thing?', 'What kinds of *argument*, if any, could support such a claim?' The difference between substantive ethics and meta-ethics can be summarized as a difference between 'first-order' and 'second-order' discussions. At the first level, that of substantive ethics, our discussions are directly concerned with practical questions of conduct, but we can then move the discussion to a second level, from which we look back at the first level, and raise questions about what it was that we were doing at that first level.

That distinction is a useful one. It becomes suspect, however, when it is accompanied by the further suggestion that the proper concern of philosophy is solely with meta-ethics, and not at all with substantive ethics. That is what many contemporary philosophers would assert. It is not the business of the philosopher, they say, to tell people how to live. People can, and should, make such decisions for themselves. The only contribution which the philosopher can usefully make is to help them to clarify the terms which they use, and the arguments which they employ, in making such decisions.

Why this philosophical modesty? Part of what is involved here is a desire on the part of philosophers not to set themselves up as preachers, a desire that people should decide for themselves how to live instead of being told by self-appointed experts. These liberal attitudes are ones which I would share. It does not follow, however, that a philosophical engagement in substantive ethics is bound to take the form of preaching. It does so only if we think of philosophers as a race apart, and assume that when they set out their views about the nature of human good, they are implying that no one else is capable of having such views. We do not have to accept these assumptions. Philosophy as I understand it is, on the contrary, a shared enterprise in which everyone is, at least potentially, a participant, and when I, as a professional teacher of philosophy, set out certain theories of substantive ethics, I do so not in order to preach, but in order to contribute to that common enterprise.

There is a second factor which helps to explain the prevalent philosophical modesty. Many philosophers would say that they cannot establish correct theories about how one ought to live, because *no one* can do so. There is, they would say, no such thing as a 'correct' view about how one ought to live, since beliefs about such matters cannot properly be said to be either true or false. Rather, they should be understood as expressions of feelings or attitudes, choices or commitments, and if people differ from one another in their basic attitudes about what is good or right, there is in principle no way of resolving the disagreement, no 'correct' answer to be arrived at.

This is a doctrine, known as ethical subjectivism or ethical scepticism, which we shall have to consider in due course. It is itself a meta-ethical doctrine. Clearly, if correct, it sets severe limits on what can be done in the way of substantive ethics. It does not rule out substantive ethics entirely, for it is still open to the ethical subjectivist to try to set out in a systematic and coherent way his own ethical attitudes, in the hope that they will appeal to others also. The great ethical philosophers of the past have all aimed to do at least this. But most of them have aimed at more. They have assumed that by the use of philosophical argument, and by appealing to shared human experience, they can provide a rational justification for a systematic theory of what would constitute right conduct or a good life for human beings.

For the purposes of this book, at any rate, I want to suggest that we cannot decide whether ethical subjectivism is or is not inescapable until we have made the attempt to work out a substantive ethical theory. The only way to find out whether reason and experience can objectively establish a view of the good life is to trust to them and see how far they will take use. This brings me to my own view of the relation between substantive ethics and meta-ethics. I have said that the distinction is a useful one. I also believe, however, that each enterprise can be properly carried out only in close conjunction with the other. Again, this has been the practice of the great philosophers of the past. In aiming to give a rational account of the good life, they have also been self-conscious about the nature of their procedures, their terminology and their modes of argument. In other words, they have been engaged in substantive ethics but have combined this with meta-ethical reflections on the status of their own substantive ethics. By contrast, many modern philosophers isolate meta-ethics from substantive ethics. As a result they not only produce extremely arid and dissatisfying moral philosophy, but also produce meta-ethics which is bad even as meta-ethics, just because it is isolated from substantive considerations and is therefore based on artificial and over-simplified examples of ethical beliefs.

I have said that I intend to examine the ethical theories proposed by some of the great philosophers of the past. This procedure needs some defending. When we contemplate the history of philosophy and find a succession of theories, each of which has been refuted by subsequent philosophers, and none of which has survived criticism intact, we may feel that the best thing to do with this history is to turn our backs on it. This tends to be the reaction of newcomers to the study of philosophy, who are likely to feel that they should waste no time on past theories which everyone now agrees to be untenable. Perhaps then we should dispense with the history, and concentrate on developing those approaches on which contemporary philosophers agree— although this resolve may itself succumb to a historically-induced scepticism, in view of the frequency with which philosophers have turned away from the past, declared a fresh start, and claimed that now at last they have found the correct approach, only to be superseded by the next such claim.

The one philosopher who has attempted to work through this scepticism, and to arrive at some positive response to it, is the nineteenth-century

German philosopher Hegel. In his *Lectures on the History of Philosophy* he notes how, faced with the diversity of past philosophies, and the fact that they all seem to refute one another, we may feel

> the necessity for applying to philosophy the words of Christ, 'Let the dead bury their dead; arise, and follow me.' The whole of the history of philosophy becomes a battlefield covered with the bones of the dead; it is a kingdom not merely formed of dead and lifeless individuals, but of refuted and spiritually dead systems, since each has killed and buried the other.[1]

For all that, Hegel wants to place the study of the history of philosophy at the centre of his philosophical method, and to insist that 'no philosophy has ever been refuted'. What have been refuted are the claims of particular philosophical systems to be final and complete in themselves. Past philosophies have typically erred by being partial and one-sided, treating as all-embracing a certain explanatory principle which has an appropriate application within its own proper philosophical sphere. The task of the history of philosophy is, therefore, to identify the important principle to be retained from each of the major philosophies of the past, to allot to it its appropriate place as an element within the whole, and to identify its proper relations to the other necessary philosophical principles.[2]

   The method must not be misunderstood. It is not simply a matter of mixing together all past philosophies in the hope that the resulting pot-pourri will contain something to satisfy everyone. As Hegel insists, the history of philosophy is as much a negative as a positive enterprise. It is essentially a critical activity. Only through the criticism of past philosophies can one determine the positive form in which each is to be retained, its appropriate limits and its appropriate place within the whole. None of them can be accepted as it stands; the transforming role of criticism is essential.

   We may indeed feel that we need to go even further than Hegel in emphasizing the role of negative criticism. He perhaps fails to recognize sufficiently the way in which the positive contributions of past philosophies coexist with distortions arising from the limited social perspective of the philosopher in question. Every philosophy contains an ideological component—an element which is to be explained as a rationalization of the limited interests and perspective of the philosopher's own social class. Part of the task of examining the history of ethical theories is therefore to distinguish the ideological components from the contributions to a shared understanding of the human good. No doubt our own ethical discussions will likewise contain their elements of ideology, but if we are aware of the danger we can, at least to some extent, seek to limit its effects.

   To the idea that one can simply and indiscriminately lump together all previous ethical philosophies a further corrective must be mentioned. What are we to count as 'past philosophies'? Not every single recorded instance of human reflection on the nature of the good life. Quite apart from the inconceivability of ever completing such a survey, the very idea of a *history* of philosophy involves the discrimination of the significant from the insignificant and, beyond that, the identification of those major contributions which should form the core of the historical tradition. We need to recognize here the operation of what Raymond Williams has called 'the selective tradition'.[3] Any cultural tradition (not only philosophical but literary, artistic, or scientific) is formed and defined by a process of selection. When we speak, for example, of 'the nineteenth-century English novel', we are talking not of every novel written in England during that period, but of certain general lines of development exemplified by what have come to be seen as the most significant contributions to the genre. Nor is the process of selection ever completed once and for all. Each new generation offers its own re-definition of the tradition. 'In a society as a whole, and in all its particular activities, the cultural tradition can be seen as a continual selection and re-selection of ancestors. Particular lines will be drawn, often for as long as a century, and then suddenly, with some new stage in growth, these will be cancelled or weakened, and new lines drawn.'[4]

So it is also in moral philosophy, and in this book I make my own selection of what I see as the significant lines of development. In a very broad sense my approach in this book is a Hegelian one. Through a critique of some major ethical theories I work towards a positive position which retains what is valid in them. However, though my approach is historical, what I have to offer is not a history of ethics. It is *too* selective for that. I have not attempted a general interpretation of the tradition, but rather have picked out what I take to be a few of the major contributions to Western ethical thought. I begin with the two great philosophers of Greek antiquity, Plato and Aristotle. I then leap two thousand years to some representative philosophers of the eighteenth and nineteenth centuries, who continue many of the themes and preoccupations of the Greeks, but within a Christian culture which also produces significant differences in their thought. I shall look at the ethical philosophies of David Hume, Immanuel Kant, and John Stuart Mill, and at Hegelian ethics as represented by the British Hegelian philosopher F. H. Bradley. Part II ends with Friedrich Nietzsche, the iconoclast of the tradition, who reacts against the values inherited from Christianity and harks back to the values of the ancient world in order to call into question the very idea of 'morality'. In Chapter 9 I link him with Marx and Freud, two other thinkers who have forced us to ask whether the moral point of view is a tenable one at all.

In Part III my approach is rather different. I deal there with ethics in the twentieth-century academic tradition. Though I again select representative figures, and though my treatment of them must necessarily, in the space available, be extremely sketchy, in one way it is less selective. It is too soon to pick out major twentieth-century figures with the stature of Hume and Kant and Mill (and in any case I am not sure that there are any). I nevertheless try to impose a shape on this body of work, to trace lines of development and continuities with the historical tradition, and to offer an assessment of where this now leaves us.

One further word about the organization of this book. It is not complete in itself. I do not provide a comprehensive paraphrase of the major writers whom I discuss. There is no substitute for reading their own words. At the beginning of each chapter in Parts I and II I suggest a basic text, which I assume that the reader will look at in conjunction with my own chapter. All of them are readily available. My own discussions will include suggestions about how to read the texts, as well as critical comments on them, but I do not aim to take the place of the texts themselves.

I begin, then, with the Greeks. Why choose such a remote starting-point? The simple answer is that the work of Plato and Aristotle remains unsurpassed. We can learn as much about ethics from them as from any of their successors, and although, from a contemporary vantage-point, it is unlikely that any philosopher would describe himself unqualifiedly as a Platonist or as an Aristotelian, the position towards which I shall work in this book is as close to them as to anyone else.

There is another reason for starting with the Greeks. Ethics itself, as a form of intellectual enquiry, at least in the West, begins with them. In the thought of the Greek philosophers we can trace the beginnings of philosophical reflection on the nature of the good life and right conduct. Although the philosophies of Plato and Aristotle contain the first comprehensive and systematic ethical theories, it is among their predecessors that we find the origins of ethical thought, and in the remainder of this chapter I shall sketch these beginnings before turning to Plato and Aristotle themselves.

The emergence of critical philosophical thought about ethics can be traced to the ideas of the Sophists, a group of thinkers active in the Greek world of the fifth century BC. The Sophists were not primarily philosophers. They were itinerant teachers who travelled from city-state to city-state offering, for a fee, all manner of teaching—in mathematics, music, astronomy, and language, but above all in rhetoric. It was their ability to teach the art of rhetoric that gave the Sophists their popularity, for in the political life of the time, and especially in a democracy like Athens, the key to political success lay in the ability to persuade with a speech in the assembly or the lawcourts, and ambitious young men were eager to acquire this skill.

Although the Sophists were not primarily philosophers, certain philosophical ideas came to be associated with them, largely because of their need to justify their own activity. The accusation to which they were obviously exposed was that in teaching people the art of persuasion they were enabling them to make others believe what was in fact false. If the Sophists' pupils in rhetoric were concerned only to propagate those beliefs which happened to suit their own convenience, then all concern for truth seemed to have vanished. A typical response on the part of the Sophists was to question the very ideas of truth and falsity. Thus Protagoras, the most famous of the Sophists, held that 'man is the measure of all things, of what is, that it is, and of what is not, that it is not'. Whatever seems to me to be the case, is true for me, and whatever seems to you to be the case, is true for you. No belief can be said to be true or false in itself, for there is no objective truth. In this way Protagoras and other Sophists hoped to evade the criticism that they encouraged a contempt for truth.

This line of thought was applied also to morality. According to Protagoras, moral ideas are a matter of convention. 'Convention' is here contrasted with 'nature', and the distinction between nature and convention is perhaps the most important philosophical idea associated with the Sophists. In asserting moral laws to be human conventions they were influenced especially by the growing awareness of cultural diversity. With the growth of trade over the previous two centuries, leading to greater contact with other peoples, the Greeks had become increasingly aware of the ways in which customs vary from society to society. The historian Herodotus delights in listing such differences: the Egyptians do this, the Thracians do that, here they cremate their dead and there they embalm them, in this society they practise polygamy and in that one they practise incest. From these facts of diversity it was inferred by thinkers such as the Sophists that what we call morality, justice, virtue, and the like are nothing other than a set of humanly created conventions.

The view that morality is conventional rather than natural does not necessarily entail a rejection of morality. On the contrary, among the more conservative Sophists it led to a stress on the importance of conventions. Protagoras' moral relativism took the form of asserting that whatever is thought right in a particular society *is* right for that society. Every society needs a set of moral conventions simply in order to function as a community. Without it the community would disintegrate as its members all went their separate ways. Although some conventions may be more effective than others, what matters most is not their precise content but the fact that they are shared and adhered to.

Among the younger Sophists and their more radical followers, however, the nature/convention contrast was put to a very different use. The conclusion was drawn that if moral constraints are mere conventions, they should be cast aside. What was rational was to live according to nature rather than according to convention. The idea of acting in accordance with nature was variously interpreted, but a common interpretation was that it meant pursuing one's own self-interest, and refusing to be tied down in this pursuit by moral inhibitions.

The more conservative and the more radical Sophists both recognize that standards of right and wrong can be questioned. Their response is either to deny them the status of truth, or to reject them altogether. In so doing they inaugurate the activity of ethical philosophy. What they do is to make human conduct problematic. Questions about how to act can no longer be answered by an automatic appeal to accepted norms. It becomes necessary to face the question, '*Why* should I act in this way rather than that?', to look for acceptable *reasons* for different kinds of actions, and to consider whether such reasons are in fact ever obtainable.

Plato and Aristotle take up this challenge. They retain many of the values of traditional morality, but they do not retain them uncritically. They attempt to place them on a rational foundation. In particular, both of them retain the traditional Greek conception of the virtues—qualities such as courage, moderation, wisdom, piety, and justice. The core of the ethical systems of both Plato and Aristotle is the attempt to justify the virtues in terms of human happiness, to show that they are good qualities to possess, because a life lived in accordance with the virtues is the happiest and most rewarding kind of life. If they can do this, they will have shown that nature and convention are not antithetical, that conventional values have their basis in nature. In the next three chapters we shall consider how successful Plato and Aristotle are in this enterprise.

Notes

1. G. W. F. Hegel, *Lectures on the History of Philosophy*, trans. E. S. Haldane and Frances H. Simson (London, 1894), 17.
2. Ibid. 36–9.
3. Raymond Williams, *The Long Revolution* (Harmondsworth, 1965), 66–70.
4. Ibid. 69.

PART I

The Ancients

2

Plato
The Health of the Personality

Reading: Plato, *The Republic*

Numerous translations are available. I shall quote from the translation by H. D. P. Lee in the Penguin Classics series. Page numbers refer to the marginal numbering which is standard in all texts and translations of *The Republic*. With the possible exception of Book X, *The Republic* is a unity and should be read as a whole. However, for our present purposes the most important sections are 327a–367e (the preliminary discussion), 434d–445e (definition of justice in the individual), 474b–480a (the theory of forms), 504a–521b (analogies of the sun, divided line, and cave), and 543a–592a (the various kinds of injustice).

Socrates

Almost all of Plato's philosophical writings take the form of dramatized discussions, and in most of them the main participant is Socrates. The life and thought of Socrates exercised an enormous influence on Plato. In the minds of many of his contemporaries Socrates was identified with the Sophists. He was not, however, a professional teacher, indeed he claimed he had nothing to teach. He simply questioned people. He would engage in discussion those of his fellow citizens who had a reputation for piety, courage, moderation, or some other virtue; he would ask them 'What is piety?', 'What is courage?', or 'What is moderation?', and by following up their answers with further persistent questioning, would reveal that they could give no satisfactory account of the virtues they were supposed to possess.

Like the Sophists, Socrates thereby raises the basic questions of ethics. What is the good life, and why should we live it? But in contrast to the Sophists, Socrates' intent was much less negative and much more serious. He was not concerned to dismiss the possibility of ethical knowledge. On the contrary, he maintained that though he himself did not possess it, such knowledge was attainable, and was by far the most important thing to strive for.

Nevertheless, one can see how Socrates could have come to be linked with the Sophists, and how his activities would have been resented as disruptive by the conventionally upright citizens of Athens. In 399 BC he was brought to trial on a charge of corrupting the young and introducing new divinities. He was found guilty, and put to death. The manner of his death, as that of his life, remained for Plato an enduring inspiration.

The form of Plato's dialogues presents us with a problem. In a work like *The Republic* all the important philosophical ideas are put into the mouth of Socrates. Do these ideas represent the philosophy of the historical Socrates, or the philosophy of Plato? The question is a disputed one, which we cannot deal with here. I shall simply assume what is at present the most widely accepted view, that, though in some of his earlier and shorter dialogues Plato may give us a fairly accurate picture of the historical Socrates, in major works like *The Republic* the philosophy presented is Plato's own, using Socrates as his mouthpiece.

Plato's Aims in *The Republic*

The theme of *The Republic* is the nature of justice. The Greek word is *dikaiosuné*. In English versions of Plato the term is standardly translated as 'justice', but the Greek concept is somewhat wider than that. The English word 'justice' primarily refers to ethical principles regulating the distribution of social benefits and burdens. It suggests the idea of people receiving their fair share or their appropriate deserts, and is closely linked also with the idea of law. *Dikaiosuné* sometimes carries similarly specific connotations, but is also used more widely so that it almost amounts to something like 'the disposition to act rightly'—to act rightly, that is, in one's dealings with other people, for *dikaiosuné* is the social virtue *par excellence*. Often we could translate it as 'morality' and not be far off the mark. As Plato says, typical manifestations of injustice would be committing sacrilege or theft, betraying one's friends or one's country, breaking promises, committing adultery, and neglecting one's duties to one's parents and to the gods. I shall abide by the standard translation 'justice', but the reader should bear in mind the wider connotations.

The account of justice in *The Republic* is built upon a comparison between the just individual and the just society. The work therefore deals not only with ethics or moral philosophy in the strict sense, but also with social and political philosophy (and indeed with metaphysics, the theory of knowledge, the theory of art—it is Plato's most comprehensive treatment of all his various philosophical interests). Much of the work is taken up with Plato's account of the organization of his ideal society, and with a discussion of how the existing societies of his day deviated from this ideal. How successfully Plato integrates his moral philosophy with his social philosophy is a matter for debate, to which I shall return. For the time being I shall concentrate on the more specifically ethical parts of *The Republic*.

The preliminary discussion of justice can be related to the Sophists' contrast between 'nature' and 'convention'. The old man Cephalus and his son

Polemarchus are the spokesmen of convention. They can define justice only in terms of conventional examples: telling the truth and paying one's debts (Cephalus); or, at a slightly more theoretical level, giving everyone his due, benefiting one's friends and harming one's enemies, or perhaps benefiting the good and harming the bad (Polemarchus). When Thrasymachus impatiently bursts into the discussion, it is as the advocate of nature against convention. His views are typical of the more radical Sophists. He thinks that conventional justice and morality consist of rules promulgated by the ruling group in society, to keep everyone else in check and to promote the rulers' own interests. The conclusion which he draws is: don't be fooled, disregard justice whenever you can get away with it, pursue your own interests and not those of other people. He believes that the only rational and natural mode of conduct is the pursuit of self-interest, and that this requires a rejection of conventional justice.

The position subsequently put forward by Glaucon, and elaborated by his brother Adeimantus, can usefully be seen as a compromise between nature and convention. They present it not as their own view, but as one which is very widely held. (For brevity's sake, however, I shall refer to it as 'Glaucon's view'.) According to this common opinion, they say, the way of life advocated by Thrasymachus would be the best if one could get away with it. If one possessed the mythical ring of Gyges, which could render one invisible, this would be possible. But as things are, if you simply pursue your own interests and entirely disregard the interests of others, inflicting harm and injury on them whenever it suits you, then others will act in the same way towards you, and you are likely to end up the loser. When people realize this, they come to an understanding with one another that each will as far as possible refrain from inflicting harm on others, provided everyone else likewise refrains. Justice, then, is indeed a convention, but it is the best available approximation to that 'self-interest which all nature naturally pursues as good'. Adeimantus adds that conventional justice has the further advantage of securing the favour of the gods as well as that of our fellow humans. Again this is an unfortunate but inescapable fact of life; if we could manage without the favour of the gods we would do so, and would then not need justice.

These ethical positions, put forward by Thrasymachus and by Glaucon and Adeimantus, set the scene for the dialogue. Socrates will confront them and attempt to refute them. It cannot be emphasized too strongly that they are not merely 'straw men'. Commentators on *The Republic* are tempted to treat Thrasymachus, in particular, as someone who is quite obviously wrong. We should, on the contrary, take very seriously the possibility that he may be right. Certainly the position presented by Glaucon as the popular view is as widely held in our own day as it was in his. The question, 'Why should I pursue my own interests?' seems redundant; such action has an obvious rationality. On the other hand the question, 'Why should I heed other people's interests?' does seem to require an answer. And in view of the obvious rationality of pursuing my own interests, the most plausible answer would seem to be that it is rational for me to heed other people's interests, just in so far as I need to do so for the sake of my own interests. This is the plausibility in Glaucon's view. And if there is that degree of truth in it, then there may be an equal degree of truth in Thrasymachus' view. For, though there are some cases where we cannot get away with injustice, there are surely other cases where we can, and is it not then rational to do so? We do not have to choose between total justice and total injustice. If the only test of rationality is self-interest, then it must be rational to lie or cheat or steal or harm others, when no one else will know and one can save one's reputation—in a shady business deal, perhaps, or minor pilfering from one's place of work, or a host of other everyday situations where a little bit of injustice would come in handy.

Can Thrasymachus be answered? Should we want to answer him? Plato, through Socrates, intends to do so. His response to Thrasymachus, and to the Sophists generally, is threefold.

1. He rejects the antithesis of nature and convention. He wishes to link the two more closely than Glaucon does. Conventional justice is not simply the best available approximation to the dictates of nature. It is itself grounded in nature, that is, in human nature. If we understand our own nature as human beings, we shall see that the life of conventional justice is thoroughly in accordance with that nature.

2. He rejects the opposition between conventional justice and personal benefit. A life lived in accordance with conventional justice will itself be the happiest and most worthwhile kind of life. Again the link between justice and well-being is closer than that posited by Glaucon. For Glaucon the relation between justice and happiness is that of means and ends; justice is not desirable in itself, but it secures happiness as a *consequence*, because it ensures that other people will be just towards oneself. For Plato the life of justice is *by its very nature* the happiest life.

3. He rejects Protagoras' view that there are no objective ethical truths or values. Since justice is grounded in human nature, we can establish as an objective truth that there are good reasons for living the life of justice.

In Plato's attempted refutation of the Sophists, the crucial role is played by the definition of justice at 434d–445e. Justice in society has been defined as a harmonious relation between the three main social classes: the guardians, the auxiliaries, and the economic class. When each class performs its proper function—when the guardians rule, the auxiliaries defend the society against its enemies, and the economic class engages in production and exchange—the society as a whole will be a harmonious unity and will be perfectly just. Socrates now suggests that to these social classes there correspond three parts of the soul, three aspects of the human personality. These are reason, spirit, and desire. By 'spirit' is meant those emotional capacities which variously express themselves in such phenomena as anger, strength of will, conscience, and shame. Though the noun 'spirit' may have misleading connotations, the adjective 'spirited' captures something of the right meaning. 'Desire' seems to mean primarily the physical appetites, the desires for food and drink and sexual satisfaction, but this raises questions of interpretation which we shall have to look at later.

Socrates proposes that, as justice in society is a harmonious relation between classes, so justice in the individual consists in a harmonious relation between the different aspects of the personality. Reason must rule, spirit must assist reason by providing the required emotional qualities of self-control and strength of will, and through their combined efforts desire must be inhibited so that it seeks no more than the satisfaction of essential physical needs. And just as bodily health exists when the different physical organs are all in a state to perform their proper function (heart, lungs, sense organs, etc., all functioning properly), so also we can say that when the three parts of the self are performing their proper functions this will constitute mental health. Goodness, then, is the health and harmony of the personality.

How does this enable Plato to answer the Sophists? Consider the three tasks which we identified for him.

1. The reconciliation of nature and convention Here, I think, Plato is weakest. If human goodness or justice is analogous to health, this will indeed serve to ground it in nature. Moral goodness will be something which human beings need in the way that they need physical health, as a requirement of their very nature. What is more questionable is the claim that this 'natural' justice will coincide with justice as conventionally understood. Plato claims that it will. At 442e–443b he takes it to be simply obvious that the person who is just, in the sense of having a properly harmonized soul, will not embezzle money, commit sacrilege or theft, betray his friends or his country, break promises, commit adultery, dishonour his parents, or be irreligious. At 589c–590c slightly more elaboration is provided. There it is said that 'the things that are conventionally dishonourable', such as getting money unjustly, self-indulgence, obstinacy and bad temper, luxury and effeminacy, flattery and meanness, are so regarded because they involve subservience to physical appetites. One might doubt, however, whether injustice always stems from such a source, and we shall have to consider later whether Plato adequately establishes the link between typically unjust actions and his own psychological analysis.

2. The linking of justice and benefit Here the appeal of the analogy with health is obvious. Physical health is quite clearly advantageous to its possessor, and preferable to illness. The proper functioning of his or her physical organs is something which any human being needs, and is intrinsically pleasurable. So if justice can be equated with psychic health, we can see how this will help Plato to establish that the just life is intrinsically happy and desirable.

3. **The objectivity of values** We can see too how the analogy with health will help Plato to assert the objective character of ethical values. What counts as health or illness seems to be objectively determinable, and it seems plausible too to maintain that the desirability of health is not merely a matter of subjective preference.

A great deal, therefore, hangs on whether Plato can successfully maintain the analogy with physical health. I want now to examine this analogy in more detail.

Justice as Mental Health

Anthony Kenny has pointed out interesting similarities between Plato's theory and Freudian psychology.[1] Both of them offer an account of mental health in terms of a harmony between the three parts of the personality. Freud, in his later works, divided the psyche into the ego, the super-ego, and the id. The ego and the id correspond very closely to Plato's reason and desire. What Freud understands by 'the super-ego' is rather narrower than Plato's 'spirit'. The super-ego is a specifically moral phenomenon. It is, in effect, the conscience created by the internalization of parental and social authority. It is akin to Plato's 'spirit', however, in that its characteristic function is to assist the ego (reason), by providing the emotional force which will keep in check the id (desire).

In a later chapter I shall say a little more about Freud in his own right, and his relevance to moral philosophy. At this point the comparison between him and Plato is useful because it alerts us to the general significance of Plato's theory. As Kenny says, 'the concept of mental health was Plato's invention',[2] and in introducing it into ethical theory, Plato was the forerunner of those who in our own day have suggested that ethical questions can be illuminated by a psychology of mental health and illness. Kenny himself is deeply suspicious of the whole enterprise. He says:

> It is characteristic of our age to endeavour to replace virtues by technology. That is to say, wherever possible we strive to use methods of physical or social engineering to achieve goals which our ancestors thought attainable only by the training of character . . . The moralistic concept of mental health incorporates the technological dream: it looks towards the day when virtue is superseded by medical know-how. But we are no more able than Plato was to make ourselves virtuous by prescription or pharmacology: and renaming virtue 'mental health' takes us no further than it took Plato in the direction of that chimeric goal.[3]

Why should the assimilation of moral virtue to mental health be thought objectionable? It may firstly seem simply implausible to suppose that someone who behaves immorally or unjustly must therefore be mentally sick or insane. Do we not know all too many people who, though ruthlessly unjust, seem also to be quite disconcertingly free of mental disharmony or disturbance, and whose mental faculties function all too effectively? Here we have to recognize, however, that we are not dealing with a simple dichotomy between total insanity on the one hand and total psychic health on the other. The comparison of Plato with Freud should remind us of Freud's insistence on the continuous spectrum that extends from psychic harmony to mental breakdown. The analogy with physical health should point us towards the same recognition. Most of us are neither sick nor perfectly healthy. We are healthy enough to function at a basic level, but not fully fit, and we can recognize the desirability of improving our health to the level of positive physical harmony and well-being. Similarly with psychic health. Plato's account attempts to establish, on the continuum between health and insanity, a close affinity between the thoroughly unjust person and the madman, and then to locate lesser degrees of injustice as intermediate points on the spectrum. This is done in the survey of unjust societies and individuals in Books VIII and IX, and especially in the discussion of the tyrannical character-type at 571a–576b. The latter discussion begins with a striking concurrence with Freudian theory—the assertion of the existence of a class of 'lawless desires', such as inclinations to incest, sadism, or bestiality, which are normally repressed but tend to manifest themselves in dreams. In the tyrannical person, who corresponds to the society ruled by a tyrant and is the extreme of injustice, these desires are no longer repressed but acted out, and one of them is set up as 'a master passion in him to control the idle desires that divide his time between them'. This master passion acquires a total dominance over the mind, and the other desires subserve it like worker bees feeding and fattening a drone, until 'the master passion runs wild and takes madness into its service, . . . all discipline is swept away and madness usurps its place'. The reference to madness is then supported by a comparison between the tyrannical character of sexual desire, the behaviour of one who is drunk, and the fantasies of omnipotence typical of the madman.

For Plato, then, the main similarity between injustice and insanity lies in the *obsessive* or *compulsive* nature of the desire which dominates such a person. A particular desire has grown out of all proportion, and lost touch with reality. If Plato can indeed establish that this is the typical feature of injustice, the continuity with insanity will be clear, and especially with that form of mental illness known as obsessional neurosis, which consists precisely in a person's behaviour being dominated by a compulsive wish, fear, or belief whose expressions are wildly irrational. To substantiate the relevance of this to injustice (in the wider sense), think of the way in which our relations to others are distorted by our own obsessions, so that we cannot respond objectively to the other person's needs and desires, or treat the other as a person in his or her own right. Take, for example, the case of racial prejudice, and think of the way in which racist attitudes are typically grounded, not in any real features of the denigrated race, but in the insecurities and frustrations of the racist himself, leading him to project on to a scapegoat emotions and fears which have no rational foundation. Or think of the nature of possessive jealousy or infatuation in sexual relations, and of how in such cases the supposed 'love' takes on an exploitative character because it is a fantasy emotion, out of touch with any rational or objective awareness of the 'loved' one's real qualities. In both cases our description draws on Plato's notion of psychic imbalance, on the idea of reason, emotion, and desires having their proper roles, and of their becoming distorted and destructive when they cease to be in harmony with one another, when emotions and desires become irrational, fantasy-ridden, and obsessive.

These examples may prompt a second objection. It may be said that the analogy between physical and mental health is misleading because, whereas what we count as physical health or illness can be determined simply by the physical facts, what we count as mental health or illness will be determined by our prior evaluations. We regard the racist as 'sick' only because we already, on independent grounds, morally object to racism—so the objection would run. And this would be an objection both to the idea of mental health in general, and in particular to the idea that it can provide an objective foundation for ethical theory.

In response to this objection we should look more closely at the status of the concept of physical health. For here too what we count as health will to some extent vary with prior values. What counts as physical health for an Olympic swimmer will differ from what counts as health for a university lecturer. The latter would be delighted with a physical condition which the former would call being hopelessly unfit. Again, what counts as physical health will vary not only in relation to different values and tasks, but also in relation to different social and physical environments. A different kind and degree of physical fitness would be needed in a pre-industrial and an industrial society, for instance, or in an Arctic climate and a temperate climate. Nevertheless there remains a central core of objectivity to the concept of physical health, and it seems plausible to suppose, as Plato does, that this objective core is provided by the notion of 'function'. A person is in a state of physical health when his or her physical organs perform their proper functions, and these 'proper functions' are determined by what it is for the person as a whole to function effectively. A hunter will need to be more fleet of foot and possess more acute vision than an office worker, but any human being needs to be able to walk and needs to be able to see. Underlying the notions of what it is to function effectively in this or that particular context or role, we have a general notion of what it is to function effectively as a human being.

The Platonic claim would be that a notion of mental health can be built on the same foundation. A certain basic harmony between the different aspects of the personality is likewise needed, if one is to function effectively as a human being. If one's emotions and desires are not guided by reason, one lives in a fantasy world. If one's rational capacities are not motivated by emotions and desires, one lapses into a state of meaninglessness. These, then, are require-ments for *any* meaningful and effective human life, whatever more particular values a person may happen to live by. And they are requirements which are satisfied to different degrees, so that a person may, without being mentally ill, nevertheless fall short of real psychic harmony.

A third objection to the ethical employment of the concept of mental health might be that it attempts to make morality a matter for experts, just as ques-tions of physical health are entrusted to the expertise of qualified doctors. Many of us would find this repellent, as Kenny does when he comments that, 'if every vicious man is really a sick man, then the virtuous philosopher can claim over him the type of control which a doctor has over his patients'.[4] There can be no doubt that Plato would welcome this implication. His justifi-cation for the role of the philosopher-kings in his ideal society is precisely that they need to act as physicians to the souls of those who cannot cure themselves.

All the same, we do not necessarily have to accept this implication, and we can reject it without having to abandon the concept of mental health. We can separate the question of whether that concept is a useful one in ethics from the question of whether it would commit us to the rule of experts. One way in which we might try to sever the two claims is by questioning the status of experts even in matters of physical health. Of course, there exists an objective body of knowledge about the causes of illness and the means to health, and of course doctors are better qualified than laymen. But we may also feel that in our own society medical knowledge has become too much the prerogative of experts, that it carries with it too much of an assumption of authority, and that the result is that ordinary people feel intimidated and incapable of acting for themselves in the matter of their own physical well-being. Thus the inference that, if goodness is a kind of mental health, it must become the business of experts, can be blocked at this first step. But we could also block it by stressing the differences between physical and mental health. We can retain the central features of the comparison between physical and mental health while recog-nizing that there are also differences, and that these differences may make it even more dangerous to entrust mental health than physical health to experts. For example, a supposed expert's assessment of the mental health of others, though it may in principle be capable of objective determination, is in practice much more likely to be distorted by biases and privileged interests. Or again it could be argued that the capacity to direct one's own life is itself an essential component of full psychic health, and that the notion of having such a condi-tion provided for one by experts is a contradiction in terms—a claim which could not be made in the same way about physical health. We could, then, accept Plato's assertion of the importance of mental health for the good life, while rejecting the further inference about the need to entrust such matters to experts. It should also be added, however, that *in particular cases* that inference *may* be valid; the compulsive sadist or the compulsive rapist, for example, may need not moral guidance but expert treatment by a psychotherapist.

The point made in the last paragraph can be generalized further. We can and should distinguish between the general claim that moral goodness is a kind of psychic health and harmony, and Plato's particular version of what this health and harmony consists in. Plato's psychology, like his politics, has an authoritarian cast. He believes that, for the proper inner harmony to be achieved, reason, in alliance with spirit, must exercise a strict control over the desires, inhibiting some, and eliminating others. Just as we might question Plato's authoritarian politics from a democratic standpoint, so also we might question Plato's authoritarian conception of psychic health, and attempt to make a case for what might be called a more 'democratic' character-structure.

The reference to Freud could again help us here. Freud's account of mental health and illness exhibits a much greater ambivalence about the repression of desires. Like Plato, Freud sees such repression as inescapable, both within society and within the individual, if civilized human life is to be viable. However, Freud also recognizes that, beyond a certain point, excessive repression becomes harmful and self-defeating. Desires which are repressed do not simply disappear, they continue to exist, but remain unconscious. If the repression is too severe, the thwarted desires find expression in substitute satisfactions. Just because their activity is unconscious, they become all the more difficult to control, and the ways in which they find expression, and resist the attempts to block them, may well give rise to mental illness. Thus the control of the desires which Plato equates with mental health can, on Freud's account, itself be a cause of mental illness, and conversely mental health may actually require the gratification of those instinctual desires which Plato wants to inhibit.

It is not entirely clear what Plato means by 'desire' in his partition of the self. Sometimes, and especially when the division is first introduced at 437d–439e, it seems to include all the desires, hunger and thirst simply being the most conspicuous. Plato's scheme would then embody a classic opposition of reason and emotion ('spirit' and 'desire' together constituting 'emotion'), of a kind which I shall consider in the next chapter. Subsequently, however, what seems more likely is that Plato wants to confine 'desire' to only certain desires. Reason has its own characteristic emotions and desires, aiming at their own special pleasures (580d–581c), and 'desire' so-called is limited to the instinctual physical desires for food and drink and sex. On this interpretation, Plato's assumption is that it is these physical desires which are essentially opposed to reason.

We might, however, question this assumption. The physical desires do not have to be irrational. Sexual desire, for example, need not be a blind and uncontrollable craving. Such desires can have their own rationality, they can be discriminating, directed at their appropriate objects. We might therefore retain from Plato the conception of goodness as psychic health, and retain also the analysis of this health as a harmony between the parts of the personality, but look for a less authoritarian, less repressive conception of what this harmony would consist in.

The relevance to ethics of the concept of mental health and of Freudian theory are matters to which I shall refer again later in the book. So far I have been concerned to lend an initial plausibility to Plato's use of the concept. We now need to look further at how it helps him to answer the Sophists.

Justice and Happiness

We saw that Plato wishes to meet Thrasymachus' challenge by showing that the just life is the happiest and most fulfilling. Initially this is held to have been demonstrated at 445a, as a direct consequence of a definition of justice as mental health. For 'men don't reckon that life is worth living when their physical health breaks down, even though they have all the food and drink and wealth and power in the world. So we can hardly reckon it worth living when the principle of life breaks down in confusion, and a man wilfully avoids the one thing that will rid him of vice and crime, the acquisition of justice and virtue in the sense which we have shown them to bear.'

The claim is further substantiated in Book IX (from 576b), where three arguments are offered.

1. The first is a further elaboration of the appeal to the idea of mental health. Plato has suggested that the tyrannical personality is one which is dominated by a single obsessive and compulsive desire. It follows, he claims, that though such a person may appear to be happy when that desire is gratified, he is in reality enslaved to the desire. The crucial point here is that satisfaction of the desire does not necessarily mean satisfaction of the person, as a whole self. Plato is appealing to the idea of the self as a unity, not just a bundle of desires, and consequently whether a person is happy must be determined by considering not his or her superficial satisfactions, but the deeper harmony that underlies them.

2. The second argument appeals to the idea that each of the three parts of the personality has its own characteristic pleasures. There are the pleasures of reason, of spirit, and of desire. Persons in whom reason is the dominant faculty (who will be those who live the just life) will value most highly the pleasures of reason, and likewise those dominated by spirit or desire will value their own respective pleasures. The question, then, is how to decide between these three estimates of the value of the different kinds of pleasure. Plato argues that the person dominated by reason possesses in the greatest measure the very qualities of knowledge and rationality which are needed to make a correct estimate. Moreover, only such persons have fully

experienced all three kinds of pleasure and are in a position to judge between them, whereas the person dominated by desire knows only his own kinds of pleasure, and cannot appreciate the value of higher kinds. Therefore, when the person dominated by reason asserts from his experience that his own kind of life, the life of justice, is the happiest, he must be right. Plato's important insight here is that, in considering the quality of a person's life, we have to ask not only whether he or she is happy in the sense of being satisfied with his or her existing experiences, but also whether that person could be happier if his or her life were enriched by new kinds of experience.

3. Plato's final argument is that our pleasures are unreal when we take pleasure in things which are themselves unreal. For Plato it follows that physical pleasures, the pleasures of food and drink and sex, are unreal, since the physical world is unreal. The only fully real world is the world of ideal forms known by the intellect, and therefore the only true pleasures are the pleasures of reason. Here we are entering Plato's metaphysics, to which I will turn in a moment. However, there is a more general question which Plato's argument poses, separable from the metaphysical issues. What is the status of pleasures which are based on illusion? Suppose that I am sustained in my life by a belief that I am widely respected by my colleagues and acquaintances, and this belief is essential to my happiness, and suppose that the belief is quite false—that I am in fact regarded by people with contempt, although they carefully shield me from a knowledge of it. Can I really be said to be happy, if my happiness depends on this illusion? Plato's answer is unequivocal: if my happiness is based on a false belief, it is a false happiness, that is, it is not really happiness at all. Can we accept such a simple answer? There are problems in doing so, for against Plato one is inclined to say that if a person really does *feel* happy, then as a matter of plain psychological fact that person surely *is* happy, whether or not he or she ought to be. And yet one is also inclined to agree with Plato, at least to the extent that there is something defective or degenerate about a happiness based on illusions, however secure those illusions are from being shattered.

In general, this section of *The Republic* offers a subtle and complex conception of happiness, which is clearly distinguished from the mere satisfaction of immediate desires. We have seen that, according to Plato, whether one is truly and fully happy will depend not only on the degree of immediate satisfaction, but on the degree of unity and harmony in one's life, on the range of one's experience, and the extent to which one has acquaintance with different possibilities, and on the depth and veracity of one's knowledge of oneself and one's world. For Plato, the mindless pleasures of the media-drugged zombie (like the prisoners in the cave at the beginning of Book VII, sitting and watch-

ing the flickering images on the wall) are not true happiness. We shall appreciate more fully the richness of Plato's account of happiness when we come to
compare it with other accounts, such as those of some Utilitarian philosophers, but in the meantime we can also see that it stands in marked contrast to
the conceptions of happiness invoked by Thrasymachus, by Glaucon and
Adeimantus, and by many of the Sophists.

Objective Values and the Theory of Forms

As the third of Plato's responses to the Sophists I listed his assertion of the
objectivity of ethical values. Implicitly this is embodied in Plato's account of
justice as mental health. When articulated as an explicit theory, it becomes
Plato's famous 'theory of forms' or 'theory of ideas'. What does this theory
assert?

To begin with let us take it that among these 'forms' or 'ideas' Plato includes
values such as goodness, justice, and beauty. Minimally, then, the theory is the
assertion that there *are* such things as goodness, justice, and beauty. More substantially, what Plato maintains is that goodness itself is something *distinct*
and *separate* from the many individual things which are good, that in addition
to all the various just individuals and just acts and just societies, and in addition to all the various beautiful sights and sounds, there are also justice itself
and beauty itself. This *separation* of the one quality from its many exemplifications is understood by Plato in a strong sense. It amounts to a separation
between two distinct worlds, the everyday physical world and the world of the
forms. The language of 'two worlds' is to be found especially in the analogy of
the cave (514a–521b), where the interior of the cave represents the everyday
physical world, and only the enlightened few can ascend to the world of true
reality outside the cave, which is the world of the forms.

This talk of the separation of two worlds should not be understood too
crudely. It is not a spatial separation between two different locations—the
world of the forms is not literally 'up there' above the heavens. This would be
too crude, because the forms, not being physical things, are not in space at all.
This indeed is the real nature of the separation. The many good things exist in
the physical world of space and time, whereas goodness itself is not a physical
thing, and does not exist in space or time. It makes no sense to say of it that it
exists 'here' or 'there', that it existed or will exist at this or that time.

This, then, is one aspect of the separation, a distinction between a spatio-
temporal existence and a non-spatio-temporal existence. But Plato also has
other reasons for emphasizing the separateness of the forms. In the first place,
it indicates the contrast between the perfection of the forms and the imperfection of their exemplifications. Justice itself cannot be equated with the
sum of individual just persons and societies, because none of these are ever

fully and perfectly just. Even the best of them fall short of the ideal in some respect.

Plato regularly puts this in terms of a contrast between 'being' and 'becoming'. The world of forms is the world of being, the world of physical exemplifications is the world of becoming. In part, 'becoming' signifies literal change. Individual good things come into existence at a certain time and cease to exist at a later time, and their goodness is therefore transitory. But their instability is also a matter of changes of aspect. Any particular good thing will also, *at the same time*, be bad in some respect, that is to say, it changes according to how you look at it. To say that it 'becomes' is therefore to say that it is never fully and completely good in all respects, and in that sense is variable. The 'being'/'becoming' contrast also serves to indicate that *objectivity* of the forms which was our starting-point. Any particular good thing is subject to becoming, not only in the sense that it is good in some respects and not others, but also in the sense that it will seem good to some people and not others. Goodness itself, however, cannot vary. It is what it is, independent of the beliefs of individual human beings. Presented with the adage that 'beauty is in the eye of the beholder', Plato would say that this may be true of the beauty of individual things, but cannot be true of beauty itself. Accordingly Protagoras' dictum that 'man is the measure of all things' is the reverse of the truth.

A further aspect of the separation of forms and their exemplifications is the contrast between the kinds of knowledge we have of each. Individual good things, since they exist in the physical world, must be known by the senses. However, since their goodness is necessarily an imperfect approximation to an ideal, we could not recognize them as good unless we already had a (perhaps unconscious) prior knowledge of the ideal itself. We could not derive our knowledge of goodness itself from our sensory experience of its instances, just because these are all imperfect. Sense-experience can awaken our knowledge of goodness, but that knowledge must be something which we already possessed prior to all sense-experience. Strictly speaking, therefore, when we speak of 'coming to know' goodness through our acquaintance with individual good things, this 'coming to know' must really be a kind of 'recollection', a re-awakening of that innate knowledge of goodness which we already possessed at birth, before all our sensory experience, and which has lain dormant in us since then. This innate knowledge, since it is not sensory perceptual knowledge, must be what we know by pure reason, by thought, by the intellect alone. In modern philosophical terminology, it is a priori knowledge, as contrasted with the empirical knowledge acquired through sense-experience. The forms are therefore objects of pure thought, and in that respect the modern English word 'idea' (which derives directly from one of Plato's own Greek terms for 'form') is an appropriate one by which to refer to them. In calling goodness, justice, and the rest 'ideas', however, we should not give the impression that they exist only 'in the mind'. They are known by the mind, but can exist quite independently of any mind. Goodness would be what it is, even though no human minds had ever existed or had ever thought about it.

I have referred to two kinds of knowledge. According to Plato, however, the so-called knowledge acquired through sense-experience is not genuine knowledge at all. Knowledge can never be false, and therefore beliefs cannot count as knowledge if it is possible for them to be false. Sense perception fails to meet this requirement, for our senses often deceive us. Therefore, if perception can turn out to be erroneous, it cannot be knowledge. It is merely *belief*. The only real knowledge is knowledge of the forms, purely rational knowledge which, when we have it, is direct and indubitable.

The 'separation' of forms from their instances amounts, then, to this. The forms are not physical things and do not exist in space or time. They are perfect, as contrasted with the imperfection of their instances. And they are apprehended not by the senses but by rational thought, which provides our only genuine knowledge rather than mere belief.

So far I have presented the theory of forms simply as a theory of ideal values. However, Plato also recognizes other kinds of forms. There are mathematical forms—for example, forms of geometrical entities such as 'triangle', 'circle', and 'straight line', and of mathematical relations such as 'equality'. There are forms of so-called 'natural kinds', and especially of biological species and genera such as 'man', or 'horse', or 'oak-tree'. The theory of forms is therefore not just a theory of ethical knowledge, but a theory of knowledge in general, and it is elaborated as such in the analogy of the divided line (509d–511e). Plato there distinguishes between four stages of awareness: (i) the use of images as a way of apprehending physical things; (ii) direct empirical acquaintance with physical things; (iii) the use of physical things as images of the forms; (iv) direct intellectual knowledge of the forms.

Rather than discuss further Plato's theory of knowledge in general, I want now to raise some doubts about it as a theory of *ethical* knowledge. This can be done by asking: what kind of ethical knowledge does Plato himself provide in *The Republic*? Into which of the four sections of the divided line does it fall? What about the account of justice, for example, in terms of the parts of the soul? Is this to count as direct intellectual knowledge of the form of justice, or is it the use of a physical image as a means of knowing the form? Does it belong in the third or the fourth section of the line? The question is difficult partly because Plato was unsure where to locate the soul in his metaphysical scheme. He sees the soul as akin to the forms and the intelligible world, and yet individual souls cannot themselves be forms, since they are all imperfect exemplifications of the general form 'soul'.

However, if we look at what is actually going on in Plato's account of justice in the soul, we must surely conclude that it belongs in the third rather than the fourth stage of the line. It involves constant reference to the facts of the empirical, physical world. The division into the parts of the soul is established by appeal to the observed facts of mental conflict. The proper relationship between the parts of the soul is presented through an analogy with physical health. The connection with justice is supported by descriptions of the kinds of observable actions in the physical world which would be produced by a condition of psychic harmony or conflict. All of this must presumably count as appealing to physical images of justice. We may well conclude that nowhere in *The Republic* does Plato himself go further than the third stage of the line.

What I now want to ask is whether he could ever conceivably do so. What would an account of justice be like which made no reference to the physical world? How could one possibly define justice or any other ethical quality, except in terms of the kinds of actions it involves and how it requires us to live in the world of our perceptual experience? It is difficult to see what could possibly count as knowledge of the form all by itself, and Plato is able to offer us nothing other than the idea of some kind of mystic vision, about which nothing can be said. This, then, is the consequence of Plato's radical separation of forms from their exemplifications. If justice or goodness really were quite separate from their instances, we could have no knowledge of them.

The conclusion which I propose is that when Plato's view of the objectivity of values is elaborated as the fully-fledged theory of forms, it leads us ultimately to a dead end. When it is presented as a thesis about the objective desirability of a healthy and harmonious state of the personality, it is much more fruitful. The most valuable parts of *The Republic* are those which lead in the direction of what is known as ethical *naturalism*—the view that a knowledge of how human beings can best live can be derived from the empirical facts of human nature and the human situation. These are the parts of *The Republic* which deal with the relationship between justice, happiness, and mental health. I have tried in this chapter to exhibit what is plausible and attractive in these ideas. There remain more fundamental questions which we need to ask about the whole enterprise, and I shall consider these in Chapter 4. But since they are questions which arise also for Aristotle's ethical theory, I turn first to Aristotle.

Notes

1. Anthony Kenny, 'Mental Health in Plato's Republic', in *The Anatomy of the Soul* (Oxford, 1973), reprinted from the *Proceedings of the British Academy*, 1969.
2. Ibid. 1.
3. Ibid. 26–7.
4. Ibid. 23 f.

3

Aristotle
The Rationality of the Emotions

Reading: Aristotle, *The Nicomachean Ethics*

I shall concentrate especially on Books I–IV and X. The translation to which I shall refer is Aristotle, *Ethics*, translated by Hugh Tredennick and introduced by Jonathan Barnes, in the Penguin Classics series.

Aristotle and Plato

Aristotle's *Nicomachean Ethics* was not a work written for publication. He did write such works, but none of them have survived. All of his philosophical works which have come down to us, including the *Nicomachean Ethics*, are in the form of lecture notes, simply for Aristotle's own use when he gave his lectures in his school, the Lyceum, and arranged and organized by later editors after Aristotle's death. Two versions of his course of lectures on ethics have survived, the other version being known as the *Eudemian Ethics*. The *Nicomachean Ethics* seems to have been the later and more definitive version, and is usually referred to simply as the *Ethics*.

Aristotle was for twenty years a pupil of Plato, from the time when at the age of seventeen he entered Plato's teaching establishment, the Academy, until his departure after the death of Plato in 347 BC. This apprenticeship shaped Aristotle's preoccupations, in respect both of his intellectual debts to Plato, and his divergences from him. As a rough guide, we can say that Aristotle's substantive ethics continues in a broadly Platonic direction, but that his meta-ethics takes a radically different turn. His disagreements with Plato stem from his rejection of the theory of forms. He developed a number of critical arguments against the theory, including the criticism to which I subscribed in my previous chapter, that Plato's radical separation of forms from particulars makes it difficult to see how we could ever have knowledge of them. Aristotle adds that even if such knowledge could be obtained, it could have no relevance for ethics. Knowledge of the Platonic forms would be knowledge of something eternal and unchanging, whereas ethical knowledge would have to be a kind of knowledge which could guide our *actions*, and would therefore have to be a knowledge of things that can be changed. Again, knowledge of the forms would be a knowledge of universals, whereas in ethics what we need is a knowledge of particulars, since it is in particular situations that we have to decide how to act. Of course, in ethical philosophy we aim at more than just a knowledge of particulars, but any universal claims which we try to produce will be generalizations from our experience of particular situations. As such they will be rough and ready approximations, and in ethics we must not look for a greater degree of accuracy and exactness than is appropriate to the subject. Every discipline has its appropriate standards of precision; the carpenter, for example, does not measure a right angle with the same accuracy as a geometrician. Accordingly in ethics we can expect generalizations which are true only for the most part, and which derive from the accumulated experience which we have built up from everyday life and particular situations. Ethical philosophy presupposes this shared experience, and is therefore not a fit subject for the young and inexperienced. This conception of ethical knowledge is stressed especially in a number of degressions and asides in Book I of the *Ethics*, and is linked with the criticisms of the Platonic theory of forms in ch. 6 of Book I.

What Aristotle retains from Plato is the general nature of the enterprise in substantive ethics. Like Plato, Artistotle wants to show that there are objectively valid reasons for living in accordance with the traditional virtues, and like Plato, he attempts to justify the virtues by examining the nature of human beings, in order to argue that a life lived in accordance with the virtues will be the happiest life. In Aristotle's version of the argument there are three main steps:

1. The ultimate end of human action is happiness.
2. Happiness consists in acting in accordance with reason.
3. Acting according to reason is the distinguishing feature of all the traditional virtues.

The first two steps are to be found in Book I of the *Ethics*, and the third step is the theme of Books II to IV. I shall examine in turn each of the three steps.

Happiness

The first stage of Aristotle's argument, then, is the claim that the ultimate end of human action is happiness. The Greek term conventionally translated as 'happiness' in the *Ethics* is *eudaimonia*, but this is another case where we should note differences of nuance between Greek and English terms. The English word 'happiness' refers primarily to a psychological state, a state of feeling. Whether one *is* happy is largely (though not entirely) a question of whether one *feels* happy. *Eudaimonia*, on the other hand, is more an objective condition of a person, and there is more room for a contrast between *feeling* happy and genuinely *being* happy. *Eudaimonia* thus has some of the connotations of 'well-being' or 'flourishing'. It is easier, too, for Aristotle to distinguish between 'happiness' and 'pleasure'. We should not, however, exaggerate the differences between the Greek and English vocabularies. On the one hand, there have been plenty of English philosophers who have asserted an important difference between 'happiness' and 'pleasure', and even, though less easily, between 'being happy' and 'feeling happy' (where locutions such as 'true happiness' may help). On the other hand, there were Greek philosophers ready enough to equate 'happiness' with 'pleasure' (such as some of the Sophists, and later the Epicureans).

Differences between Greek and English, then, cannot by themselves account for Aristotle's position. Equally important is the influence of Plato. Like Plato, Aristotle accepts that happiness cannot be divorced from pleasure. One who is happy will necessarily find pleasure in his way of life. The converse however is not true, and here too, Aristotle follows Plato. The fact that a person experiences pleasure does not entail that the person is happy. According to Aristotle's account in Book X, pleasure is a state of mind which supervenes upon human activities. When we are fully committed to and involved in an activity, we take pleasure in it. 'The pleasure perfects the activity' (1174b 23). From this it follows that pleasures take their character from the activities which they complete, and the value of the pleasure will be determined by the value of the activity. If we take pleasure in good activities, the pleasure is good pleasure, but if the activity is bad, the pleasure is bad also. If a person takes pleasure in corrupt and perverse activities, such as crude sensual indulgence, the existence of the pleasure is not an element of positive value in the situation, which could be set against the negative value of the activity. Rather, the very fact that the person takes pleasure in the activity is a measure of how corrupt he or she is, and the pleasure is itself a corrupt pleasure. Therefore pleasure cannot itself function as a criterion of value. We need an independent criterion to determine the value of different kinds of life, and to determine which constitutes genuine happiness, and this criterion can then serve to determine also the value of different kinds of pleasure.

Aristotle, then, shares with Plato a rich conception of happiness, which is distinguished from mere immediate satisfaction of desires. This, and the wider connotations of *eudaimonia*, help Aristotle to treat almost as a truism the claim that the ultimate end of human action is happiness. At I.4 (1095a 17) he says that there is 'pretty general agreement' that the highest good is happiness, and at I.7 (1097b 22) he says that this may look like a platitude. We can appreciate his point, if we think of the assertion as having some of the obviousness of the statement that the ultimate end is well-being.

The crucial step, then, is not the introduction of happiness as the ultimate end, but the assumption which is prior to this and which Aristotle does not even question—the assumption that human action is to be understood in terms of ends and means. This is baldly stated in the first sentence of the

Ethics: 'Every art and every investigation, and similarly every action and pursuit, is considered to aim at some good.' No argument is offered. And once this framework of ends and means is presupposed, the stage is already set for the idea that if we want to know what the highest *good* is, we have to ask, 'What is the ultimate *end* of human action, what is it that all our actions finally *aim* at?'

There are two aspects of the relation between happiness and the ends/means framework which need to be clarified, both because Aristotle is liable to misrepresentation on these two points and because he is himself somewhat confused on them. In the first place, it is important to notice that Aristotle is *not* saying that happiness is the *only* thing which is an end in itself, and that everything else which human beings desire is desired as a means to happiness. That thesis has been maintained by other philosophers and is therefore easily read into the *Ethics*, but is not Aristotle's position. In I.7, at 1097b1, he says of happiness that

> we always choose it for itself, and never for any other reason. It is different with honour, pleasure, intelligence and good qualities generally. We do choose them partly for themselves (because we should choose each one of them irrespectively of any consequences); but we choose them also for the sake of our happiness, in the belief that they will be instrumental in promoting it.

Here it is quite clear that, according to Aristotle, honour, pleasure, intelligence, and the virtues are all aimed at for their own sake, and that he therefore recognizes a plurality of things which are all good in themselves.

What is also clear from the passage, however, is that he wants to give happiness a special status within this plurality. What are his grounds for doing so? Honour, pleasure, intelligence, and the virtues are, he says, not only aimed at as ends in themselves, but are also aimed at for the sake of happiness, whereas happiness is never pursued for the sake of anything else. And because these other things are both ends and means, whereas happiness is never a means to anything else, Aristotle claims that this makes it a 'more final' end (1097a 30), and thus the supreme good.

The argument is, however, a *non sequitur*. The fact that intelligence, for instance, *can* be desired as a means to happiness, in no way shows that when it *is* desired as an end in itself, it is at all inferior to happiness as an end. This would be equivalent to saying that because people enjoy drinking both milk and Coca Cola, and also drink milk (but not Coca Cola) for its additional nutritional benefits, it follows that they enjoy milk less than Coca Cola. That would be nonsense, but Aristotle's own argument is no more respectable than that. So far, then, he has not shown that honour, pleasure, intelligence, and the virtues are at all inferior or subordinate to happiness. If he had recognized this, and had given all these things a place in the good life in their own right, independent of happiness, he might have ended up with a significantly different account of the good life.

To deal with this difficulty, Aristotle could perhaps invoke another remark which he makes in the same chapter—and this is the second point that needs to be clarified. Still speaking of happiness, he says: 'What is more, we regard it as the most desirable of all things, not reckoned as one item among many; if it were so reckoned, happiness would obviously be more desirable by the addition of even the least good, because the addition makes the sum of goods greater . . .' (1097b 16–19). The key phrase here is 'not reckoned as one item among many'. This seems to mean that happiness is not to be regarded as one more good thing in the same list as honour, pleasure, intelligence, and the various virtues. Rather, happiness is a good in so far as it is that of which all the other goods are constituents. It is not a separate good from them; they are the things which go to make up happiness. This would provide a way of making sense of the claim that happiness is 'more final', and is therefore the 'supreme' good. The idea would be that happiness is more basic than the other goods, not as being something better of the same kind, but as being the framework into which the various particular goods fit.

To illustrate the point further, compare the case of having or lacking a meaning in one's life. Suppose someone says, 'I thought I had everything I wanted—a well-paid job, a lovely family, a nice house—but none of it seems to make sense, it all seems meaningless'. In wanting to have a meaning in his life, such a person is not looking for one more item of the same order as all the others, as though he should say 'I've got the job, I've got the family, I've got the house, all I need now is the meaning.' What he wants is that all the other things should add up to something, that they should fit together in a coherent way which would endow them all with real value. And this, perhaps, is how Aristotle likewise sees happiness, as the shape or pattern into which the various items fall.

Such an idea might also assist Aristotle in a further respect. When he says that happiness is the highest good, he means, of course, *one's own* happiness. For any human agent, the ultimate end must necessarily be that person's own happiness. This presents Aristotle with the problem of what significance to give to our relations to other people. Is the fulfilment of our obligations to others, or the exhibiting of concern for others, not a good in itself? I shall look more closely at this question in the next chapter, but for the moment we can simply note that the concept of happiness as an overall framework might help. It would enable Aristotle to say that our relations to others are *constituents* of our own happiness, and this might seem more satisfactory than saying that our relations to others are merely *means* to our own happiness.

The Human Function

We have seen that for Aristotle the identification of happiness as the highest good is something of a truism. The more important task, he thinks, is to find out what happiness consists in, and his answer forms the second step in the three-stage argument. He sets out to show that happiness consists in acting in accordance with reason, and he does so by appealing to the idea of the *function* of a human being. Just as a good sculptor or a good carpenter is one who succeeds in performing the proper function of a sculptor or carpenter, so also we can determine what a good human life is by looking for the function of a human being. Do human beings, then, have a function? Yes, says Aristotle, for 'just as we can see that eye and hand and foot and every one of our members has some function, should we not assume that in like manner a human being has a function over and above these particular functions?' (1097b 30.) To determine what this function is, we have to look at what is *distinctive* of human beings. Life is something shared by all plants and animals, so the proper function of a human being cannot be mere biological survival and growth. Nor can it be a mere life of sensations, for this is shared by animals of all kinds. What is distinctive of the human species is the possession of reason, and the exercise of this must therefore be the proper function of a human being.

To many of Aristotle's modern readers, the idea of a 'human function' has seemed very implausible. His analogies fail to convince. Sculptors or carpenters have a function because they are the occupants of social roles, and the functions which attach to these roles are defined by the institutional arrangements of an organized society. Being a human being, however, is not just a matter of filling a social role, nor is the human race an organized society. It may be that we all fill social roles, but we are not, as human beings, fully defined by them. The analogy with bodily organs fares no better. An eye or a hand or a foot has a function because it belongs within a system of interdependent parts, which is the human organism. There is, however, no corresponding organism of which human beings are all parts. The only plausible candidate for such an organism would be a human society, considered as a system of interdependent roles. That, however, simply takes us back to the previous analogy. It might help to strengthen the view that as members of society we have functions, but not that as human beings we have functions.

A third possible analogy which Aristotle could have utilized would be the analogy with artefacts. A knife or a chair has a function, a good knife is one which cuts, and a good chair is one which is comfortable to sit in. Again, however, the analogy with a human being fails. The counter-argument has been forcibly stated by the modern French philosopher Jean-Paul Sartre, in his lecture 'Existentialism and Humanism'. 'If', says Sartre, 'one considers an article of manufacture—as, for example, a book or a paper-knife—one sees that it has been made by an artisan who had a conception of it . . . Thus the paper-knife is at the same time an article producible in a certain manner and one which, on the other hand, serves a definite purpose, for one cannot suppose that a man would produce a paper-knife without knowing what it was for.'[1]

Now a human being, Sartre thinks, can analogously be thought of as exist-ing for a purpose only if he is likewise the product of a divine artisan. If that were the case, God as artisan would define the purpose and create human beings to serve it. If, on the other hand, there is no God, the analogy is no longer available. Human beings are then free to choose what they will be and what purposes they will recognize. There can be no pre-given purpose which human beings exist to serve.

Sartre here implies that within a theistic context the notion of a human function or purpose might indeed make sense. This possible development of Aristotelian ethics was in fact taken up by Catholic theology, most notably by the medieval philosopher Thomas Aquinas. It then becomes the basis of a so-called 'natural law' morality. Two examples will illustrate the role of 'function' in Catholic morality. Since human beings have been created by God to live and to perpetuate their own being, suicide is wrong. And since human beings have been given sexuality in order to reproduce and perpetuate the species, contra-ception, frustrating this proper purpose of sexuality, is wrong. In each of these examples, the appeal is to a purpose with which human beings have been endowed by God, and the violation of which is therefore held to be morally wrong.

The Christian version, then, is a possible way of retaining Aristotle's notion of a human function. Even then, however, there are problems. It is not clear how we are to identify, from among all the possible purposes which human beings and their capacities can serve, those which are their proper and natural purposes. No doubt the proper purposes of human beings are those for which they are intended by God, but how do we tell which those are (other than by appealing to revelation)? To take the case of sexuality, human beings undeni-ably *can* employ sexuality for purposes of sheer pleasure; why then is not that, but reproduction, held to be the 'natural' purpose of sexuality?

Some philosophers have defended Aristotle by suggesting that the word 'function' is not the appropriate translation of the Greek term *ergon*. The latter means literally 'work' or 'task'. Therefore, it has been said, Aristotle is not claiming that human beings have a 'function' (which would require the improper analogy with social roles, or organs, or artefacts), but simply that they have something like a 'characteristic activity'. This, however, will not suf-fice as a defence, for the difficulty lies not just in the concept of 'function', but in the general pattern of argument which underlies it. The premise of that argument is that a certain kind of activity is *distinctive* of the human species, and the conclusion of the argument is that that kind of activity is the *best* for human beings. We may doubt whether Aristotle can infer the conclusion from the premise via the concept of 'function', but if we deprive him of that concept, the problem still remains whether there is any other way in which he can get from the premise to the conclusion. Replacing the concept of 'function' with that of 'characteristic activity' is no solution; indeed it leaves the argument even more obviously incomplete, for the problem is precisely that of showing why the fact that an activity is 'distinctively' or 'characteristically' human is any reason for engaging in it. It is distinctive of us as human beings that we are the only species capable of destroying all life on this planet, by means of a nuclear war, but that is no reason why we should do it. Why, then, from the fact that rational activity is distinctively human, should it follow that we ought to live according to reason?

I want to mention one other criticism which has been directed at Aristotle's concept of the 'human function'. In this case, however, not only do I consider the criticism invalid, but I think that by looking at it we can begin to discover what is of positive value in Aristotle's position. The criticism is an *ad hominem* one. It points to the fact that Aristotle, as well as recognizing a human function, ascribes a characteristic function also to women and to slaves. In his *Politics* (Book I Ch. 5) he claims that some human beings are slaves by nature. Rationality is distinctive of all human beings, but natural slaves possess it in a lesser degree, and so likewise do women, since their distinctive functions also are different. The proper function of women is to obey men. And the proper function of natural slaves is to obey those who are by nature masters, since the former possess sufficient reason to understand rational principles, but not to formulate them for themselves. For Aristotle, then, the fully human life can be lived only by the free-born male citizen.

That is what the concept of a 'natural function' leads to—or so, at least, Aristotle's critics would claim. From these examples, they would say, we can see that the concept serves to legitimate the functions assigned to human beings, and to particular groups of human beings, in particular societies. The so-called natural function is really a specific social role, treated as though it were sacrosanct and eternal.

Does Aristotle's idea of a human function, however, inevitably have to commit him to such a view of women and of slaves? I think not. The very same concept could have been used by him to criticize the existing roles of these groups. Women and slaves, he could have said, are human beings with distinctively human capacities. It is therefore quite wrong that they should be assigned to roles which prevent them from realizing these capacities. In treating them as fit only to obey, we are treating human beings as less than fully human. Now of course, Aristotle does not say this. The point is, however, that his ethical vocabulary could lend itself as readily to this as to what he in fact does say. The concept of a fully and distinctively human life does not have to legitimate existing social roles, it can equally well serve as a socially critical concept.

Moreover, not only is it the case that Aristotle *could* have argued in this way. It is also the case that we might well *want* to argue in this way. The fact that a certain kind of life is 'less than fully human' might well be a valid reason for criticizing the fact that people either choose or are compelled to live such a life.

The idea at work here is that if people are unable to make full use of their distinctively human capacities, their lives are thereby impoverished. Notice further that the critical force of this idea may hold good, even if the person concerned is content with such a life. If someone's life is taken up with the menial tasks of a slave, or with the mindless and mechanical operations of the modern production line, or the kitchen sink, then although he or she may acquiesce in or even have come to enjoy such a life, we might still want to describe it as dehumanized. The concept of a fully human life is, therefore, closely bound up with the Platonic and Aristotelian conception of genuine happiness as more than a sum of immediate satisfactions.

I do not think that Aristotle has adequately worked out such a concept. In due course we shall have to consider what more can be made of it, and we shall look at alternative versions offered by Mill and by others. Something more is needed than the bald Aristotelian argument that because a certain activity is distinctively human, it is therefore constitutive of a good human life; nor does the concept of 'function' render the argument any more valid. What more is needed, we shall have to decide.

The Doctrine of the Mean

I turn now to the third stage in Aristotle's overall argument. Having claimed that the highest good is happiness, and having attempted to link happiness with the idea of acting in accordance with reason, Aristotle now has to analyse the traditional virtues, such as courage and moderation, as various forms of action in accordance with reason. With this step he will have completed his attempt to show that the life of the traditional virtues is the best kind of life.

This third step takes the form of Aristotle's celebrated 'doctrine of the mean'. Virtue, he says, consists in observing the mean between excess and deficiency, and this idea of 'following the mean' is the particular sense which we should give to the requirement of acting in accordance with reason. The doctrine is introduced in Book II, in a preliminary way in Chapter 2, and then more substantially in Chapters 6 to 9. It is applied to the analysis of the particular moral virtues in Books III and IV, and a cursory attempt is also made to apply it to the virtue of justice in Book V (at 1133b 30).

The doctrine of the mean has been popularly and superficially understood as a counsel of moderation. It is supposed that the people who observe the mean are the people who never exhibit strong emotions and who never go to extremes. They will never be greatly elated, nor greatly dejected. They will never fall violently in love nor out of love. They will never show great enthusiasm for any object or enterprise, but neither will they show any great aversion. In political life they will define their position as midway between the main contending parties. In everything they will observe a sober caution.

Many of Aristotle's more philosophical commentators have protested against this popular reading. The doctrine of the mean is not, they say, a doctrine of moderation, and Aristotle is not saying that we should never feel anything strongly. They would point especially to II.6, at 1106a 26, where Aristotle distinguishes between 'the mean in relation to the thing' and 'the mean in relation to us'. The 'mean in relation to the thing' would be a mid-point between the available extremes. If, for example, we had to choose a portion of food, and the biggest portion available was ten pounds, and the smallest was two pounds, then to aim at the mean in relation to the thing would be to choose a six pound portion. Therefore if Aristotle were advocating that we should always observe the mean in relation to the thing, the popular reading would be correct. However, Aristotle is emphatic that this is not what he is advocating. He is saying that we should observe the mean in relation to us. How, then, are we to understand this? Aristotle explains:

> It is possible, for example, to feel fear, confidence, desire, anger, pity, and pleasure and pain generally, too much or too little; and both of these are wrong. But to have these feelings at the right times on the right grounds towards the right people for the right motive and in the right way is to feel them to an intermediate, that is to the best, degree; and this is the mark of virtue. (1106b 18–23)

To observe the mean in this sense will not necessarily involve always choosing a mid-point, for sometimes the right way to feel anger, or fear, or whatever will be to feel it very strongly. In some circumstances, feeling a moderate degree of anger, to the extent that one is moved to raise one's voice, may be to feel too much anger, but in other circumstances the same degree of anger may be too little. It all depends on the circumstances, and all that the principle of 'the mean in relation to us' requires us to do is to exhibit the degree of anger appropriate to the circumstances.

The trouble is that the doctrine now begins to seem vacuous. When, we might ask Aristotle, should I feel fear? His answer is: at the right time. For what reasons? On the right grounds. Towards whom? Towards the right people. The principle of 'the mean in relation to the thing', as a principle of moderation, would at least have given us a significant answer to the questions. We therefore have the following dilemma. The doctrine of moderation seems unattractive and implausible, but it is at least a substantial doctrine, and we know what it would be to follow it. On the other hand the doctrine of the mean, in its proper Aristotelian sense, may appear to be acceptable only at the cost of saying nothing substantial at all. Let us therefore see if we can, after all, give rather more substance to it.

I take the doctrine to be a thesis about the proper relation between reason and feeling. I use the word 'feeling' widely, to include emotions, desires, and inclinations in general. In concentrating on feelings I may seem to be misrepresenting Aristotle, who says that the mean applies to both feelings and actions

(1106b 16–17). His subsequent discussion, however, suggests that it is intended to apply to actions in so far as they are themselves expressions of feelings. That, at any rate, I regard as the most fruitful way of interpreting him. On this interpretation, then, an action which accords with the mean will be an action which is an expression of feelings which accord with the mean.

Now, the first and most basic point which Aristotle is making is that in so far as our actions are expressions of our feelings, the difference between right and wrong actions is very much a matter of degree. The judgement that an action is wrong will not typically be a qualitative judgement, to the effect that the action expresses a wholly improper kind of feeling. Rather, it will be a quantitative judgement, to the effect that the action expresses a feeling which, though acceptable enough if felt to the right degree, is in the present context excessive or deficient. Basic human feelings such as fear, pleasure, generosity, pride, ambition, and anger cannot, according to Aristotle, be called wrong in themselves, but only if they are felt to the wrong degree. Thus to say that, in the matter of actions and feelings, what is right is the mean, is, at the very least, to make the negative point that what is wrong is excess and deficiency.

To indicate the fuller significance of Aristotle's position, however, I want to contrast it with two other views of the relation between feeling and reason. The first of these is Plato's discussion of the relations between the parts of the soul. I say 'Plato's', but in fact his position is ambiguous. In general, as we have seen, Plato thinks that the proper relation between reason and feeling is that reason should rule, and the feelings should obey. Aristotle says the same (at the end of Book I, at 1102b 30–1). To bring out the contrast between them, therefore, we need to clarify what each of them means by this formulation. The general picture we get from Plato is that the rule of reason consists in reason checking and inhibiting the feelings. This, however, is where the ambiguity emerges, for it is not clear whether he wants to urge the inhibition of *all* the feelings by reason, and certainly, as we saw, he sometimes recognizes that reason has its own characteristic emotions and desires. But the physical desires, at any rate, need to be firmly repressed, and the overall impression we obtain from the *Republic* is of a fundamental opposition between reason and feeling. They are, respectively, the man and the beast in us, and the man must tame and control the beast.

As a contrast with Plato, consider the views of D. H. Lawrence. Lawrence is even more wayward and ambiguous than Plato, and I shall have to oversimplify again. But at least sometimes, Lawrence presents the proper relation between reason and feeling as this: that reason should keep out of the way, and leave room for the free and entirely spontaneous expression of the feelings.

Let us call these two views the 'Platonic' position and the 'Lawrentian' position, and let us retain the inverted commas to signal that we may not be doing justice to Plato or to Lawrence. Plato may not have been 'Platonic' and

Lawrence may not have been 'Lawrentian', but other people have been, and the two positions are recognizable ones. Common to them both is the idea of a necessary antagonism between reason and feeling. Either reason must check the feelings, or it must yield to them; one or the other must give way. I want to suggest that we can usefully see Aristotle as questioning the necessity of this antagonism. For Aristotle, feelings can themselves be the embodiment of reason. It is not just a matter of reason controlling and guiding the feelings. Rather, the feelings can *themselves* be more or less rational. Reason can *be present in them*.

What does it mean to say that feelings can be more or less rational? Essentially it is a matter of their being more or less appropriate to the situation. Take the case of anger. Suppose I become furious because someone fails to say hello to me. I fly off the handle, in a way which is quite inappropriate, and entirely out of keeping with such a cause. Here my anger is irrational. Suppose, in another case, that I become furious because I see a gang of children heartlessly taunting and bullying a younger child. Here my anger may be quite appropriate; the cause may be genuinely appalling. In these two cases, then, my anger is irrational and rational respectively.

To speak of, and to advocate 'rational anger' may sound excessively intellectualist. Notice carefully, however, what is meant here. It is not that my anger is the product of an independent rational decision. I do not first ask myself what my response should be, reflect on and assess the situation, and then decide to become angry. My anger may be entirely immediate and automatic. Nevertheless, my feelings may be rational in the sense that they are sensitive to the real nature of the situation. They are not, for instance, distorted by extraneous considerations, as they might have been in the first example. It might have happened, perhaps, that I had had a row with my family before leaving home, and that this was why I vented my anger on the poor unfortunate who failed to greet me. I would then be insensitive to the real nature of the occurrence, in treating it as an occasion for anger. In contrast, it is when my feelings are not blinded and distorted in this sort of way that they can be said to be sensitive to the situation. And it is in this sense that they are rationally appropriate.

This, I think, is what Aristotle is referring to when he says that observing the mean is having feelings on the right occasion, for the right reason, to the right degree, and towards the right person. Aristotle's ideal is that of the rational emotional life. And we can perhaps accept a limited sense in which it is a doctrine of moderation. Not only does it involve the avoidance of whatever would on the particular occasion be an excess or a deficiency. It could also, at the general level, be described as a position intermediate between the 'Platonic' ideal of reason inhibiting and checking the feelings and the 'Lawrentian' ideal of non-rational emotional spontaneity. In another sense, however, it is not a mid-point between these two positions, but is fundamentally opposed to both of them, since it rejects their shared assumption of a necessary antagonism between reason and feeling.

This still leaves the problem: how are we to tell where the mean lies? How can we know when, and to what degree, and on what grounds to feel anger, or fear, or pleasure, or whatever? Aristotle's only answer appears to be: we should feel these things as and when a good person would feel them. He says: 'So virtue is a purposive disposition, lying in a mean that is relative to us and determined by a rational principle, and by that which a prudent man would use to determine it' (1106b 36—the word 'prudent' here translates the Greek *phronimos*, meaning a possessor of practical wisdom). This does not look much more helpful. It seems open to an obvious circularity since the *phronimos* is the person who gives the right answers, and the right answers are those which are given by the *phronimos*. Why does Aristotle nevertheless think that this is sufficient, and that we neither need nor can say more than this?

For answer we must look to his theory of moral knowledge. Practical wisdom or moral knowledge is what Aristotle calls *phronesis*, the kind of knowledge possessed by the *phronimos*. We have previously seen that Aristotle emphasizes the difference between practical and theoretical knowledge. The essential feature of practical knowledge is that it is concerned with particulars, not with universals. To possess it is to know what to do here and now. It is not a matter of appealing to rules and general principles, not a matter of logical argument or intellectual ability. It consists simply in knowing, in a particular situation: this is what I should do.

How is this knowledge acquired? From practical experience and by habituation (II. 1). What Aristotle means, I think, is this. One's moral education consists in being told in particular situations that one's behaviour is appropriate or inappropriate. On one occasion one may be told 'You lost your temper too easily, your anger was out of all proportion to the situation'. On another occasion one may be told 'You reacted much too meekly, you shouldn't take things lying down'. In this way one builds up an intuitive sense of when, and to what extent, anger is appropriate. Now, a crucial point is that the matters about which one acquires this sense are very much matters of degree. This is why one cannot formulate any precise rules about them. It is impossible to say in any very informative way what the different degrees of anger are, and how severe a situation has to be to warrant them. (The impossibility will, I think, be apparent to anyone who tries to do it.) The same goes for the other emotions. Nevertheless, one can come to know when and how far to feel anger, or fear, or pleasure, or pride. This is why Aristotle thinks it impossible and unnecessary to say any more than that the mean is 'at the right time, to the right degree, on the right grounds and towards the right person', and that the standard is fixed by the *phronimos*. The knowledge which enables us to understand this is acquired not by learning theoretical principles, but by moral training, by being properly brought up in a morally civilized community.

This, then, is Aristotle's picture of the life of reason. However, I should add that at the very end of the *Ethics* a completely new picture suddenly emerges. Throughout most of the work we are given the impression that the life of reason is what I have called 'the rational emotional life', the life guided by *phronesis*. Then, at X.7, we are abruptly told that the highest happiness will consist in rational activity in a quite different sense, namely the activity of intellectual contemplation. This ability does not belong in the everyday social world where the moral virtues have their place. It is pursued in retreat from that world, in the lonely splendour of the philosopher. The two pictures can, if we wish, be made formally consistent with one another. The life of the moral virtues is the fully human life, and that is why Aristotle devotes most of his attention to it, whereas the contemplative life is more properly divine than human, and only a few can attain to it. Nevertheless the switch is disconcerting.

I believe that the strength of both Plato and Aristotle lies in their attempt to work out a naturalistic ethics, based on an understanding of human nature. This leads them both to offer an account of the psychological foundations of the traditional virtues, and to formulate this in terms of the relations between the different aspects of the personality. Aristotle's version I take to be the more acceptable, incorporating as it does a more satisfactory understanding of the relation between reason and feeling. Each of them uses his psychological theory to forge a link between the virtues and happiness, and each of them produces a subtle and suggestive account of what constitutes happiness.

This whole approach common to Plato and Aristotle has nevertheless met with certain fundamental criticisms. I shall consider these in the next chapter.

Note

1. Jean-Paul Sartre, *Existentialism and Humanism*, trans. Philip Mairet (London, 1948), 26.

4

Egoism and Altruism

Prichard's Objection

The central enterprise upon which Plato and Aristotle are engaged is the attempt to show that the traditionally good and virtuous way of life is one which we have reason to follow, since it is the happiest and most fulfilling. It has been argued by some philosophers that the whole enterprise is in fact radically misconceived. A classic statement of this criticism can be found in H. A. Prichard's 1928 lecture, 'Duty and Interest'.[1] Prichard's central argument is this: if justice is advocated on the grounds that it is advantageous to the just person, it is thereby reduced to a form of self-interest. In that case it will not really be *justice* that we are advocating. The just person—the morally good person as conventionally understood—is someone who keeps his promise simply because he has promised, who pays his debt simply because he owes it, who refrains from lying simply because it would be dishonest. He is essentially different from someone who does these things because it will make him happier or better off. Therefore, if Plato or Aristotle were to succeed in persuading someone to be 'just' or 'virtuous' because he would thereby be happier, he might induce him to perform the appropriate actions, but would not really have made him into a morally good and just person.

Prichard's argument is formulated in terms of the concept of 'duty'. For Prichard, duty is not really duty unless it is done for duty's sake. The same criticism could be reformulated, just as powerfully, in terms not of 'duty' but of 'altruism'. Within our own moral culture, largely as a product of the Christian tradition, an altruistic concern for others is widely held to be a, or even the, supreme value. If, however, in caring for other people, I do so because I think that it will make my own life happier, then it would seem that it is not really a concern for others which motivates me, but a concern for myself. From the above standpoint, the action then ceases to be morally admirable.

Notice exactly what is being claimed here. It is not being suggested that Plato and Aristotle exclude altruistic qualities from the good life, and advocate a selfish disregard for the interests of others. That would be the position of someone like Thrasymachus. We have seen that, for Plato, justice is essentially an altruistic virtue requiring respect for others' interests, loyalty to one's parents and friends and country, the honouring of one's promises and agreements, and so forth. Justice likewise figures in Aristotle's list of the virtues, as does generosity. Aristotle also has a lengthy discussion of friendship, and gives concern for one's friends a central place in the good life. So the criticism is not that Plato and Aristotle exclude altruisim. It is that, because they justify it by reference to the agent's own happiness, they reduce it to a kind of enlightened self-interest, and so deprive it of its moral value.

This is likely to be seen as a searching criticism. And yet it also seems very plausible to defend altruism in the manner of Plato and Aristotle. For, surely it just is the case that a life lived in harmony and co-operation with others, sharing sympathetically in their hopes and sorrows, is the most fulfilling and rewarding. Is it not a basic fact of human experience that a life of mutual aid and consideration is more satisfying than one of hostility and enmity? And if so, is this not as good a reason as one could require for living such a life? We are thus faced with a dilemma between what look like two equally persuasive positions, that of Prichard on the one hand and that of Plato and Aristotle on the other. Can the dilemma be resolved?

We might begin to resolve it by emphasizing how the Platonic and Aristotelian position differs from the view presented by Glaucon and Adeimantus in *The Republic*. Glaucon and Adeimantus, it will be recalled, suggest that most people regard justice as a sort of mutual insurance policy. In this view, to live justly is not advantageous *in itself*, but it does have desirable *consequences* for the agent, since he earns the goodwill of others (not to mention that of the gods). This, then, is the popular view, but Glaucon and Adeimantus are dissatisfied with it. They ask Socrates to demonstrate that justice is a good to the just person, not simply in virtue of the consequences, but in its very nature. This is what Socrates in *The Republic* proceeds to do. The position is, of course, Plato's own, and it is also in its broad character that of Aristotle, who likewise claims not that the virtues are *means* to happiness, but that 'happiness *is* an activity of the soul in accordance with perfect virtue' (*Ethics* I.13, my italics). I shall refer to the two opposed positions as 'Glaucon's view' (although Glaucon himself does not advocate it), and 'the Socratic view' (which is shared by Plato and Aristotle).

According to Glaucon, then, justice is a good to the just man, because if you act justly towards others they will act justly towards you, and so you will be better off. According to the Socratic view, justice does not simply have advantageous consequences, it is *itself* the greatest benefit. For Glaucon, justice is an *instrumental* good; it enables you to get what you need in order to live well. For the Socratic view, justice is an *intrinsic* good; it *is* living well. According to Glaucon, then, there is an *external* relation between justice and benefit. According to the Socratic view, the relation is an *internal* one.

A further important difference follows. In Glaucon's account, justice is recommended in the light of a preconceived idea of what happiness consists in, what the agent's proper interests are. We are presumed already to have an idea of what happiness is—it is, perhaps, the acquisition of wealth and the wielding of power, and the like—and the argument proceeds on that assumption. In the Socratic account, no such idea of happiness, of the agent's interests, is assumed. On the contrary, happiness is itself re-defined in the course of the argument. If we are convinced by the Socratic account, then, in the light of our understanding of justice, we are brought to change our idea of happiness. Thus, for Glaucon, we first know what our interests are, and then come to see how justice contributes to them. For Plato and Aristotle, we must first understand what justice is, and only then can we come to see what our true interests are.

Plato's own analysis of Glauconian virtue comes in Book VIII of the *Republic*, in the account of the oligarchic personality. The person who acts justly, as an external means to his own self-interest, is there said to be ruled by desire rather than by reason. The desires which would lead him to cheat and steal and harm others are simply held in check by other desires which are equally self-interested. His is the 'shopkeeper' morality, the ethic of 'Honesty is the best policy':

> the high reputation for honesty which he has in other business transactions is due merely to a certain respectable constraint which he exercises over his evil impulses, for fear of their effect on his concerns as a whole. There's no moral conviction, no taming of desires by reason, but only the compulsion of fear. . . . This sort of man, then, is never at peace with himself, but has a kind of dual personality, in which the better desires on the whole master the worse. . . . He therefore has a certain degree of respectability, but comes nowhere near the real goodness of an integrated and united character. (554c–e)

Aristotle does not employ the vocabulary of 'health' and 'illness', but he too appeals to the psychological facts. Like Plato, he analyses the virtues in terms of the right relation between reason and feeling. He argues that the happiest and most fulfilling life is that of the person in whom this right relation obtains, because he will be living the fully human life of reason.

I think that when the Platonic and Aristotelian position is properly spelled out in this way, and clearly distinguished from the Glauconian position, Prichard's criticism loses a good deal of its force. That objection seems persuasive largely because we feel that if someone treats others as *means* to his own happiness, then however much this may lead him to respect their interests, his attitude towards them can hardly be described as an altruistic one. Rather, it is an instrumental attitude to others. If Plato and Aristotle, however, are presenting a proper concern for others as *constitutive* of one's own happiness, their account of the altruistic virtues may appear no more suspect than the altruism of one who simply enjoys helping others.

Moral Egoism

Nevertheless there remain difficulties, and I think that they can be brought out if we consider the following example. Suppose that someone, perhaps a neighbour of mine, is in trouble and needs help; he needs, perhaps, someone to talk to, with whom to share his troubles, and from whom to ask advice. Suppose now that I put to myself the question: why should I help him? The Glauconian answer would be: 'By helping him, you will put him in your debt and increase the chances that he may help you some day, and you will improve your reputation in the eyes of others so that they too will be well disposed towards you.' Such an answer exhibits a purely instrumental attitude to the other person. It is not an attitude of genuine concern for him, but one which regards him simply as a means to one's own benefit. The Platonic and Aristotelian answer would be: 'I should help him because a life of sympathetic concern for others is the most rewarding and fulfilling kind of life.' This, as I have been stressing, is an importantly different answer. It does not represent, in the same kind of way, an instrumental attitude to the other person. But now contrast it with a third possible answer: 'Because he needs help'. This answer is different again. And when we compare it with the second answer, we must surely agree that it is this, the third answer, that represents most fully the attitude of genuine responsiveness to the other's needs. As such, it suggests that there is still something unsatisfactory about the Platonic and Aristotelian answer.

These remaining doubts may be strengthened if we look particularly at some of Aristotle's discussions of particular virtues. Consider this description of the person who exhibits liberality (i.e. generosity at the individual level):

> He will avoid giving to any and everybody, so that he may have something to give to the right people at the right time and in circumstances in which it is a fine thing to do. (IV.1. 1120b 3–4)

Clearly the motivation which Aristotle envisages in such a person is not that he wants to make sure that the right people get the help they need, but that he wants to ensure that he himself has the best opportunities to exhibit generosity. We find something very similar in Aristotle's account of the so-called 'great-souled' or 'magnanimous' person, whose virtue has seemed peculiarly offensive to many modern readers.

> The magnanimous man does not take petty risks, nor does he court danger, because there are few things that he values highly; but he takes great risks, and when he faces danger he is unsparing of his life, because to him there are some circumstances in which it is not worth living. He is disposed to confer benefits, but is ashamed to accept them, because the one is the act of a superior, and the other the act of an inferior. When he repays a service he does so with interest, because in this way the original benefactor will become his debtor and beneficiary. (IV.3 1124b 6–12)

It appears that he will reserve his courage not for when it is most needed but for when he can be most courageous, and he will regard the activities of giving and receiving, and of paying one's debts, as a veritable competition in virtue. Think back to our previous three-way comparison. Aristotle's virtuous individual does not cultivate the altruistic virtues as means to his own interests. He cultivates them for their own sake. But he cultivates them very much *as states of himself*, and in this he is in marked contrast with the third of the three individuals we imagined. He is preoccupied with himself, he focuses on the sort of person he wants to be, instead of focusing on the needs of the other person and responding to them in their own right. He is not an egoist in a straightforward sense, but he exhibits what we might call a kind of 'moral egoism'.

Part of the trouble here is Aristotle's emphasis on *ends*, which I noted in the previous chapter. This commits him to saying that, if virtuous activity is not wanted for the sake of further consequences, then it must itself be an end, something which we aim at. This already has the effect of detaching the virtuous activity from the circumstances (including other people's needs) which require it; the circumstances become an opportunity to achieve the end of performing the virtuous activity, instead of the activity being a response to the circumstances. The question then is: can either Plato or Aristotle avoid this, so long as they want to retain the link between virtue and individual happiness? Our own happiness is surely an end; therefore if virtuous activity is constitutive of happiness, and if this is a reason for performing it, do we not have to say of the virtuous activity also that it is an end in itself?—and does this not automatically put us in the position of 'moral egoism' which I have been ascribing to Aristotle?

There is one way in which we might try to avoid it, and might retain *both* the idea of one's own happiness *and* the idea of other people's needs as reasons for altruistic activity. We might do this by distinguishing between two levels of reason-giving. We could perhaps distinguish between the question, 'What action should I perform (here and now)?', and the question, 'What kind of life should I lead?' What makes these distinct? Consider the circumstances in which I might put the second question to myself. I might come to be struck by the narrowness of my life, by the extent to which I am preoccupied with myself, and to which my experience is thereby impoverished. I might decide that I need to think consciously about being more attentive to others, and giving more play to my own sympathetic responses. My reason for trying to change my life in this way might be that my life would thereby be enriched. But the change might involve precisely the cultivation of habits of thinking about others' needs as such, rather than about how my helping them can enrich my own life. In other words, I might become more the sort of person who, on particular occasions, helps others just because they need help.

This distinction between two levels of reasoning may help to make something like a Platonic or Aristotelian position more acceptable. I shall return to it later. For the time being, I want to leave the discussion in this inconclusive state. I have argued that Plato and Aristotle do not reduce the virtues to self-interest in any straightforward and obvious sense. I have also suggested that there is a more subtle and problematic form of egoism to be found in their ethics. Whether this is a ground for criticism of them, is a question which must now wait until we have worked out a clearer view of the whole problem of egoism and altruism, and this will require that in subsequent chapters we do two things.

The Social Dimension

First, we need to look more closely at the *social* dimension of human life. At this point I shall simply assert dogmatically that a satisfactory account of the ethical significance of altruism depends upon a satisfactory treatment of the role of social relations in the life of the individual. In saying this, I am implying that Plato and Aristotle do not provide an entirely adequate treatment. In the case of Plato, there is a profound ambivalence. On the one hand, *The Republic* combines moral philosophy and social philosophy to a quite unusual degree. The account of justice in the individual is paralleled by the account of justice in society, with its lengthy description of the ideal state. The problem, however, is whether the two accounts are ever really integrated with one another. The relation between them is basically one of *analogy*. The account of justice in the individual does not proceed by looking at the individual in a social context, but simply by arguing that, since justice in society must be harmony between the parts of the state, so by analogy justice in the individual must be a harmony between the parts of the personality. What we need to know, however, is not only how the justice of the individual is *analogous to* the structure of society, but how it is actually *affected by* the individual's existence in society. Plato says surprisingly little about this, but he does say something, and his answer would appear to be this. Ordinary people, in whom the rational part of the soul is not very strong or well developed, can in fact achieve justice only in a well-ordered society. In such a society they would make up the economic class, and presumably also the auxiliary class. At the end of Book IX Plato says of them:

> To ensure that people of this type are under the same authority as the highest type, we have said that they should be subjected to that highest type, which is governed by its divine element; but this control is not exercised, as Thrasymachus thought, to the detriment of the subject, but because it is better for every creature to be under the control of divine wisdom. That wisdom and control should, if possible, come from within; failing that it must be imposed from without, in order that, being subject to the same guidance, we may all be brothers and equals. (590c–d)

In other words, if justice means being under the control of reason, and if one's own reason is not strong enough, then the reason of the rulers must do the job instead. For such a person, therefore, justice is possible only in a just society.

What of those whose own reason is powerful enough to play the commanding role? They would, of course, be the guardians in a just society. Could they, however, achieve justice in themselves without filling that social role? Plato's answer is that they could, and that they most probably would have to do so. Book IX concludes with Glaucon suggesting that the good man is unlikely to enter politics, to which Socrates replies:

> 'Oh yes, he will, very much so, in the society where he really belongs; but not, I think, in the society where he's born, unless something very extraordinary happens.'
>
> 'I see what you mean,' he said. 'You mean that he will do so in the society which we have been describing and which we have theoretically founded; but I doubt if it will ever exist on earth.'
>
> 'Perhaps,' I said, 'it is laid up as a pattern in heaven, where those who wish can see it and found it in their own hearts. But it doesn't matter whether it exists or ever will exist; it's the only state in whose politics he can take part.' (592a–b)

Plato is here expressing his doubts about the practical feasibility of the just society, and his confidence that even in its absence it is possible for some individuals to be just. He also thinks, however, that even if such a society could be created, it would add nothing to the justice of the just individuals. They would take on the role of guardians, not in order to complete their own justice, but with reluctance, and solely for the sake of the rest of society. When, in the analogy of the cave, Socrates says that the philosophers must return to the world of the cave, Glaucon protests:

> 'But surely that will not be fair. We shall be compelling them to live a poorer life than they might live.'
>
> 'The object of our legislation,' I reminded him again, 'is not the welfare of any particular class, but of the whole community. . . . You see, then, we shan't be unfair to our philosophers, but shall be quite justified in compelling them to have some care and responsibility for others. . . . But of course, unlike present rulers, they will approach the business of government as an unavoidable necessity.' (519d–520e)

The implication is that the truly just individual does not need society; he can live a just life in any society or in none.

There is something of the same ambivalence in Aristotle. Although the bulk of the *Ethics* envisages the virtues being exercised in society, the introduction of the contemplative life at the end of Book X forms a kind of Platonic postscript. Despite his rejection of Plato's other-worldly metaphysics, Aristotle retained an attraction to the Platonic ideal of the self-sufficient philosopher living the life of the pure intellect. He concedes that:

> the wise man, no less than the just one and all the rest, requires the necessaries of life; but, given an adequate supply of these, the just man also needs people with and towards whom he can perform just actions, and similarly with the temperate man,

the brave man, and each of the others; but the wise man can practise contemplation by himself, and the wiser he is, the more he can do it. No doubt he does it better with the help of fellow-workers; but for all that he is the most self-sufficient of men. (1177a 28–b1)

Neither Plato nor Aristotle, then, does full justice to the place of social relations in the good life. Until we have worked out a more satisfactory account of the nature of our relations with others, we cannot deal adequately with the question of the ethical significance of altruism. I shall return to this suggestion later in the book, and especially in Chapter 8.

The Christian Tradition

The other thing which we have to do in order to deal with the problem of egoism and altruism is to look at the alternative to the Platonic and Aristotelian position, and that means looking at the Christian tradition, and at those ethical philosophies which have been influenced by it. I shall not in this book provide any substantial discussion of Christian ethics, nor indeed of the relation between ethics and religion in general. (My neglect of this area is to be explained partly by limitations of space, and partly by my own religious scepticism.) Nevertheless, it is clear that Christianity places altruism at the centre of the good life. This altruistic morality is formulated directly in, for example, the so-called Golden Rule, 'All things whatsoever ye would that men should do to you, do ye even so to them' (Matt. 7: 12), or in Jesus' commandment 'Thou shalt love thy neighbour as thyself' (Matt. 22: 39).

Even more striking, when seen against the background of Greek ethics, is the positive value which Christianity attaches to qualities such as meekness and humility, in contrast to self-assertion and worldly success. This is a central theme of Jesus' Sermon on the Mount, which begins with the Beatitudes: 'Blessed are the poor in spirit . . . Blessed are they that mourn . . . Blessed are the meek . . .' etc. There is some similarity with Plato here—with the ascetic strand in Plato which advocates a turning away from material goods and physical pleasures, for the higher life of communion with the world of the forms. Christianity and Plato share a 'two worlds' metaphysics, a division between the world of the flesh and the world of the spirit. The contrast with Aristotle, however, is absolute. Consider Jesus' doctrine of non-resistance to evil: that if anyone strikes you on the right cheek you should turn to him the other, and that if anyone would take your coat you should give him your cloak as well (Matt. 5: 38). Of these examples Aristotle would say: here anger is appropriate.

Similarly, contrast the Christian praise of humility and meekness with the qualities of Aristotle's 'great-souled' or 'magnanimous' person. The virtue which the latter exhibits is what we might call self-respect or self-esteem, taking a pride in oneself and one's achievements. It is linked with the virtue of 'truthfulness' (IV.7), by which Aristotle means being honest and open about oneself, acknowledging one's merits as well as one's faults. In Aristotle's ethics there is no room for false modesty.

Which of these two contrasting ethical views is the more acceptable? There is no immediate and obvious answer to the question, and it is not enough simply to consult our culturally-formed prejudices. We have to look at how the two views can be defended, and consider whether those defences can stand up to critical scrutiny. A full assessment of Christian morality is impossible without a consideration of the metaphysics on which it depends, and that is a task beyond the scope of this book. Only against the background of the 'two worlds' view which I have mentioned can one make sense of the idea that worldly success is of no value when set against a timeless spiritual world, and that our object must be to transcend all worldly aspirations so as to bring the soul nearer to God. All I am able to say here is that I cannot accept the metaphysics, and therefore cannot accept the morality which goes with it. (In Chapter 9, when discussing Nietzsche's criticisms of Christian morality, I shall note briefly how these include in their target the interconnections between Christian metaphysics and Christian ethics.[2])

What I do want to consider at length is the broader ethics of altruism which Christianity has fostered. I shall look at it not in a form which ties it to the Christian religion, but as it occurs in subsequent ethical philosophies which bear the imprint of the Christian tradition, and which take something like the Golden Rule, or 'Love thy neighbour as thyself', as the central principle of ethics. The claims of this altruistic morality have to be weighed against those of the Platonic and Aristotelian ethics which, though it does not exclude altruism, assigns the central place to the agent's own happiness. The philosophers whom we shall consider believe that the ethics of altruism can be defended. They defend it, not by appealing to divine revelation, or to a divine command which has to be accepted on authority, but by appealing to human reason and/or experience. Let us see whether they can make good their claim.

Notes

1. Included in H. A. Prichard, *Moral Obligation and 'Duty and Interest'* (London, 1968).
2. Nietzsche's attack on the 'two worlds' view is to be found especially in his *The Twilight of the Idols*. There are English translations in *The Portable Nietzsche*, ed. and trans. Walter Kaufmann (New York, 1954), and in *The Twilight of the Idols and the Anti-Christ*, trans. R. J. Hollingdale (Harmondsworth, 1969).

PART II

The Moderns

5

Hume
Sympathy

Reading: David Hume, *Enquiry Concerning the Principles of Morals*
(first published 1751)

Since there is no uniform system of page numbering, references will be to para-graph numbers, and I suggest that the reader should number the paragraphs in his or her own copy. I shall use roman numerals to refer to Sections of the work, and arabic numerals to refer to the paragraphs within the Sections. For example, 'II.1' means paragraph 1 of Section II. The only Sections to which numbered para-graph references will be given are II, III, V, IX, and Appendices I and III.

An earlier and more difficult presentation of Hume's ethical theory is to be found in Book III of his *A Treatise of Human Nature* (1739), which I shall occasionally mention.

David Hume, the eighteenth-century Scottish philosopher, can hardly be enlisted in the Christian tradition. He was the author of one of the great works of religious scepticism, his *Dialogues Concerning Natural Religion*. A central question of his ethical theory, however, is the one which I posed at the end of the previous chapter, of how a concern for one's own interests is extended by morality into a concern for the interests of others. Hume's answer employs the concept which he variously refers to as 'sympathy', or 'humanity', or 'fellow-feeling', and an examination of this concept will prove a useful point of entry into his moral philosophy.

Virtues and Vices

We need first to avoid certain misunderstandings. Hume does not use the term 'sympathy' in the narrow sense in which it is now commonly used, to mean something like 'compassion' or 'pity'. He means by it a capacity to be moved or affected by the happiness and suffering of others—to be pleased when others prosper, and distressed when others suffer. He insists that sym-pathy, thus understood, is an independent human tendency which exists in its own right.[1] Various of his philosophical predecessors had claimed that sym-pathy was analysable as a form of self-love, and had erected their ethical sys-tems upon that claim.[2] Hume repudiates the claim.

Another possible misunderstanding should also be noted. When Hume discusses the role of sympathy, he is not talking about it as itself a morally admirable quality. He is not concerned to persuade us that we ought to exhibit sympathy or humanity, or even to claim that we do in fact admire it. He is not entirely consistent in his vocabulary, but on the whole when he wants to talk about altruistic qualities as virtues, he uses the term 'benevolence'. 'Sympathy' is not itself the name of a virtue. The terms 'sympathy' and 'humanity' denote not an *object* of moral approval, but the *source* of moral approval. Hume's central claim is that when we ascribe moral praise or blame, that praise or blame derives from an attitude of sympathy. The fact that we feel sympathy towards others is what explains why we judge as we do.

Like Plato and Aristotle, Hume assumes that moral judgements are primarily judgements about virtues and vices. We morally praise people in so far as they exhibit virtues, and blame them in so far as they exhibit vices. Only secondarily are our moral judgements concerned with individual actions. We praise or blame actions because they reveal morally admirable qualities in the agent. The difference from Plato and Aristotle emerges when we look at what Hume counts as virtues. According to Hume, what makes various qualities 'virtues' is that they are useful or agreeable, either to their possessor or to others. He agrees with Plato and Aristotle to this extent, then, that the virtues would not be virtues unless possession of them were in some sense an advantage. It may be a direct advantage—that is, possession of such qualities may be immediately pleasing, in which case he describes the qualities as 'agreeable'; or it may be an indirect advantage—that is, possession of such qualities may help to promote states of affairs which in their turn are pleasurable, and these are the qualities which Hume describes as 'useful'. He parts company from Plato and Aristotle, however, in that he thinks that not only qualities useful or agreeable to their possessor, but also qualities useful or agreeable to others, are regarded as virtues.

Typical examples in Hume's list of virtues are:

Qualities useful to others: benevolence, justice, fidelity.
Qualities useful to their possessor: discretion, industry, frugality, strength of mind, good sense.
Qualities agreeable to their possessor: cheerfulness, magnanimity, courage, tranquillity.
Qualities agreeable to others: politeness, modesty, decency.

Such a list has much in common with those of Plato and Aristotle, but the prominent place given to benevolence marks a decisive shift from the standpoint of the Greeks. Benevolence is given a chapter to itself in the *Enquiry*, and in that chapter Hume remarks that 'the epithets *sociable, good-natured, humane, merciful, grateful, friendly, generous, beneficent*, or their equivalents . . . universally express the highest merit which *human nature* is capable of attaining'. (II.1.) It may be doubted whether Plato and Aristotle would concur with the phrase 'highest merit', and they would certainly disagree with Hume about *why* we regard such qualities as virtues.

Hume, then, thinks that we admire the virtues because we feel sympathy and humanity. Benevolence, for example, is a quality the exercise of which promotes the happiness or well-being of people in general, and because, through sympathy, we take pleasure in this general happiness or well-being, we are led to admire the quality which promotes it. Similarly, industry is a quality which makes for happiness on the part of its possessor, and it is through sympathy with that happiness that we admire industry in those who possess it. The relationship between sympathy and the virtues is, however, not quite as simple as this, and Hume proceeds to add complications. He recognizes that the strength of people's sympathy varies according to circumstances, whereas moral judgements are made (or at least purport to be made) in accordance with fixed and unvarying standards. The same qualities ought to call forth the same judgements of praise and blame, though our level of sympathy may rise or fall. When we contemplate the virtues of someone in a remote time or place, for example, we may be pleased at the thought of the happiness which these virtues helped to produce among his or her fellows, but our sympathy will be much weaker than it would be if we were contemplating the happiness of those close to us. Hume deals with this problem by suggesting that our immediate feelings are 'corrected' by general standards. He sees this adoption of a general point of view as a practical contrivance, whereby human beings are able to communicate more effectively, and introduce a greater degree of uniformity into their judgements.

> Sympathy, we shall allow, is much fainter than our concern for ourselves, and sympathy with persons remote from us much fainter than that with persons near and contiguous; but for this very reason it is necessary for us, in our calm judgements and discourse concerning the characters of men, to neglect all these differences and render our sentiments more public and social . . . The intercourse of sentiments, therefore, in society and conversation, makes us form some general unalterable standard by which we may approve or disapprove of characters and manners. (V.42)

We might reformulate Hume's position as follows. Moral judgements are not a *direct* expression of our feelings of sympathy. Rather, the operation of sympathy enables us to adopt certain *criteria* for the ascription of moral praise and blame, and moral judgements are then made by the application of these criteria.

A further complication is introduced in the case of certain of the virtues, and again the complication involves the further extension of our judgements by general rules. Of the virtues in question, the most important is justice, which Hume discusses in Section III and Appendix III of the *Enquiry*. By 'justice' we are to understand a set of social rules which govern the distribution of the goods which society makes available. Hume assumes that the most effective way of distributing such benefits is to protect all members of society in the enjoyment of whatever property they happen to possess. To act justly, in short, is to respect the property rights of others. In the *Treatise*, Hume had *simply* assumed this. In the *Enquiry* he sees the need to argue against alternative conceptions of justice. It might be felt that justice requires more than the maintenance of property rights, since the existing distribution of property may itself be unjust. Some members of society may own vastly more than others, simply because they happen to have inherited it, or because their property has been augmented by the vagaries of the market. Is this not unjust? Would it not be more just if property were apportioned to people according to what they deserve, or alternatively if it were distributed equally among all the members of a society?

Hume rejects both the idea of 'justice as desert' and that of 'justice as equality' on the grounds of their disutility. Attractive though it may be to reward people as they deserve, 'so great is the uncertainty of merit, both from its natural obscurity and from the self-conceit of each individual, that no determinate rule of conduct would ever result' (III.23). People would never agree about what they deserved, and the result would be chaos. Likewise the pursuit of equality is 'at bottom impracticable', and persistence in it against the odds 'would be extremely pernicious to human society' (III.26). People differ in their talents and abilities. Consequently, they naturally tend towards inequality, and any attempt to obstruct the tendency will either prove futile, or require extremely authoritarian measures to prevent people rising above others. Unjust though it may appear, therefore, the most useful conception of justice is that which guarantees to people what they already have.[3]

What all these conceptions of justice have in common, nevertheless, is that they generate a system of rules for the distribution of social goods. And it is their connection with a system of social rules that gives justice and other similar virtues a special status in Hume's theory. A particular act of justice, taken in isolation, may well have harmful consequences, and a particular act of injustice may have beneficial consequences. If I were to rob the rich and give to the poor, for instance, the rich would scarcely miss what I took from them, and the poor would gain far more than the rich would lose. Nevertheless, though the individual act of theft may be useful, the act is of a kind which, if generally practised, would be extremely harmful. What has to be assessed, according to Hume, is not the individual act but the system as a whole. When we make this assessment we find, according to Hume, that a system of rules which guarantees everyone security of possession is more useful than any alternative system. And this is what entitles us to say that justice, understood as a disposition to respect people's property, is a virtue. In the *Treatise*, Hume had described justice and similar virtues as 'artificial virtues' (in contrast to 'natural virtues') because they presupposed the existence of a set of social conventions. He abandoned this terminology in the *Enquiry*, in order to avoid the other associations which might be invited by a description of justice as 'artificial' or 'unnatural'. Nevertheless, the distinction between 'natural virtues' and 'artificial virtues' remains a useful way of marking the special status which Hume ascribes to the latter.

Hume, then, envisages three stages by which our judgements are extended:

Stage 1. Sympathy induces us to take account of the happiness and suffering of others as well as our own.

Stage 2. General standards correct the operation of sympathy, so that we attach the same moral importance to the happiness or suffering of anyone, ourselves or others, close to us or remote from us.

Stage 3. In some cases we need to take into account not merely the utility of particular acts, but the usefulness to society of a whole system of general rules and conventions.

Each of these three is a move from a limited to a more generalized standpoint. Together they challenge the Platonic–Aristotelian view that one's moral assessments are necessarily made from the standpoint of a concern for one's own well-being. How successful are they? I shall now examine each of them in turn, taking them in the reverse order.

Justice

Hume's account of justice is an example of a position often referred to as 'rule-utilitarianism'. Utilitarianism in general will be the subject of Chapter 7. For the moment it will be sufficient to define utilitarianism as the theory which states that actions are right in so far as they produce happiness or prevent suffering, wrong in so far as they produce suffering or prevent happiness. It differs from Hume's overall ethical theory in applying the utility-test to actions rather than to qualities of the agent.

Utilitarianism itself, however, has its variants, and some utilitarians have wanted to defend the variant known as 'rule-utilitarianism' in contrast to 'act-utilitarianism'. The utilitarian assessment, they say, should be applied not to individual actions but to moral rules. We should ask not 'Which actions will produce the greatest happiness?' but 'What are the moral rules, observance of which would produce the greatest happiness?' We then have a two-tier system of moral justification. Individual actions are to be assessed by asking, 'Is this action in accordance with an acceptable moral rule?' Moral rules in turn are to be assessed by asking, 'Will the observance of this rule produce more happiness than the observance of any alternative rule?' Hume, then, is putting forward essentially the same position when he suggests that the utility of justice resides not in the utility of individual just acts but in the utility of the general system of property-rules.

The question which arises for any two-tier system of moral justification is: can the two tiers really be kept separate? Critics of rule-utilitarianism have argued that they cannot, and the same criticism may, I think, be applied to Hume's account of justice. Consider his admission that someone who stole from the rich in order to give to the poor could, in the particular case, do more good than harm. Hume thinks that the rules of property ought nevertheless to be observed because of the utility of the overall scheme. How might our benevolent thief take issue with Hume?

He might first accuse Hume of assuming that rules must always be very simple and general. Simple rules, he may say, cannot do justice to the complexity of particular situations. If it is normally in the interests of society that property should be respected, but if there are also exceptional circumstances where one can do more good than harm by stealing, then the rules of justice should incorporate the exceptional circumstances as well as the normal case. In place of the simple rule, 'Do not steal', we may need the more complex rule, 'Do not steal unless you are stealing from very rich people who do not need what you take from them, and giving it to poor people who can make much better use of it.' And once we make our moral rules more complex, the gap between general rules and individual acts disappears. However detailed the relevant features of the individual act may be, they can always be incorporated into a rule, albeit a highly complex one. Thus rule-utilitarianism turns out to be indistinguishable from ordinary 'act-utilitarianism', and the two-tier structure collapses.

Hume may reply that our moral rules *ought* to be kept simple and general, and that the reasons for doing so are themselves reasons of utility. If the rules for the protection of property have all sorts of exceptions built into them, the security which they are supposed to provide will vanish. Everyone will regard his or her own case as exceptional, and the discretion which the rules allow will be exploited to the point of chaos.

But now, our objector may say, this argument for keeping rules clear and simple is itself an act-utilitarian one. What is being claimed is that, if the rule against stealing allows for exceptions, any particular agent who is contemplating an act of theft will be biased in his or her own favour, will be incapable of reviewing the consequences accurately and objectively, and will probably end up doing more harm than good. But that is a claim about the consequences of an individual act. Moreover, if it is recognized as such, it may in some circumstances become a debatable claim. There is indeed a risk that people will make exceptions in their own favour, and this is a risk of which I ought to be conscious when I am inclined to regard my own case as exceptional, but if, in a particular case, I can be confident that I have reviewed the circumstances objectively, and that I really will do more good by stealing, ought I not to make the exception and commit the act of theft, even though the necessarily simple rules forbid me to do so?

Not so, Hume will reply, for the question you should put to yourself is not 'What will happen if *I* keep or break the rule?' but, 'What will happen if *people in general* keep or break the rule?' 'The benefit resulting from [virtues such as justice] is not the consequence of every individual single act, but arises from the whole scheme or system concurred in by the whole or the greater part of society' (Appendix III.3). General rules safeguarding property are morally desirable, because if everyone abides by them this will be highly useful to society, and though the consequences of someone's breaking them on a particular occasion might be good, the consequences of a general infraction of them would be disastrous.

If general rules are regarded in this way as rules whose *general* observance would be beneficial, a gap really does open up between the general rule and the individual act. Rule-utilitarianism becomes a genuinely distinct theory, different from act-utilitarianism. But it achieves the distinctness only by leaving it unclear why anyone should accept it. To the question 'What would happen if everyone did that?' there is an obvious answer—'But *not* everyone is doing it.' It is plausible enough that the *actual* consequences of an action should be relevant to whether one ought to perform it. It is quite unclear why the entirely *hypothetical* consequences of innumerable *other* actions should be relevant. It may be true that if people in general disregarded the rule against stealing, security of property would disappear, and social life would break down. But since social life has not broken down, and the property system continues to be perfectly viable, why should I not make use of the fact to do some good by stealing from those who have more than they need?

In short, any rule-utilitarian is caught in the following dilemma. Either the reasons for following a (perhaps complex) rule are simply reasons for performing a certain kind of act, in which case the gap between rule and act disappears, and rule-utilitarianism ceases to be a distinctive theory; or there is a real gap between rule and act, in which case it is quite unclear why one should stick to the system of rules when breaking them can do more good. What Hume needs to explain is how one may come to be *committed* to certain social rules, despite the advantages of breaking the rules on particular occasions. This in turn requires an explanation of how one comes to be committed to the social institution or community whose rules they are. Some more satisfactory account is needed of the relation between the individual and society, and we shall look at a possible source for this in Chapter 8.

General Standards

Let us now revert to Stage Two of Hume's scheme, the correction of sympathy by general standards. Hume, we saw, presents this as a matter of practical convenience: human beings could not converse effectively on moral matters if their judgements reflected the varying strength of their feelings of sympathy. As a factual claim this is unconvincing. Hume is presumably impressed by the fact that our moral language includes not only the direct expression of personal sentiments ('I admire Brutus') but also the impersonal ascription of objective qualities ('Brutus was a good and noble citizen'). But why should we not manage perfectly well with a moral vocabulary confined entirely to the former? There may be good reasons why we need also the language of objective qualities, but Hume does not tell us what these reasons might be. Moreover, even if we do need it, could we not employ such language in a way which mirrored the variability of our feelings? Other areas of discourse operate perfectly well in that way—the language of tastes, for example. One person may say, 'I find cream cakes rather sickly', and another may say, 'I don't find them sickly at all'. The question, 'Are cream cakes *really* sickly?' has no clear sense, in the absence of any 'general unalterable standard' by which it can be answered, but it does not follow that communication has broken down. The person who finds cream cakes sickly will act on that basis, his less sensitive interlocutor will do likewise, and no further problem need arise. If ease of communication is the only consideration, I do not see why moral language should not operate in the same way. I shall suggest in a later chapter that ease of communication is *not* the only consideration, and that Hume's point can be restated more convincingly. Hume himself, however, fails to do so.

Sympathy

I turn finally to Stage One, the claim that our judgements of moral approval or disapproval are generated by our feelings of sympathy. This claim is vital to Hume's ethical theory. It is what sets him apart from the egoistic perspective of Plato and Aristotle. What are we to make of it?

The difficulties emerge when we ask, 'What if someone fails to feel sympathy?' Hume does not raise this question. He simply assumes that sympathy is universal. If we bear in mind what he means by 'sympathy', this assumption is less implausible than it might appear. He is not assuming that everyone is always motivated by feelings of kindness and concern for others. His claim is merely that everyone is to some degree affected by other people's happiness or suffering. However little they might be moved to act on it, Hume would claim, no one can be totally indifferent to the contemplation of others' pleasures and pains. Though even this limited claim is not strictly true, we may, I think, concede this much to Hume, that someone who is incapable of sympathy in this rudimentary sense would normally be regarded as an instance of a psychopathic condition. We are envisaging not just someone who acts inconsiderately or cruelly towards others, but someone who is literally incapable of responding to other people as human beings. An actual example of such a condition would be the autistic child who 'treats people as if they were inanimate objects, exploring their shape as he would a toy or a piece of furniture.

He appears to feel and behave as if alone in a world uninhabited by other persons.'[4]

Sympathy, we may allow, is, if not universal, at any rate a feature of any normal human being. This, however, will not take Hume very far in answering our question. If sympathy is something possessed by even the most cruel and ruthless of characters, it must be compatible with a wide range of behaviour. How much weight, then, ought it to carry in determining our actions? One might suppose Hume's view to be that it should be a decisive influence on our judgements about how to act. But why *should* it have this dominant role? Again Hume evades the question. Indeed, he would see it as a question which is simply not his concern. His task, he would say, is to describe and explain how we do in fact make our moral judgements, not to tell us how we *ought* to make them. He is not in the business of recommending, but merely of recording.

There is a further reason why he can avoid addressing the question. Recall that the kinds of moral judgements he is concerned with are judgements about personal qualities rather than judgements about actions. He thereby avoids offering any account of how we make difficult decisions about how to act. Take the case of a woman who is confronted with the choice of whether to walk out of a marriage which has stunted and oppressed her. If she does so, she may be exhibiting the qualities of courage and self-respect. If she decides to stay, perhaps out of an enduring loyalty to her husband, or a concern for her children, she may be exhibiting the qualities of fidelity or benevolence. But it is no comfort to her to know that whatever she does, she will be exhibiting morally admirable qualities. She still has to decide what to do. Should sympathy be the decisive consideration? If so, does that mean she should be influenced by other people's needs and interests at the expense of her own? Why should she? Why indeed should sympathy play any effective role at all in her decision? Why should she not simply act out of self-love on this occasion? Hume offers no way of answering these questions.

We can imagine possible answers. Hume could say that if her judgement about what to do is to be a moral judgement, it will be guided by sympathy, since the defining feature of moral judgements is precisely the fact that they stem from sympathy. Such an answer, however, would merely beg the question. Even supposing that moral judgements are by definition those which are guided by sympathy, why should one's judgement about what to do be a *moral* judgement rather than some other kind of practical judgement? Why should one decide on the basis of sympathy rather than on some other basis such as self-love?

A further answer which Hume might supply is that only by judging on the basis of sympathy, can one produce a judgement with which other people can agree. He says:

When a man denominates another his *enemy*, his *rival*, his *antagonist*, his *adversary*, he is understood to speak the language of self-love, and to express sentiments

> peculiar to himself and arising from his particular circumstances and situation. But when he bestows on any man the epithets of *vicious* or *odious* or *depraved*, he then speaks another language, and expresses sentiments in which he expects all his audience are to concur with him. He must here, therefore, depart from his private and particular situation and must choose a point of view common to him with others; he must move some universal principle of the human frame. (IX.6)

This universal principle is the sentiment of humanity or sympathy.

> And though this affection of humanity may not generally be esteemed so strong as vanity or ambition, yet, being common to all men, it can alone be the foundation of morals or of any general system of blame or praise. (ibid.)

Hume is still talking here about judgements of personal qualities, rather than judgements of actions. One could, however, suggest in the same vein that judgements about what to do should take the form of moral judgements, based on sympathy, because those are the kinds of judgements on which people can agree.

Again the answer would beg the question. Why give priority to judgements on which people can agree? Hume has allowed in this passage that people can speak the language of self-love and be perfectly intelligible to one another. Why, then, should we not act on self-love, and forgo the luxury of other people's concurrence with our judgement about what to do?

The problem, then, is this. It may be that the distinctive feature of moral judgements is their connection with sympathy, and it may be that sympathy is an almost universally shared sentiment. This, however, constitutes no reason why we should form judgements from a moral point of view rather than some other, or why we should act on such judgements. And when Hume himself eventually tackles the problem directly, he abandons his reliance on sympathy and reverts to an appeal to self-love. Part II of the *Enquiry's* Conclusion begins: 'Having explained the moral *approbation* attending merit or virtue, there remains nothing but briefly to consider our interested *obligation* to it, and to enquire whether every man who has any regard to his own happiness and welfare will not best find his account in the practice of every moral duty.' The implication is that the way to demonstrate the obligation is to show that the path of moral duty is the path most conductive to one's own happiness and welfare. Accordingly, Hume proceeds to remind us that possession of the social virtues puts one on good terms with one's fellows, and that 'no society can be agreeable or even tolerable where a man feels his presence unwelcome and discovers all around him symptoms of disgust and aversion' (IX.18). Even in the case of justice, 'where a man, taking things in a certain light, may often seem to be a loser by his integrity', the fact remains that 'inward peace of mind, consciousness of integrity, a satisfactory review of our own conduct . . . are circumstances very requisite to happiness.' (IX.22–3.)

As with Plato and Aristotle, the appeal to self-interest is not a crude one.

The argument is not that possession of the virtues is *instrumentally* advantageous, bringing compensatory benefits in its wake, but rather that possession of them is *itself* a state of happiness and well-being. Such an argument nevertheless remains unsatisfactory, for reasons which we considered in the previous chapter. And by reverting to the appeal to self-love, Hume shows that his use of the concept of sympathy does not after all enable him to succeed where Plato and Aristotle failed. We remain confronted by the same dilemma. Either the moral desirability of altruistic actions remains unjustified, as when Hume asserts that we just do as a matter of fact adopt the standpoint of sympathy, and form our judgements accordingly; or some further justification is offered, which then reduces altruism to a form of self-love. Hume oscillates between these alternatives, but never transcends the opposition between them.

Reason and Sentiment

So far I have been contrasting Hume with Plato and Aristotle on the problem of egoism and altruism. In the remainder of this chapter I shall examine a second contrast with the Greeks—on the problem of moral knowledge. Plato and Aristotle, it will be recalled, disagreed on the nature of such knowledge. Plato's explicit doctrine viewed moral knowledge as a purely intellectual acquaintance with abstract universal forms. Implicit in Plato's own practice, however, we found a rather different view, much more in line with Aristotle's position: that moral knowledge is to be derived from an empirical study of the facts of human existence. This position I referred to as *ethical naturalism*.

Hume's disagreement with Plato and Aristotle is as radical as it could be. Quite simply, he denies that there can be such a thing as moral knowledge. Moral approval and disapproval derive from sentiment rather than from reason.

As a first step to a fuller understanding of this stark claim, we need to look at what Hume means by 'reason' and 'sentiment'. In other philosophical contexts 'reason' is sometimes opposed to 'experience' and equated with pure thought, the operation of the intellect without any reliance on the senses. In the present context, however, Hume uses 'reason' (for which he sometimes substitutes the term 'understanding') in a more comprehensive sense, to mean our capacity to judge of truth and falsity, that is, to obtain any kind of knowledge, whether from pure thought or from experience. Whereas the sphere of reason, then, is that of knowledge, the sphere of sentiment is that of feelings and emotions, and Hume insists on the sharp division between the two.

> The distinct boundaries and offices of *reason* and of *taste* are easily ascertained. The former conveys the knowledge of truth and falsehood; the latter gives the sentiment of beauty and deformity, vice and virtue. (Appendix I.21)

Reason, he allows, has a role to play in our moral thinking. Through the use of reason we discover the consequences of various human qualities and actions. Take the case of justice. Hume claims that the upholding of justice, that is, of clear and simple property rules, will make for good order and prosperity in any society. Conversely, the violation of such rules will make for chaos and destruction. These are straightforward factual claims, and the establishing of their truth or falsity is the province of reason. Even if they can be shown to be true, however, this is not sufficient to establish that justice is a virtue. That conclusion follows only if it is also accepted that order and prosperity are desirable, and that chaos and destruction are undesirable. These further assertions are not factual claims, and they cannot be established by reason. To accept them is to feel a certain kind of sentiment. As we have seen, Hume thinks that the sentiment in question is the feeling of sympathy or humanity, which leads us to approve of the virtues because of their useful and agreeable features. He also thinks that everyone shares this feeling. Nevertheless, he would have to agree that if someone did not feel the requisite sympathy, if someone revelled in chaos and destruction, and therefore regarded justice as a vice and injustice as a virtue, we could not show him to be mistaken. We could not do so, not because it would be beyond our powers, but because *nothing could count as* his being mistaken. Moral utterances are simply not the kind of thing that could be either true or false.

A passage in Hume's *Treatise*, much quoted by recent philosophers, has commonly been interpreted as making the same point. The passage runs as follows:

> In every system of morality which I have hitherto met with, I have always remarked that the author proceeds for some time in the ordinary way of reasoning, and establishes the being of a god, or makes observations concerning human affairs; when of a sudden I am surprised to find that instead of the usual copulations of propositions *is* and *is not*, I meet with no proposition that is not connected with an *ought* or an *ought not*. This change is imperceptible, but is, however, of the last consequence. For as this *ought* or *ought not* expresses some new relation or affirmation, it is necessary that it should be observed and explained; and at the same time that a reason should be given for what seems altogether inconceivable, how this new relation can be a deduction from others which are entirely different from it. (*Treatise* Book III Part 1, Section 1)

Here Hume seems again to be saying that moral assertions are not statements of fact, and therefore cannot be derived by reason from other statements of fact. Given any set of 'is'-propositions, one will proceed from them to the acceptance of an 'ought' only if one has the appropriate sentiment.

That is the traditional interpretation. It has however been questioned, and with the questioning goes a reinterpretation of Hume's general account of reason and sentiment. It has been pointed out that Hume does not, in this passage, say that the derivation of an 'ought' from an 'is' is impossible, only that it 'seems altogether inconceivable'. Perhaps, therefore, he is to be taken literally: the derivation *seems* inconceivable, but with care it can be done. 'Ought'-propositions do follow from 'is'-propositions, but only from certain kinds of 'is'-propositions. And Hume's 'reason'/'sentiment' doctrine is then reinterpreted as the claim that the 'is'-propositions from which 'oughts' do follow are statements of fact about human sentiments. Such a claim is perhaps to be found in these sentences of the *Enquiry*:

> The hypothesis which we embrace is plain. It maintains that morality is determined by sentiment. It defines virtue to be *whatever mental action or quality gives to a spectator the pleasing sentiment of approbation*; and vice the contrary. We then proceed to examine *a plain matter of fact*, to wit what actions have this influence. (Appendix I.10—my italics in final sentence)

Here Hume does seem to be saying that, by establishing the relevant facts as to which actions and qualities produce a certain kind of sentiment, we can arrive at moral conclusions about which qualities and actions are good or bad, virtuous or vicious. If this is what he means, then he turns out to be an ethical naturalist after all.

Now we can agree that Hume is indeed, in one sense, a proponent of ethical naturalism. He sees ethics as a part of the study of human nature and insists that the proper method in ethics is the experimental method. What we need to do is to investigate the facts about what people's moral sentiments are actually like. But the question is: in what sense can these facts be called 'moral facts'? I want to suggest that they are moral facts only in a limited sense. When we establish that people feel a sentiment of approbation towards, say, acts of kindness, we do not thereby establish that kindness *is* a virtue, but only that people *regard* it as a virtue. The 'moral fact' which has been established is a second-order moral fact, not a first-order moral fact. It is true that, in the passage just quoted, Hume says that he *defines* virtue, as 'whatever mental action or quality gives to a spectator the pleasing sentiment of approbation'. This would imply that 'Kindness is a virtue' simply *means*, 'Kindness elicits from people a sentiment of approbation', and that therefore in establishing the latter, one is also establishing the former. I think, however, that Hume must be taken to be speaking loosely when he offers this as a 'definition'. The two cannot strictly mean the same, for it is essential to his theory that whereas 'Kindness elicits approbation' is a fact discoverable by reason, 'Kindness is a virtue' is not a deliverance of reason but an expression of sentiment. That, surely, is what the distinction between reason and sentiment is all about.

Hume's Arguments

Assuming that the traditional interpretation is correct, let us look at the arguments which Hume offers in defence of his position. There are five of these.

1. 'Reason', says Hume in the first argument, 'judges either of *matter of fact* or of *relations*' (Appendix I.6). But whatever fact or whatever relation we consider, it can be sometimes virtuous and sometimes vicious. Therefore virtue and vice cannot be identified with any particular facts or relations.

Reversing Hume's order, let us take first the case of 'relations'. Consider, he says, the example of ingratitude. This may be defined as occurring when A shows ill-will to B after B has shown good-will to A. The relation exhibited here is, according to Hume, the relation of *contrariety*; A's ill-will is contrary to B's good-will. The wrongness of ingratitude cannot, however, consist in this relation of contrariety, for the same contrariety would exist if A displayed good-will towards B in response to B's ill-will towards A, but in such a case the action, far from being wrong, might even be regarded as praiseworthy.

It is clear that Hume is using the term 'relation' in a special and limited sense. A natural response to the example would be to insist that 'returning ill-will for good-will' is a *different* relation from 'returning good-will for ill-will'. Hume takes them to be instances of the same relation, contrariety, because he assumes that the relations we should be looking for are purely *formal* or *logical* relations. Why should he make this assumption? Because the opponents he has in mind are philosophers who have expressly declared that moral right and wrong do consist in certain formal relations. Samuel Clarke, for instance, writes in his *Discourse on Natural Religion* of 1705 that:

> In respect of our Fellow-Creatures, the Rule of Righteousness is, that in particular we so deal with every Man, as in like Circumstances we could reasonably expect he should deal with Us . . .[5]

Clarke explains that:

> The Reason which obliges every Man in Practice, so to deal always with another, as he would reasonably expect that Others should in like Circumstances deal with Him, is the very same, as That which forces him in speculation to affirm, that if one Line or Number be equal to another, That other is reciprocally equal to It. Iniquity is the very same in Action, as Falsity or Contradiction in Theory, and the same cause which makes the one absurd, makes the other unreasonable.

He thus asserts precisely the view which Hume attacks, that wrongness in such cases is identical with the formal relation of contrariety. Against such a view, Hume's counter-example may be a sufficient refutation. It remains possible, however, that other more concrete, non-formal relations are constitutive of moral wrongness. Why should not ingratitude itself, for example, be such a relation? In Hume's categorization, 'ingratitude' would count as a 'fact' rather than a 'relation'. What does he say about it under that head?

His use of the term 'fact' seems also to be unnecessarily restricted. When we examine the crime of ingratitude, he says, and look for the facts,

> nothing is there, except the passion of ill-will or absolute indifference. You cannot say that these, of themselves, always and in all circumstances are crimes. No, they

are only crimes when directed towards persons who have before expressed and displayed good-will towards us. Consequently, we may infer that the crime of ingratitude is not any particular individual *fact* . . . (Appendix I.6)

But why should not someone's having displayed ill-will *in return for good-will*
be itself a fact? In asserting that the only fact here is the display of ill-will,
Hume seems to be assuming that a fact must be something which can be taken
in at a glance, without any reference to a wider context. In particular, the context of relationships within which an action is performed has been excluded
from Hume's category of 'facts', just as it was excluded from his category of
'relations'. It is, then, not surprising that neither any 'fact' (in this restricted
sense) nor any 'relation' (in this restricted sense), can be equated with moral
right or wrong. It remains perfectly possible that facts or relations in some
wider sense might be identifiable as moral facts or relations.

2. Hume's second argument is virtually a restatement of the first. In moral
deliberations, he says, 'we must be acquainted beforehand with all the objects
and all their relations to each other.' This is the province of reason, to determine the relevant facts and relations.

> But after every circumstance, every relation is known, the understanding has no
> further room to operate, nor any object on which it could employ itself. The appro-
> bation or blame which then ensues cannot be the work of the judgement, but of the
> heart, and is not a speculative proposition or affirmation, but an active feeling or
> sentiment. (Appendix I.11)

Hume here assumes that when all the facts and relations are known, and when
therefore, by definition, reason can do no more, some further step is still necessary. In other words, he assumes what he assumed in the first argument, that
facts and relations cannot themselves have a moral significance. This is simply
to beg the question. To take the previous example, in establishing all the facts
and relations, may we not establish that a particular act is one of ingratitude,
and is this not to say that, whatever sentiments people may feel about it, the act
is wrong? What need is there for any further step?

3. Hume's next ploy is to compare moral approval with the perception of
beauty, and to suggest that since the latter is a matter of sentiment and taste,
the former must be likewise.

> Euclid has fully explained all the qualities of the circle, but has not in any proposi-
> tion said a word of its beauty. The reason is evident. The beauty is not a quality of
> the circle. It lies not in any part of the line, whose parts are equally distant from a
> common centre. It is only the effect which that figure produces upon the mind . . .
> (Appendix I.14)

Hume again begs the question—or rather, two questions. The reason why
Euclid says nothing about the beauty of the circle is not as evident as Hume

supposes. It may be not that 'the beauty is not a quality of the circle', but simply that it is a different *kind* of quality from the geometrical qualities with which Euclid is concerned. For all that Hume has said, it remains perfectly plausible to suppose that the beauty is something objectively present in the circle, and that someone who fails to appreciate its beauty has failed to see something which is there to be seen.

Even if Hume is right about beauty, he begs a further question in supposing that moral qualities must be like aesthetic ones. We might allow that judgements of beauty are ultimately matters of personal taste, but still insist that moral judgements are different. The distinction is a plausible one. If someone insists on painting all the walls of his house a uniform black, we might simply say, 'Well, if that's how you like it, it's up to you'; but if someone goes in for sadistic child-murder we are hardly likely to produce the same response. The example suggests a difference between aesthetic judgements and moral judgements, and Hume has given us no reason for denying the difference.

4. The brief fourth argument is merely a particular application of the first. Rightness or wrongness cannot consist in any particular relations, he argues, since the same relation may exist between inanimate objects as between moral agents, and be virtuous or vicious in the latter case but not in the former.

> A young tree, which over-tops and destroys its parent, stands in all the same relations with Nero when he murdered Agrippina and, if morality consisted merely in relations, would no doubt be equally criminal. (Appendix I.17)

Like the first argument, this depends entirely on Hume's specialized use of the term 'relations' to mean 'formal relations'. Without that restriction we could perfectly well insist that the relation of Nero to Agrippina is *not* the same as that of the tree to its parent. Nero wills the death of his mother, the tree does not, and that is why the one act is wrong and the other is not.

5. Only in Hume's last argument (and then only towards the end of his formulation of it) does a substantial point emerge. Moral responses must be the product of sentiment rather than reason, he says, because sentiment, unlike reason, has a necessary connection with *action*. In pronouncing something to be virtuous or vicious, we are not engaging in mere theoretical speculation, we are inclining ourselves and others to act in a certain way. This is something which reason by itself cannot do.

> Reason, being cool and disengaged, is no motive to action, and directs only the impulse received from appetite or inclination, by showing us the means of attaining happiness or avoiding misery. Taste, as it gives pleasure or pain, and thereby constitutes happiness or misery, becomes a motive to action, and is the first spring or impulse to desire and volition. (Appendix I.21)

Hume here supplies the missing ingredient which is needed in order to give force to the previous arguments. Facts cannot by themselves have a moral significance, because a moral response is a commitment to action, whereas reason by itself is wholly inactive. This is why, when reason has done all its work, some further step is still necessary, and this step has to take the form of a sentiment, because sentiments are the mental processes which motivate us to action.

Hume's whole thesis concerning reason and sentiment, then—his denial of the idea of moral truth and falsity, and his denial that reason can establish moral conclusions—depends upon his claims about the connection between morality and action, and about the inactive character of reason. I shall assess these claims when, in Part III, I have looked at some latter-day versions of them.

Notes

1. In the *Treatise* Hume shows some inclination to analyse 'sympathy' into its component psychological mechanisms (see *Treatise* Book III, Part III, Section I). In the *Enquiry*, however, he is content to state that 'It is needless to push our researches so far as to ask why we have humanity or a fellow-feeling with others. It is sufficient that this is experienced to be a principle in human nature. We must stop somewhere in our examination of causes . . .' (footnote to V.17).
2. The classic example is to be found in Thomas Hobbes's *Leviathan*, published in 1651.
3. For a defence of equality against Hume and his modern followers, see my article 'Does Equality Destroy Liberty?' in Keith Graham (ed.), *Contemporary Political Philosophy* (Cambridge, 1982), and my book *Free and Equal* (Oxford, 1987).
4. Philip Barker, *Basic Child Psychiatry* (London, 1971), 69.
5. L. A. Selby-Bigge (ed.), *British Moralists* (Oxford, 1897), ii. 23.

6

Kant
Respect for Persons

Reading: Immanuel Kant, *Fundamental Principles of the Metaphysic of Morals* (first published 1785)

I shall concentrate entirely on Sections I and II. Quotations are from the translation by Thomas K. Abbott, available in the Library of Liberal Arts. References are to paragraph numbers. The paragraphs of Section I should be numbered from 1 to 22, and the paragraphs of Section II from 1 to 90. Abbott occasionally deviates from the paragraph divisions in the original text. In the First Section he runs together paragraphs 17 and 18; paragraph 18 should begin at the words 'Let the question be. . .'. And in the Second Section he runs together paragraphs 88 and 89; paragraph 89 should begin at 'An absolutely good will . . .'.

The Protestant Ethic

With the ethics of Immanuel Kant we are firmly in a Christian context, that of eighteenth-century German Protestantism. Kant's parents were adherents of Pietism, a tendency (not an independent sect) within the Lutheran church. This background was an important influence on Kant, and his moral philosophy has its starting-point in certain general features of Protestant Christianity. The sociologist Max Weber, in his classic study of the Protestant ethic, says of its Lutheran origins:

> at least one thing was unquestionably new: the valuation of the fulfilment of duty in worldly affairs as the highest form which the moral activity of the individual could assume. . . . The only way of living acceptably to God was not to surpass worldly morality in monastic asceticism, but solely through the fulfilment of the obligations imposed upon the individual by his position in the world. That was his calling.[1]

As Weber here indicates, the attitude of 'worldly asceticism' stands in contrast to the monastic tradition of 'other-worldly asceticism'. Unlike the latter, it does not conclude from the devaluation of the things of this world that the individual should withdraw from worldly affairs in order to seek spiritual perfection. The world of social and economic obligations is the world in which one has been placed by God to live a good life. On the other hand there is no suggestion, as there would be for Aristotle, that in engaging in these activities one is directly achieving one's own fulfilment as a human being, and giving expression to the highest potentialities of human nature. Worldly activities provide the setting in which one is required to exhibit moral goodness, but the actual content of these activities has no intrinsic value. The fulfilment of one's duty may have beneficial consequences for oneself and for others (Weber's thesis identifies the Protestant ethic as the explanation for the economic success of the early capitalists), but its value primarily consists not in its effects but in its being a manifestation of the inner spiritual state of the person.

In these features of the Protestant ethic we can locate the source of Kant's stress on 'duty for duty's sake'. Kant is the first philosopher to put the concept of 'duty' at the very centre of ethics. Traditionally the concept refers to the requirements that are imposed on one by one's occupancy of particular social, economic, and political positions—one's duties as a parent, as an employer or employee, as a citizen, as a holder of political office, and so on. Kant extends the concept from these specific 'duties' to a generalized 'duty', and proposes that moral goodness consists in the performance of this generalized 'duty' for its own sake. But in detaching the concept from specific roles and offices, Kant also seeks to detach it from any idea of utility. The fulfilment of 'duty' becomes simply an abstract moral requirement, not something required for the effective functioning of human social institutions. Duty is to be performed entirely for its own sake, not in order to promote human happiness or fulfilment. The background of the Protestant ethic can help us to understand the emergence of this idea.

My reason for referring to the Protestant background to Kant's thought is not just as an exercise in the history of ideas. The First Section of Kant's *Fundamental Principles* establishes the main outlines of his ethics by appealing to the evidence of 'common understanding', 'the moral knowledge of common human reason'. What is this common moral understanding? I would suggest that it is, in effect, the ethics of Protestant Christianity. That is to say, it does not possess the universal quality which Kant might want to claim for it. It is the ethical common sense of a particular society and a particular historical epoch. We therefore need to identify the historical and social limits of this conception of morality, in order properly to assess Kant's argument. The whole of his moral philosophy in fact seems to me to depend very heavily on this appeal to what he regards as the ordinary moral consciousness. Not only does the First Section explicitly set out from this point. The argument of the Second Section appears to presuppose the conception of morality set out in the First Section. I am not sure whether Kant thinks that he is, in the Second Section, providing independent arguments for the validity of that conception of morality. Whatever his intentions, however, I would claim that he fails to do so. At most he supplies hints as to how we might work out an independent justification; in the main, what I find in the Second Section is a further clarification and elaboration of the ethical theory which has previously been derived from the ordinary moral consciousness. Nor does the Third Section supply the required independent justification. In it, Kant sketches the metaphysics which is needed to explain the possibility of morality. In a world where everything that happens is causally necessitated, human beings can nevertheless possess the free will which morality presupposes because, as selves, they belong to the realm of *noumena* (or 'things in themselves'), as well as to the world of *phenomena* (or 'appearances'). In this way Kant attempts to demonstrate that morality is *possible*, but not that it is *necessary*—that is, he has still not told us why we ought to understand morality in this way, and why we ought to act in accordance with such morality. Ultimately he sets out no answer to this question, other than the claim that his account of morality is that of the ordinary moral consciousness. And if this consciousness is effectively the consciousness of Protestant Christianity, we may find it more questionable than Kant does.

First Section

Let us now look more closely at how, in the First Section, Kant derives his ethical theory from the ordinary moral consciousness. He begins with the assertion that nothing is unconditionally good except a good will, whose worth is entirely separable from the value of the results it brings about. This initial claim derives its plausibility from the widely held idea that moral evaluations focus primarily on people's *intentions*. People are not morally blamed if, through no fault of their own, their good intentions lead to unfortunate results. If A dives into the sea to rescue B, who is being carried away by the current, but because the current is stronger than she thought, fails to effect the rescue and is herself drowned, she will have done no good and have produced only additional loss of life and the additional grief of her family and friends; nevertheless, in virtue of her intentions and her efforts to realize them, she is liable to be morally praised rather than criticized. Note however that in the obvious examples of this kind the intention must itself be described as an intention to perform or effect something. Results are thus not irrelevant; the contrast is between the *intended results* and the *actual results*, and the former are the objects of praise or blame.

At paragraph 8 Kant introduces the central concept of 'duty', the term by which we are to refer to the good will when it is seen as being in opposition to inclinations. Actions have moral worth only if they are done from duty, not from inclination, and since 'inclination' contrasts also with 'reason', actions done from duty must coincide with actions governed by reason. It is not clear whether Kant wants to say that an action can have *no* moral worth if it is *at all* in accordance with one's inclinations. A charitable interpretation would, I think, have to take him to be saying something weaker: that an action motivated by inclination has no moral worth unless it is *also* motivated by a concern for duty. And presumably to say that it is also motivated by duty would be to say something like this: that as well as having an inclination to perform the action one also recognizes it to be one's duty, and on the strength of this recognition one *would have* performed the action *even if* one had had *no* such inclination. The philanthropist who enjoys helping others would not then be barred from exhibiting moral worth, provided he also had a sense of duty. On this interpretation Kant would be saying only that if someone has a direct inclination to perform the action, it is *more difficult to determine* whether he is also motivated by duty, whereas when inclination and duty conflict, the force of the sense of duty is obvious. Such an interpretation is marginally favoured by paragraph 9, and more strongly supported later when, at II.42, Kant says: '. . . the sublimity and intrinsic dignity of the command in duty are so much the more evident, the less the subjective impulses favour it and the more they oppose it'.

If Kant is interpreted in this way, his position will indeed get a certain amount of support from commonly accepted moral ideas. There does seem to be a certain plausibility in the idea that if an action is done solely because one enjoys it, it has no moral worth, because it does not involve any effort of will.

It is in paragraph 14 that Kant really begins to go beyond the ordinary moral consciousness, and radically to extend his own previous claims. He has previously maintained that the goodness of the good will is independent of the *results which are achieved*. He now claims that it is independent of the results which are *aimed at*, and that, as I mentioned previously, is very different. Again, he has previously maintained that duty is contrasted with *inclination*. What he now introduces is the much stronger claim that duty is to be contrasted with all specific *purposes*. Take our previous example of the unsuccessful rescuer. I agreed that she might be morally admired even though she failed to achieve anything. Nevertheless, as I also mentioned, this admiration is inseparable from our recognition of what it was that she tried to do. The natural assumption would be that she acted with the purpose of saving the life of another person, and it is this that makes her morally admirable. Again, to say that she acted with that purpose would not be to say that, in any normal sense, she did it out of inclination. Presumably she does not enjoy pitting her strength against a raging sea. The purpose which we attribute to her, so far from constituting an inclination, may be precisely what she sees it as her duty to do.

I suspect that in paragraph 14 Kant sees himself as simply developing further the themes of the previous paragraphs. I am suggesting, however, that in reality the case is quite otherwise. The paragraph marks a radically new departure, and cannot be supported by what has gone before. What can support it, then? Not an appeal to the common moral understanding, either, if that is supposed to be something widely shared across different societies and cultures. It can be given plausibility only by the previously mentioned features of the Protestant ethic.

If the idea of 'duty' is abstracted in this way from all specific purposes, a further problem arises, for there now seems no way of determining what this 'duty' consists in. It would appear to be completely empty. Kant's answer, in paragraphs 15 and 16, is that since all consideration of inclinations and effects is excluded, duty must be defined not in terms of its content, but as a purely formal requirement. It is the requirement of acting from respect for the moral *law*. Why 'law' specifically? Because the idea of duty involves that of acting on *principle*, following a *universal* principle, and not simply reacting to the immediate and particular situation. The vocabulary of 'moral law' carries with it religious connotations, it suggests the conception of morality as something laid down by a divine lawgiver, and thereby gives this talk of 'law' an initial intuitive plausibility. Kant, however, would certainly repudiate this conception (and does so at II.85). The moral law is not, in his view, something imposed on us from without by any arbitrary will, divine or otherwise. It is the expression of pure reason, and in so far as this law involves a lawgiver, it is legislated by any rational being. Thus, in the only sense in which the moral law is laid down by God, it is also laid down by all of us as human beings possessing reason. This idea of the moral law as something laid down by every rational agent for himself is elaborated by Kant at II.55–60.

If, in obeying the moral law, one is only obeying oneself and following one's own will, why speak of 'obedience' and 'law' at all? Because we are divided beings, split between reason and inclination. In so far as we are rational, morality is simply the expression of our own free will. In so far as we are also creatures of inclination, however, morality is something which we have to obey. The popular conception to which Kant comes closest is not that of morality as obedience to God, but that of morality as obedience to one's conscience, the obedience of the lower self to the higher self.

But now, if duty is defined as respect for the moral law, this seems merely to shift the problem. How are we to determine what the moral law commands? Kant maintains that the moral law, like the idea of 'duty', cannot be defined by its content. Consequently, he accepts, there is nothing left for it to command, other than simply that one's actions should be law-abiding. This, at first, looks like an entirely empty requirement, a law which says only, 'Obey this law'. Kant claims however that, though entirely formal, it is not entirely empty, for when we abstract from all particular content, what remains to the idea of law is the requirement of universality. A law which commands simple law-abidingness thus has the form: so act that you can will that your maxim should become a universal law.

Kant claims that everyone actually recognizes this moral law. There is a certain truth in this. We might think here of the way in which people regularly question the rightness of an action by asking; what if everyone did that? Kant's moral law also has a certain affinity with the Golden Rule: 'Act towards others in the way in which you would like them to act towards you' (although Kant points out the limitations of this principle, especially in its negative formulation, in his footnote to II.52). Whether 'common human reason' understands by these principles what Kant understands by them, and in particular whether it understands them as purely formal principles, is another question. We shall be in a better position to answer it when we have looked at his attempt to show, in the Second Section, how this moral law can guide our actions.

Second Section

Kant's most important innovation in the Second Section is to introduce the concepts of 'hypothetical imperatives' and 'categorical imperatives'. An *imperative* is the linguistic form in which a *command* is expressed. *Commands* are related to *laws* as *duty* is to the *good will*: in each case the former adds to the latter the idea of an opposition to inclination. Thus all rational beings act according to the conception of laws. A being whose will was wholly determined by reason and who had no inclinations (a non-physical being not affected by sensory stimuli) would not experience these laws as commands, and would be what Kant calls a 'holy will'. Beings such as ourselves who have both reason and inclinations, and in whom the two can conflict, do experience the laws of reason as commands, in so far as our inclinations may prompt us to deviate from them.

Hypothetical imperatives are the expression of commands which are conditional on inclinations or purposes. They have the form, 'Do this in order to achieve that'. Examples would be, 'Tear back to open', or 'Make friends if you want to be happy'. The first of these is an example of what Kant calls 'imperatives of skill', expressing commands which are conditional on purposes which one may or may not share—one may or may not be interested in opening a packet of cornflakes. The second is an 'imperative of prudence', since the command derives from the one purpose which is necessary for all human beings, the pursuit of happiness. Categorical imperatives, on the other hand, express commands which are not conditional on any purpose at all. They are not of the form, 'Do this in order to achieve that', but simply 'Do this'. It therefore follows from the account of morality in the First Section that categorical imperatives are the form in which the commands of the moral law are expressed.

Kant provides four different formulations of the categorical imperative, and has left his readers in some confusion as to how the various formulations are related to one another. A clear explanation is, however, eventually given at II.72–5. Strictly speaking, there is only one categorical imperative. It can be given an entirely general formulation (which I shall refer to as G), and it can be given three other, more specified formulations (which I shall refer to as S1, S2, and S3). The more specified formulations rephrase G in such a way as to indicate more clearly how it can be applied in practice. The four formulations are:

G. Act only on that maxim whereby you can at the same time will that it should become a universal law.

S1. Act as if the maxim of your action were to become by your will a universal law of nature.

S2. So act as to treat humanity, whether in your own person or in that of any other, never solely as a means but always also as an end.

S3. So act as if you were by your maxims in every case a legislating member in the universal kingdom of ends.

S1 is clearly only a slight variation on G. The only significant change is the extension of the phrase 'universal law' to 'universal law of nature'. The minimal interpretation of S1 would be that it simply requires us to apply G in the world as we know it. We are to consider whether the maxims of our actions, when universalized, could be consistent with the empirical facts of the natural world in which we have to act. Some of Kant's interpreters have, however, wanted to read rather more into the phrase 'law of nature', and I shall consider their suggestions in due course.

What of S2 and S3? They appear to differ more radically from G. How then can they be called reformulations of it? To make sense of this, it is helpful to see all the formulations as permutations on the concepts of *rationality* and *universality*. G and S1 require that as rational beings we should be able to universalize the maxims of our actions, that is, we should be able to will them as universal laws. S2 then requires us to universalize our conception of ourselves as rational beings, and to treat all other human beings likewise as rational beings. Finally S3 synthesizes S1 and S2, bringing together the two ideas of 'universal laws' and 'rational beings'. In so far as we are rational beings, we would all will the same things as universal laws. Therefore these universal laws are ones which would be agreed on in a hypothetical community of rational beings, and they are laws which would enjoin respect for all the members of that hypothetical community as rational beings. This hypothetical community is what Kant calls a 'kingdom of ends', and a further requirement of right action is, therefore, that it should be compatible with the laws of a kingdom of ends.

Kant says very little about how S3 would be applied in practice. He has a good deal more to say about S1 and S2, and examines their application to four examples. I shall devote the remaining two sections of this chapter to questions concerning the practical application of S1 and S2, and Kant's discussion of it in connection with his examples. First, however, a word about the overall structure of the examples.

The four examples are systematically chosen. They are: (i) the duty to refrain from suicide; (ii) the duty to refrain from making false promises; (iii) the duty to develop our talents; (iv) the duty to help others. Examples (i) and (iii) are duties to ourselves, and (ii) and (iv) are duties to others. Examples (i) and (ii) are called by Kant 'perfect duties', and (iii) and (iv) are 'imperfect duties'. Kant's explanation of the terms 'perfect' and 'imperfect' is rather perplexing. He says (in the footnote to paragraph 34): 'I understand by a perfect duty one that admits no exception in favour of inclination'. Since, however, Kant normally seems to suppose that *no* duty admits of any exception in favour of inclination, it is difficult to see how he can use this feature to distinguish between perfect and imperfect duties. It would be tempting to interpret him as meaning that perfect duties are those which admit of no exceptions *at all*, whereas imperfect duties are those which can be overridden by perfect duties or by other imperfect duties (but not by inclinations). This is tempting because Kant certainly wants to say that some duties admit of no exceptions, and since it would be highly implausible for him to maintain this of all the things which he regards as duties, he does need some distinction between duties which do and duties which do not admit of any exceptions. Such an interpretation would be in keeping with the nature of Kant's examples. Duties not to commit suicide, or to make false promises, do seem to be of a kind which he might regard as having no exceptions, whereas this could hardly even be said intelligibly of duties to develop one's talents or to help others. If an opportunity were to present itself for me to develop my talents or help someone else by making a false promise (perhaps in order to obtain money on false pretences so that I can put myself through college or give it to a friend in need), one would expect Kant to say that the duty not to make false promises should be the overriding one. This would also make sense of what he says when he comes to apply S2 to the examples, for he then classifies examples (i) and (ii) as 'necessary duties, or those of strict obligation', and (iii) and (iv) as 'contingent or meritorious duties'. Finally, it would fit in with what Kant says in other writings. All in all, the interpretation would be irresistible, were it not for the fact that it is not what Kant actually says. Perhaps, then, we should simply convict him of carelessness.

There is one other general point to be made about how Kant applies the categorical imperative to his examples. The application of it is primarily a *negative* test. Actions whose maxim does *not* accord with the categorical imperative are ones which we ought *not* to perform. If they cannot be universalized, or if they involve treating human beings simply as means, then they are morally impermissible. Kant is not saying, however, that all actions which *do* accord with the categorical imperative are ones which we *ought* to perform. That would be nonsense. There are innumerable actions which can perfectly well be universalized, and do not involve treating people solely as means, but which are certainly not obligatory. I can certainly will it to be a universal law that everyone should take up jogging. This does not mean that I have a moral duty to do so myself. All that Kant wants to say of any such actions which accord with the categorical imperative, is that they are morally permissible, not that they are obligatory. And this is in keeping with the popular conception of morality, which is commonly thought of as setting limits to what we can do, forbidding rather than requiring.

Primarily, then, the categorical imperative serves to distinguish between permissible and impermissible actions. Now Kant does want to say that there are positive as well as negative duties. How, then, can these be identified by the categorical imperative? They can be identified because positive duties of the form, 'You ought to do X', can be restated in the negative form, 'Failure to do X is impermissible'. Kant would claim that a refusal to help others in need cannot be universalized. Therefore, he would conclude, the refusal to help others is impermissible, and hence it follows that helping others is obligatory. The test remains a negative one, but it can in this way generate positive duties. Notice that of the four examples it is (i) and (ii), the 'perfect' duties, which are negative, and (iii) and (iv), the 'imperfect' duties, which are positive. This provides further support for the suggested interpretation of 'perfect' and 'imperfect'. It makes sense to say of negative duties that one should *never* commit suicide out of self-love, *never* make false promises, etc., whereas it is quite unclear what it could mean to say that one should *always*, without exception, develop one's talents or help others. Thus negative rather than positive duties can plausibly be said to admit of no exceptions.

Universalizability

I turn now to a closer examination of G and S1, the two formulations which require that the maxim of any action should be universalizable. I assume that Kant does not envisage G being applied to particular actions independently, but only via S1 (or via S2 or S3). I shall therefore concentrate on S1 and consider how effectively this can serve as a basic moral principle.

I have said that Kant does not offer any fully worked out justification for any of the formulations of the categorical imperative, other than the derivation from the ordinary moral consciousness in the First Section. There are, however, hints as to how such a justification might be devised. 'Rationality' and 'universality' are, we have seen, the two key concepts, permutation of which produces the different formulations of the categorical imperative. Now, I think there is a case for saying that of the two, 'rationality' is the more fundamental, and that the requirement of universality can be derived from that of rationality. In other words, the claim would be that it is a necessary condition of my acting rationally that my actions should be universalizable. The question, 'Why act rationally?' cannot be answered. No further reason can be given, but someone who asks, 'Why?', is already committed to the search for reasons, and has therefore already accepted the requirement of rationality. If we can show, then, that in order to be rational my actions must also be universalizable, we can provide a defence of Kant which does not have to rely upon the assumptions of the ordinary moral consciousness.

Now there is certainly a weak sense in which rationality involves universality. To be rational, my behaviour must be universalizable in the sense of being consistent. Let us take Kant's example of false promises. Kant imagines someone who 'finds himself forced by necessity to borrow money. He knows that he will not be able to repay it, but sees also that nothing will be lent to him unless he promises stoutly to repay it in a definite time' (II.36). Suppose that he decides to make such a promise, knowing that he cannot keep it. If he believes his actions to be rationally justified, then he is, as Kant says, committed to the universal principle or maxim, 'Whenever I believe that I am in need of money, I will borrow money and promise to repay it, although I know that I can never do so'. And if he cannot accept this as a universal principle, then he cannot rationally regard himself as justified in the present case, unless he can point to some additional relevant feature of the present situation which justifies his action.

This, then, is the weak sense of universalizability, as consistency. An action cannot be rational unless it falls under a universal principle which commits me to acting in the same way in all relevantly similar circumstances. Kant, however, wants a stronger sense of universalizability. He wants not just a principle of consistency, but what we might call a principle of the *impersonality of reasons*. The idea here is that reasons cannot be specific to particular individuals. If R is a valid reason for *me* to do action A, then it must also be a valid reason for *anyone* to do A in the same circumstances. Reasons are, by their very nature, reasons for anyone. Thus in the promising example, if our false promiser thinks that he is rationally justified, then he must also accept that everyone else would be equally justified in making such a promise whenever they needed money and could not repay it. And if he cannot accept this, then he cannot rationally regard himself as justified in the present case.

This is a more controversial sense of universalizability, but it does seem fairly convincing. It does seem correct that reasons, to be reasons at all, must be impersonal in this sense. Suppose, then, that we allow Kant this assumption, and accept that the categorical imperative in form G or S1 can be defended along these lines. The question now is: can such a principle, when applied to particular cases, effectively serve to distinguish permissible from impermissible actions? Can it, in other words, give concrete results?

There are two difficulties which have standardly been thought to arise for Kant at this point, and many critics would claim that they are insuperable. The first of these is the problem: *under what description* is an action to be universalizable? Any action can be described in a number of different ways. In our promising example we could imagine various possible descriptions, such as:

(a) making a promise when one cannot keep it;
(b) making a promise when one needs money and cannot keep the promise;
(c) making a promise when one needs money to pay one's way through college but cannot keep the promise;
(d) making a promise when one needs money which will eventually enable one to be of great benefit to humanity, even though one cannot keep the promise.

Whether or not the action is universalizable may depend very much on which description is taken. Kant assumes that something like description (b) would be the appropriate one, and claims that on such a description it could not be universalizable. If it were universalized, 'the promise itself would become impossible . . . since no one would consider that anything was promised to him, but would ridicule all such statements as vain pretences'. In any such case, however, a more precise description along the lines of something like (c) or (d) would be possible, and when so described, the action might well be universalizable. It is arguable that if everyone made false promises in the circumstances of (c), the general level of trust might be lowered, but not to an extent which would make promises impossible. This could be argued even more plausibly of (d). Moreover, one can imagine building more and more precise details, of an absurd kind, into the description of the action, just in order to make it universalizable, for example:

(e) making a promise when one needs money and cannot keep the promise, when it is a Thursday, and there is an 'r' in the month, and there are eighteen letters in one's name.

Given that this combination of circumstances would be fairly rare, the general level of trust would not be greatly impaired if everyone were prepared to act on this principle, and therefore one could claim that it would in fact be universalizable.

Kant's answer would be that the universalizability test is not to be applied to an action under just any description. What must be universalizable is the *maxim* of the action. I have made frequent use of Kant's term 'maxim' in stating his position, and it now needs to be explained. Roughly speaking, the maxim of an action is a statement of the agent's intention formulated as a universal principle. Such a principle is universal in the weak sense referred to above. Thus it encapsulates the agent's initial reason for wanting to perform the action—the description under which he regards it as justified, prior to the application of the categorical imperative. A description such as (e) may be a correct description of a proposed action, but it is hardly likely to be the description which features in the agent's maxim, for presumably he does not contemplate making the promise *because* it is a Thursday, and there is an 'r' in the month, and there are eighteen letters in his name. Therefore the fact that the action may be universalizable under that description is not enough to legitimate it.

Kant's insistence that the agent's own maxim must be universalizable may, then, suffice to rule out absurd and far-fetched descriptions. It is not clear, however, that it can serve as the appropriate guide for determining the one description to be chosen, and for ruling out all other possibilities. In the first place, people's maxims may not be all that determinate. If we were to ask of our false promiser, 'Is it under description (b), or (c), or (d) that he is considering performing the action?', there may be no clear answer, not because we cannot find out but because he may simply not have formulated it for himself with such precision. He may have a vague conviction that the circumstances are pressing ones and make a false promise necessary, but not have thought out exactly what it is about the situation that necessitates the false promise. Even if he has done so, however, why should that provide the appropriate way of pinning down the correct description? This seems to make the rightness or wrongness of an action depend too much on the vagaries of individual psychology. If the action is universalizable under one description and not under another, whether or not it is morally permissible will then depend on how the agent himself happens to think about it. If he formulates his reasons very carefully and contemplates the action under description (d), and if it is universalizable under that description, then we shall have to say that it is morally permissible. If he formulates his reasons only vaguely and thinks of the action only in the more general terms of (b), and if the action is not universalizable under that description, then we shall have to say that the action is morally impermissible, even though (d) might still be a correct description of it.

Kant might accept these implications. He might remind us that, in his view, the proper objects of moral evaluation are not actions but motives. Therefore, he might say, if one and the same action can be right or wrong depending on the terms in which the agent thinks of it, that is as it should be; the moral assessment varies because the motives vary. We might perhaps retort that what the universalizability test seems likely to assess is the agent's sophistication in formulating his motives, rather than their moral qualities. But let us leave this objection now, for there is another which is even more formidable. This is the problem of Kant's *formalism*.

Kant explicitly asserts that the principle of universalizability is a purely formal principle. That, for Kant, is a condition of its being an authentically moral principle, which it could not be if it were tied to a particular content. Therefore when his critics accuse him of formalism, there is as yet no disagreement. What the critics will add, however, is that because the principle is a purely formal principle, it is useless. Absolutely any action can be universalized without contradiction. The principle rules out nothing, and therefore cannot be used to distinguish between right and wrong actions. Hegel put the point succinctly:

by this means any wrong or immoral line of conduct may be justified . . . The absence of property contains in itself just as little contradiction as the non-existence of this or that nation, family, etc., or the death of the whole human race. But if it is already established on other grounds and presupposed that property and human life are to exist and be respected, then indeed it is a contradiction to commit theft or murder; a contradiction must be a contradiction of something, i.e. of some content presupposed from the start as a fixed principle.[2]

The phrase 'the absence of property' refers to an example used elsewhere by Kant, but the example of promising will illustrate the point equally well. Kant claims that the maxim of making a false promise cannot without contradiction be universalized, since if it were universalized promising itself would become impossible. Hegel's retort would be: the non-existence of promising is not self-contradictory, it is simply in contradiction with the presupposition that promising ought to exist. Thus the formal principle can generate a moral conclusion only if an additional content is smuggled in. And Hegel's criticism has subsequently been repeated by innumerable other critics of Kant.

Now Kant himself is happy to admit that the principle of universalizability cannot entail moral conclusions just by itself. It has to be applied, and in applying it we have to take into account facts about the world in which it is applied. I have already indicated that this, at the very least, is what must be meant by Kant's phrase 'universal law of nature'. In the promising example, Kant employs the assertion that if it were a universal law for people to make false promises when in difficulties, promising would become impossible because promises would never be taken seriously; and this is a factual claim which has to be combined with the principle of universalizability in order to produce the moral conclusion. This Kant would certainly accept. The real criticism, however, is not that Kant needs these factual additions, but that he also needs *additional moral or other evaluative presuppositions*—in the promising example, the presupposition that the practice of promising ought to exist. If this is the case, it must surely be a defect in Kant's ethics, and I think we shall find that it *is* the case, if we look at the various attempts to defend or supplement Kant.

a. Maxims   One suggestion is that Kant does not need to bring in any external ethical content to combine with the formal principle, because the content is supplied by the maxim itself.[3] The maxim, 'When in difficulties, make false promises', already presupposes the institution of promising, and thus the non-existence of promising which would follow from its being universalized would be in contradiction, not indeed with itself, but with the original maxim. If promising became impossible, then the maxim, 'When in difficulties, make false promises', would itself become impossible. Similarly stealing could not be universalized, for if it were, property would cease to exist, and stealing would then be impossible.

This defence can give Kant only temporary respite. He cannot, perhaps, be accused of importing the presupposition of promising, since this is already presupposed in the original maxim. Still, the fact remains that it is presupposed, and that some account has to be given of it. That is to say, an adequate ethical theory needs not just the principle of universalizability, but a full account of these institutions such as promising, property, punishment, marriage, etc., which have ethical implications built into them. This is the direction in which Hegel takes his criticism of Kant, substituting for Kant's concept of 'duty for duty's sake' a theory of the duties which attach to social institutions.

b. Natural purposes A second suggestion offered in defence of Kant involves reading more into the phrase 'universal law of nature' than I have so far done. Nature, it has been suggested, should here be understood as something *purposive*, and S1 requires that a maxim when universalized should be consistent with *purposes in nature*.[4] There are various indications that Kant was prepared to employ this concept in his ethical theory. In a passage in the First Section he argues that reason must exist for a higher purpose than the promotion of our happiness, and he there subscribes explicitly to the idea of natural purposes: 'In the physical constitution of an organized being, that is, a being adapted suitably to the purposes of life, we assume it as a fundamental principle that no organ for any purpose will be found but what is also the fittest and best adapted for that purpose' (I.5). He wants to apply the same principle not only to physical organs, but also to psychological faculties. In the first of the four examples, it is important that the contemplated action is suicide *motivated by self-love*, and Kant says that it cannot be universalized because 'a system of nature of which it should be a law to destroy life by means of the very feeling whose special nature it is to impel to the improvement of life would contradict itself' (II.35). In other words, a universal law of suicide motivated by self-love would contradict the natural purpose of self-love. Similarly, in the third example Kant argues that a rational being cannot will a universal law not to cultivate one's talents, because 'he necessarily wills that his faculties be developed, since they serve him, and have been given him, for all sorts of possible purposes' (II.37). Given him by whom? Again the answer is 'by nature', as Kant indicates when he returns to the example at II.53 and speaks of 'the end that nature has in view in regard to humanity'.

It is clear that Kant does employ the concept of natural purposes, and that in conjunction with the principle of universalizability it can generate concrete moral conclusions. It is much less clear that this vindicates Kant's ethical theory. The concept of natural purposes is not just a minor supplement to the categorical imperative. It embodies a substantial ethical position, and a highly controversial one at that. This does not mean that we should dismiss it; we have seen that it gains support from Aristotle and the Christian 'natural law' tradition. But it does mean that if Kant is going to use it he should elaborate a defence of it, and this would give his ethical theory a very different character indeed. It would be the idea of natural purposes, rather than the principle of universalizability, that would do all the work, and indeed the latter would become redundant. If suicide out of self-love, when universalized, is contrary to the natural purpose of self-love, then it is equally true that a single act of suicide out of self-love is contrary to that natural purpose, and in that case we do not need to invoke the principle of universalizability at all.

c. Intuitions The two suggestions so far considered have been attempts to defend Kant. I turn now to three attempts to improve upon Kant, rather than defend him. I shall argue that these attempts either fail to produce a workable ethical principle, or do so only by demoting the categorical imperative to a minor role. The first of these suggestions is that, though the categorical imperative cannot itself tell us what we ought or ought not to do, 'its value—a great value—lies in putting us in the right attitude, by requiring us to ignore our own particular wishes and to adopt an impersonal point of view.[5] Once we have been 'put in the right attitude', however, something further is needed, some kind of moral perception or intuition which will enable us to see where our duty lies.

The trouble with this is, as before, that the proposed addition is in fact a whole new ethical theory. Like the concept of 'natural purposes', that of 'moral perceptions' is extremely controversial, and if an ethical theory could be built up to justify it, it could function as a complete theory in itself, and Kant's own ethics could simply be left to take a back seat.

d. Utility Much the same goes for the next proposal. Some writers have suggested that the principle of universalizability needs to be supplemented with utilitarian considerations. In envisaging our maxim as a universal law we should then have to ask not, 'Does it become self-contradictory?' but 'Would its universalization lead to undesirable consequences? Would it tend to produce more suffering or less happiness that some alternative action?' Such a proposal looks attractive when applied to examples like that of false promising. Having established that the maxim to make a false promise would, if it became a universal law, make promising impossible, we have not thereby revealed any contradiction. What we can say is that such an eventuality would be highly undesirable. Human beings without the institution of promising would be at a great disadvantage, deprived of all the conveniences which that institution carries with it.

In the previous chapter we saw that Hume, in his discussion of justice, makes one such attempt to combine the concepts of utility and universalizability. I pointed out some of the difficulties. In the present chapter what needs to be added is that in any marriage of utilitarian and Kantian ethics, the utilitarian component is bound to be the dominant partner. Such a marriage would be very much at variance with the whole spirit of Kant's ethics, with its constant stress on the irrelevance of consequences and happiness. Strictly speaking, it is not incompatible with what Kant actually says in this vein. What he says is that an action has no moral worth if it is done *for the sake of* consequences such as the promotion of happiness, or the prevention of suffering. If, however, we say of an action that *when universalized* it would produce happiness or suffering, and if we perform or refrain from the action on those grounds, we are not acting *for the sake of* such consequences, since the individual action itself *would not have* those consequences. An individual act of false promising, for example, need not itself have any of those undesirable consequences which universal false promising would have. Thus Kant could consistently maintain that morally good actions do not aim at utilitarian consequences, while agreeing that utilitarian considerations should be taken into account, in determining whether the maxim of an action could be universalized. It would be logically consistent, but it would nevertheless be incongruous.

e. Inclinations A further suggestion would be that the principle of universalizability needs to be supplemented with the agent's own inclinations. One would then have to ask not, 'Can my maxim be universalized without contradiction?', but, 'Would the universalized maxim be consistent with my own inclinations? Would I *want* my maxim to be a universal law?' It is in this version that the idea of universalizability has enjoyed a considerable vogue among ethical philosophers recently.[6] As an interpretation of Kant, it would seem to have the same incongruity as the previous proposal. The idea that inclinations could play such a role in helping to determine our duty seems entirely foreign to Kant's insistence on the opposition between duty and inclination. And yet, surprisingly enough, Kant himself eventually works round to such a position. Of examples (iii) and (iv) he says that the maxim of the action could in fact be universalized without contradiction; what makes the maxim wrong is that 'it is impossible to *will* that such a principle should have the universal validity of a law of nature'. It is not clear what 'willing' means here, but in the case of (iv) it seems to amount to something very much like inclination. Kant says that the maxim not to help others in distress could without contradiction be a universal law; nevertheless one cannot will that it should be universal, because 'many cases might occur in which one would have need of the love and sympathy of others, and in which, by such a law of nature, sprung from his own will, he would deprive himself of all hope of the aid he desires' (II.38). What can this mean, if not that such a universal law would be contrary to one's inclinations?

The attraction of this option is that, although it involves supplementing the principle of universalizability with an additional source of evaluation, the latter is not an additional *moral principle*. Thus it does not require a whole new ethical theory to justify it. We do not, in fact, have to go outside the limits of

Kant's own conceptual structure. We can work within Kant's moral psychology, employing his antithesis of reason and inclination, and modifying it to state not that the requirements of reason *exclude* the inclinations, but rather that the requirements of reason (in the form of universalizability) are to be *imposed upon* the inclinations.

It is an attractive proposal, but I do not think that it will work, and my objection to it is not, as with its predecessors, that the proposed addition to Kant is too strong, but that it is too weak. I do not think that the combination of universalizability and inclinations will generate the concrete moral conclusions which it is supposed to produce. To do so would require a stronger notion of universalizability than is legitimate. I have said that the principle of universalizability is defensible in this sense: that if I believe I have good reason to act in a certain way, I am thereby committed to *recognizing that others have good reason* to act in the same way in relevantly similar circumstances. I am not, however, thereby committed to *willing* that they should act in the same way. Therefore there need be no inconsistency between my universalized maxims and my own inclinations. I can perfectly well recognize that others have good reason to act in a certain way, while wanting them not to.

To make the point clearer, consider Kant's fourth example. We are to imagine someone whose maxim is not to help others in distress. Kant claims that he cannot universalize this maxim, because if he were in distress he would want others to help him. I am suggesting that despite that fact, he *can* universalize his maxim. He can quite consistently say something like this: 'I see no reason why I should help others in distress. I accept that this logically commits me to the view that if I were in distress, there is no good reason why others should help me. Now certainly I would want them to help. If I were in a position to do so, I would try to induce them to help me. But at the same time I entirely accept that they would be rationally justified in refusing to help me.' This is perfectly consistent. And it is as far as the combination of universalizability and inclinations can take us. I have allowed that, if we are to be rational, our practical maxims must be universalizable in two senses. These are:

(i) universalizability as *consistency*—the requirement that one's reason for performing a certain action in certain circumstances must be a reason for one to perform *the same* action again in relevantly similar circumstances;

(ii) universalizability as *impersonality*—the requirement that one's reason for performing a certain action in certain circumstances must be a reason for *anyone* to perform the same action in relevantly similar circumstances.

It does not follow however, that one's practical maxims must be universalizable in a third sense, that of:

(iii) universalizability as *impartiality*—the requirement that one's reasons must give equal weight to everyone else's desires and interests, along with one's own.

The requirement of impartiality is quite distinct from the previous two, and unlike them it cannot legitimately be presented simply as a requirement of formal rationality. It is not, therefore, a defensible interpretation of the notion of universalizability.

f. Further formulations There remains one other possibility: that G and S1 can be applied to concrete cases, and produce concrete conclusions, only when supplemented with the other formulations, S2 and S3. This is not, on the whole, Kant's position. He certainly claims to be applying S1 in its own right to the four examples. Later, however, he does suggest that the relation between S1 and S2 is that they specify respectively the *form* and the *matter* of morality (II.73–4). Certainly S2 appears to be less of a purely formal principle than S1. We might therefore incline to the view that, though S1 is not a workable principle in itself, its real value is to pave the way for S2, and that with the formulation of S2 we do indeed have a viable moral principle. Let us, then, consider S2.

Respect for Persons

S2 requires us to treat human beings (including ourselves) as ends, and never only as means. The world 'only' is important. Kant is not saying that we should never use human beings as means at all. Human society would be impossible if people could never make use of one another. Every time I eat a meal, I make use of the people who produced and marketed the food, every time I ride on a bus I make use of the driver, every time I read a book I make use of the author. Examples could be multiplied. Kant's point is that we should not regard people *simply* as means to our own ends. All human beings are ends in themselves, and when the circumstances arise (which they may not), we should treat them as such. The question is, then: What is it to treat someone as an end?

Kant's choice of the term 'end' stands in need of explanation. The word normally indicates something to be brought about, something which we aim at in our actions. To regard people as ends in this sense would presumably be to aim at bringing into existence as many people as possible, and we should then have to take Kant as advocating a life of maximum sexual indulgence. This is not, I presume, what he has in mind. The only continuity between Kant's talk of 'persons as ends' and the normal meaning of 'ends', is that in both senses 'ends' are contrasted with 'means'. This however seems to leave us where we started—with the negative injunction that treating people as ends is treating them not merely as means. Perhaps we can best interpret Kant, initially, as saying that to treat people as ends is to treat people as beings who *have* ends. I should not treat human beings as mere means to my own ends, because I should recognize that they themselves have ends of their own. They have ends, because they are free, rational and autonomous agents, they can act in accordance with purposes and principles, they are persons, not things (II.48).

This is still very vague, and I shall attempt shortly to make it more precise, but first I want to look at how Kant wishes to justify S2. In general terms, I have suggested that the justification depends on a further redeployment of the concepts of 'rationality' and 'universality'. A key passage is the following:

> *rational nature exists as an end in itself.* Man necessarily conceives his own existence as being so; so far then this is a *subjective* principle of human actions. But every other rational being regards its existence similarly, just on the same rational principle that holds for me; so that it is at the same time an objective principle from which as a supreme practical law all laws of the will must be capable of being deduced. (II.49)

What this amounts to is the application of the requirement of universalizability to one's conception of oneself as a rational being. We can rephrase it as the three-step argument: (i) one necessarily regards oneself as a rational being, as an end; (ii) one therefore has to accept that everyone else is justified in regarding himself/herself as a rational being and as an end; (iii) it is therefore an objectively valid principle that everyone should be treated as a rational being and as an end. The move from (i) to (ii) is justified by the notion of universality as the impersonality of reasons. The difficulty resides in the move from (ii) to (iii), for this requires an extension of the idea of universalizability, of the kind which I criticized in connection with proposal (e) above (pp. 85–7). It requires a shift from 'universality as impersonality of reasons' to 'universality as impartiality', and there are no good grounds for thinking that one can derive the latter from the former. If I treat myself as a person, I may be logically committed to accepting that others have good reason to treat themselves as persons, but I am not logically committed to the principle that *I* should treat *them* as persons. A world of self-respecting egoists is not an irrational world.

I conclude that, to the extent that it is contained in the brief passage I have quoted, Kant's defence of S2 fails. I do not think that he has provided any further arguments, other than the appeal to the ordinary moral consciousness. Nevertheless, the idea of respect for persons, though it lacks a sound justification in Kant, is an immensely fruitful idea, and I want to bring out some of its implications.

I have said that, initially, we could understand the idea of 'treating persons as ends' to mean 'treating persons as beings who have ends'. Part of what this will require, then, is that we should be motivated by other people's ends, as well as by our own. This is asserted by Kant when he applies S2 to example (iv); 'the ends of any subject who is an end in himself ought as far as possible to be *my* ends also' (II.54). This will involve a concern for the interests of others, helping to promote their happiness and to prevent their suffering. Such a conception of morality forms the substance of the utilitarian ethic, which we shall consider in the next chapter, and it is by no means distinctive of Kant. There is, however, in Kant's position something much more distinctive. In so far as treating human beings as ends involves helping to promote their ends, this stems from something more basic, an attitude not just towards their interests, but towards the persons themselves. It is the attitude which Kant tries to capture with the concepts of 'respect' and of 'dignity'. At II.68–9 Kant contrasts 'value' and 'dignity'. 'Whatever has a value', he says, 'can be replaced by something else which is equivalent'. 'Value' is thus the kind of worth possessed by all the various individual objects of desire, such as material goods, or personal qualities such as skill, or wit, or strength. Such things are essentially replaceable. If I buy a new copy of a book and immediately lose it, and if someone then gives me a replacement copy which is exactly the same as the previous one, it will be just as good as the previous one and I will have lost nothing. Moreover, different kinds of things which have value can to some extent compensate for one another. If I have a house with a large garden which I value, this may to some extent compensate for the smallness of the rooms, or the damp in the cellar, and I may be prepared to accept the one as the price I have to pay for the other. Likewise with personal qualities, if I have certain intellectual skills this may to some extent compensate me for my lack of skill as a games player. Now all such things have value, because of the role which they play in the lives of persons. Persons are what give value to things. Persons themselves, therefore, as the source of value, must have a quite different kind of worth; 'that which constitutes the condition under which alone anything can be an end in itself, this has not merely a relative worth, that is, value, but an intrinsic worth, that is, *dignity*' (II.69). In contrast to things which have value, persons, in so far as they have dignity, are irreplaceable. If I take the lives of ten people, I cannot compensate for this by bringing into existence ten more people. As possessors of dignity, persons are the proper objects of the attitude of respect. Respect for dignity is something quite distinct from the promotion of value. Respect for other persons may, as we have seen, require me to help promote their ends, but what it does, more basically, is to set limits on my own pursuit of my own ends. It is 'the supreme limiting condition of all our subjective ends, let them be what we will' (II.55). In pursuing our own ends, we are precluded from employing means which will violate the sanctity of other persons (II.70). Respect is not the same as either inclination or fear, but it has something analogous to both. It is like inclination in being something which we freely and voluntarily will, but it is like fear in being something to which we are subject, and which thwarts our pursuit of our own ends. It is one and the same respect which we feel for persons as rational beings, and for the moral law as the law of reason (footnote to I.16).

I do not have room to explore here the more concrete moral implications of this idea of respect for persons. I mention only the most basic of them: respect for persons involves respect for their *liberty and autonomy*. An ethic which was confined to the *promotion* of ends would incline to paternalism. It would require me to promote the happiness and prevent the suffering of others even at the cost of imposing on them, if necessary, the means to their happiness. For the Kantian ethic, on the other hand, the basic requirement is a respect for the other person's own pursuit of his or her own ends through his or her own free action, and I am to help in the promotion of those ends only in ways which are compatible with that basic respect. Accordingly, Kant lays great emphasis on the notion of human *rights*, in so far as these identify basic freedoms which have to be respected (II.52). In this *Lectures on Ethics* he declared:

> There is nothing more sacred in the wide world than the rights of others. They are inviolable. Woe unto him who trespasses upon the right of another and tramples it underfoot! His right should be his security; it should be stronger than any shield or fortress. We have a holy ruler and the most sacred of his gifts to us is the rights of man.[7]

Whether human rights can be regarded as literally inviolable is a matter for argument. Certainly there are problems, for example, where rights conflict. If there is a 'right for life', for instance, what are we to say of cases where it may be necessary to kill one person in order to save the life of another? What a Kantian ethic will certainly insist on, however, is that rights cannot be violated simply for the sake of promoting desirable ends, whether for oneself or for others.

S2, I am suggesting, is a much more satisfactory formulation of the categorical imperative than S1, and a comparison between the two gives the true measure of the accusation of formalism directed against S1. What seems intuitively interesting, and even inspiring, about an ethic of universality is the idea of universal humanitarianism, the idea of refusing to discriminate between human beings, and of respecting the claims of all to have their humanity recognized. S2 makes this idea explicit, whereas S1 disguises it as a formal principle of pure reason.

On the other hand, I still want to insist that Kant has not provided an adequate justification of S2. The question '*Why* should I respect all human beings as persons?' remains unanswered. Kant's failure here is a failure to justify the strong version of universalizability, as impartiality rather than mere impersonality, and it is the same failure which vitiates also the most plausible interpretation of S1. Kant, then, unlike Plato and Aristotle, undoubtedly furnishes a morality of altruism. Like Hume, however, he presents the opposite problem. Can he, or anyone else, provide any good reason for adhering to an altruistic morality?

Notes

1. Max Weber, *The Protestant Ethic and the Spirit of Capitalism*, trans. Talcott Parsons (London, 1930), 80.
2. G. W. F. Hegel, *Philosophy of Right*, trans. T. M. Knox (Oxford, 1952), para. 135.
3. Marcus G. Singer, *Generalization in Ethics* (London, 1963), 251-3.
4. The principal advocate of this interpretation is H. J. Paton in his book *The Categorical Imperative* (London, 1947).
5. W. D. Ross, *Kant's Ethical Theory* (Oxford, 1954), 94; cf. 34-5.
6. The most influential formulation has been that by R. M. Hare in his book *Freedom and Reason* (London, 1963).
7. Immanuel Kant, *Lectures on Ethics*, trans. Louis Infield (New York, 1963), 193-4.

7

Mill
The Greatest Happiness

Reading: John Stuart Mill: *Utilitarianism* (first published 1861)

There are many editions. A useful one is the Fontana edition edited by Mary Warnock, which also contains Mill's essays on *Bentham* and *On Liberty* and parts of Bentham's *Introduction to the Principles of Morals and Legislation,* all of which are valuable additional reading for the present chapter. Warnock's introduction is also very helpful.

My references will again be to paragraphs, numbered within each chapter. There are 6 paragraphs in Chapter I, 25 in Chapter II, 11 in Chapter III, 12 in Chapter IV, and 38 in Chapter V. My occasional page references to other works by Mill and by Bentham will be to the page numbers in Warnock's edition.

Kant, Bentham, and Christianity

At the beginning of his *Utilitarianism* (paragraph 4) Mill takes his distance from Kantian ethics. He places at the centre of his own moral theory the very things which Kant wants to exclude—the assessment of actions in terms of their ends and consequences, their contribution to human happiness, and the prevention of human suffering. For all that, Mill was a great compromiser in philosophy, and he saw things of value in Kant's theory, which he wanted to retain. He draws on the alternative tradition represented by Kant in order to qualify what was, on balance, a much more positive influence on him—the philosophy of Jeremy Bentham.

Bentham's ethics can be compared in its crudity (or simplicity, according to how we view it) with the position presented by Glaucon in the *Republic*. All human action, he claimed, is motivated by the desire for pleasure and the avoidance of pain. The only rational moral theory, therefore, will be one which seeks to make such action as consistent and effective as possible. In practice each person's pursuit of his or her own pleasure will be modified, to take account of the pleasures and pains of others, by the influence of four 'sanctions'. These are the *physical* sanction (the pleasure and pain one experiences as a direct and natural consequence of one's actions): the *political* sanction (the influence of laws and political edicts on one's pleasures and pains); the *moral* sanction (the influence exerted by other people's responses to oneself and by popular opinion in general); and the *religious* sanction (the influence exerted by the prospect of divine rewards and punishments). The combined effect of all these sanctions is to induce people to pursue their own pleasure in such a way as to co-operate also in the production of pleasure and avoidance of pain for others. The task of the moralist and of the legislator is to manipulate the various sanctions, so as to maximize the happiness of all. Clearly, on this theory, I can attach to the happiness of others only an instrumental value, and my only reason for pursuing it will be for what it contributes to my own happiness. Bentham, however, thought that this reason would be an effective one. Individuals and legislators alike ought therefore to regulate their conduct by the *principle of utility*, by which 'is meant that principle which approves or disapproves of every action whatsoever according to the tendency which it appears to have to augment or diminish the happiness of the party whose interest is in question' (i.e. in the case of individual actions, the happiness of the individual, and in the case of social organization, the happiness of the community).

John Stuart Mill's father, James Mill, was Bentham's friend and collaborator, and with Bentham's help devised an ambitious scheme of education for his son. It is not surprising, therefore, that the younger Mill grew up a convinced utilitarian, but not surprising either (adolescence being what it is) that he then reacted against it. In what he later called 'a crisis in my mental history', he came to see Benthamite utilitarianism as too limited and uninspiring. Bentham's philosophy, as he subsequently wrote in his essay on *Bentham*,

> will do nothing (except sometimes as an instrument in the hands of a higher doctrine) for the spiritual interests of society . . . It can teach the means of organising and regulating the merely *business* part of the social arrangements. Whatever can be understood or whatever done without reference to moral influences, his philosophy is equal to: where those influences require to be taken into account, it is at fault. (Warnock: op. cit., 105 f.)

The principle deficiency in Bentham's conception of moral influences is that

> Man is never recognised by him as a being capable of pursing spiritual perfection as an end; of desiring, for its own sake, the conformity of his own character to his standard of excellence, without hope of good or fear of evil from other source than his own inward consciousness. (Ibid. 100)

The concession to Kantian ethics is clear here.

The insights which Bentham lacks, Mill aspires to incorporate within what is still a utilitarian framework. He remains committed to the view that 'actions are right in proportion as they tend to promote happiness, wrong as they tend to promote the reverse of happiness', and that 'by happiness is intended pleasure, and the absence of pain; by unhappiness, pain, and the privation of pleasure' (II.2). Unlike Bentham, however, he puts a much more altruistic slant on the doctrine. In keeping with his emphasis on the nobility of disinterested devotion to moral duty, he interprets utilitarianism as requiring that one's actions should aim at the general happiness, regardless of whether this will increase one's own happiness. Interpreted in this light, utilitarianism is, he thinks, essentially concordant with the ethics of Christianity. 'In the golden rule of Jesus of Nazareth,' he says, 'we read the complete spirit of the ethics of utility' (II.18). Mill was certainly not a Christian. Like many of his contemporaries, however, he wished to extract from Christianity the essential spirit of its ethics, which should continue to inspire mankind under the guise of a 'religion of humanity'. This exalted ethical religion, detached from its Christian context, would have to rest upon the somewhat fragile foundations of Bentham's hedonistic psychology. We shall now have to consider whether the resulting structure is sufficiently stable to survive.

Higher and Lower Pleasures

Mill offers two kinds of defence of utilitarianism. In Chapter II, he mounts a negative defence, attempting to eliminate misunderstandings of the theory and to meet objections to it. The point of reference here is, as with Kant's defence, the ordinary moral consciousness, and Mill wants to show that utilitarianism is essentially consistent with that commonsense morality. He does not, indeed, claim that utilitarianism in its implications coincides exactly with the accepted moral beliefs of his day. He was critical of many of those beliefs, and the utilitarian theory provided the standpoint from which he would want to criticize them. What he would claim, however, is that the general body of widely-accepted moral beliefs, when properly reflected upon, made internally consistent, and modified in the light of empirical facts, will be found to be broadly in accordance with the principle of utility, which can therefore be adopted as its underlying principle. This is Mill's approach in Chapter II. Chapter IV is different. He there attempts a more positive defence, one which is independent of the ordinary moral consciousness and is in some sense a more basic proof. Just what form this proof is supposed to take, and in what sense it is a 'proof', I shall consider in due course, but I shall begin by examining the first kind of defence.

From the standpoint of commonly accepted beliefs and values, the point on which Mill feels his utilitarianism to be most vulnerable is its hedonism—its assertion that the sole ultimate value is happiness, and that this can be equated with pleasure and absence of pain. Mill envisages the response of his critics: 'To suppose that life has (as they express it) no higher end than pleasure—no better and nobler object of desire and pursuit—they designate as utterly mean and grovelling; as a doctrine worthy only of swine' (II.3). It is to deal with this kind of objection that Mill introduces, in Chapter II, his distinction between higher and lower pleasures. Pleasures differ from one another in quality as well as in quantity, and the superior pleasures are those which befit our nature as human beings, and utilize our capacities for intelligent activity.

To appreciate the force of the distinction between 'quantity' and 'quality', we must look to a comparison with Bentham. Bentham's theory is insistently quantitative. To estimate the value of an action we must measure the value of the pleasures and pains it produces, and Bentham asks us to do this by measuring their intensity, their duration, their certainty or uncertainty, their propinquity (how long we have to wait for them), their fecundity or purity (i.e. the further pleasures or pains they are likely to cause), and their extent (the number of people who experience them). Although Bentham can hardly have taken seriously the idea of assigning precise numbers to these measurements, it is fair to say that this is the ideal to which he would aspire.

In introducing considerations of quality as well as quantity, Mill is in part reverting to the position of Plato and Aristotle. Like them, he believes that to find out what constitutes full and genuine happiness, we have to look at what is specific to the nature of human beings and distinguishes them from other animal species. Unlike Aristotle, however, he does not attempt the transition from the view of human nature to the view of human happiness by means of the essentialist argument that because certain activities are essentially human, they constitute the natural and proper purpose of human life, and provide the content of human happiness. For Mill, the connection between human nature and human happiness is not this essentialist one but a psychological one. The description of utilitarianism as a doctrine worthy only of swine is, he says,

> felt as degrading precisely because a beast's pleasures do not satisfy a human being's conception of happiness. Human beings have faculties more elevated than the animal appetites, and when once made conscious of them, do not regard anything as happiness which does not include their gratification. (II.4)

The point, then, is not that because human beings have distinctive capacities, they *therefore ought to* (or are intended by nature to) find their happiness in the exercise of them; it is that because they have these distinctive capacities, they *are not fully satisfied by* a happiness which does not involve the exercise of them.

How can Mill say this? Is it not all too apparent that many people actively pursue trivial and mindless pleasures, and are entirely content with them? Mill's answer is that though, finally, the higher pleasures can be said to be superior only because human beings prefer them, the preferences which determine their superiority must be the preferences of those who have a real experience of the alternatives. Undoubtedly there are many people whose experience has been largely confined to trivial and mindless pleasures, and who continue to pursue them fairly exclusively. What Mill would claim is that if they could properly experience some of the more demanding enjoyments which human beings are capable of, they would themselves come to find those more rewarding. The phrase '*properly* experience' is important. The pleasures of literary and artistic enjoyment, of intellectual enquiry, of creative and imaginative work, or of energetic devotion to a cause, may not reveal themselves upon an immediate acquaintance. They require application and commitment over an extended period of time, a willingness to accept temporary set-backs, and in some cases a process of education. But anyone who has really experienced what such activities have to offer will not thereafter willingly forgo them.

This would also be Mill's answer to another common reaction, that his position is an 'élitist' one. When Mill says that the superiority of the higher pleasures is decided by the 'verdict of the only competent judges', his readers are often inclined to reply: Why should I accept that verdict? If I really am passionately and exclusively devoted to so-called 'animal' pleasures, what right does anyone else have to label those pleasures inferior? Mill's answer would have to be: No right at all—other than a right grounded upon what your own judgement would be if you could really experience the alternatives. Mill depends heavily on the assumption that if they could only experience them fully, everyone really would prefer the higher pleasures. He does qualify this slightly, but significantly. He admits that there are those who, having at one time been able to appreciate the higher pleasures, subsequently neglect them and relapse into habits of apathy. But such cases are, he thinks, susceptible of explanations in social and psychological terms which will show them to be cases of degeneration.

Two other qualifications ought to be added to Mill's position, and these are ones which he does not himself add. We should, I think, qualify Mill's rather severely intellectualist account of the higher pleasures. He tends to assume that the distinction between higher and lower pleasures corresponds to that between intellectual (or at any rate spiritual) and physical activities. There is no need to assume this. There are plenty of physical activities which offer more than superficial pleasures—activities which require skill, energy, care, and commitment, and which are appreciated and enjoyed only when pursued in this way. Indeed, if we think of examples, such as activities of skilled craftsmanship, the intellectual/physical dichotomy seems positively misleading. The second qualification is that the contrast between higher and lower pleasures need not entail that the lower pleasures have to be excluded from a worthwhile life. Mill was inclined to exclude them. He tended to look on the pleasures of physical sensation as simply degrading. This, however, is not essential to his general position. The much maligned triad of food, drink, and sex are surely pleasures without which any human life is the poorer. While characterizing them as 'lower' pleasures, Mill could quite consistently have allowed a place for them, adding only that a life which was devoted overwhelmingly to them, and which detached them from any context of wider significance, however replete with pleasure it might be, would be a trivial and empty life.

With these qualifications, Mill's position seems to me to be a distinct advance on Bentham. Though tending in an Aristotelian direction, it improves also upon Aristotle, in so far as it does not rely on his essentialist argument. Many of Mill's critics, however, though agreeing with this, would add a new objection. They would say that Mill may be right to recognize qualitative differences of pleasure, but that he is inconsistent in so far as he also wants to hang on to Bentham's quantitative version of utilitarianism. He continues to refer to it, for example, as the *Greatest* Happiness Principle, and to say that an action is right if it produces *more* happiness than any alternative.

Up to a point—but only up to a point—this objection can be answered. The categories of quantity and quality are not mutually exclusive. A difference may be a qualitative one, and at the same time be a quantitative one just because it is also qualitative. If, of two pleasures, one is richer and more rewarding because it employs more of one's faculties and energies, then it will for that very reason be *more* pleasurable, and a life encompassing it will be a life of *greater* happiness, even though the pleasure will be no more intense or long-lasting. The point is that, though one can speak of 'greater' pleasure or happiness in such cases, the quantitative difference is one which can be recognized *only on the basis of the qualitative difference*. Only if we can see that the pleasure is more demanding, less superficial, and therefore more rewarding, can we see that it is also a greater pleasure. If we look for a *purely* quantitative difference, we shall not find one.

Mill, then, is not necessarily inconsistent in using both quantitative and qualitative terminology. The real trouble is that he still, to some extent, wants to combine the qualitative conception with Bentham's arithmetical, additive conception of quantitative differences. He does, on occasion (though much less than is commonly supposed), continue to speak as though one could determine the rightness or wrongness of an action simply be *adding up* the quantities of pleasure and pain it will produce, by 'calculating and weighing the effects' (II.24), and thereby determining whether the action does or does not 'tend to increase the sum total of happiness' (II.17). To that extent he is indeed inconsistent. It is not enough, however, simply to charge him with inconsistency. The criticism is facile unless it also indicates in which direction the inconsistency should be resolved. I have already indicated my own view that its resolution should take Mill more firmly in the direction of Plato and Aristotle rather than of Bentham.

Duties

I turn now to the other most widespread objection to utilitarianism, and this is that it fails to give an adequate treatment of the concept of duty. A division

is often made between *teleological* and *deontological* theories in ethics. A teleological theory is one which asserts that an action is right or wrong, in so far as
it produces good or bad consequences. Utilitarianism is one form of teleological theory, distinguished from other teleological theories by its assertion that
the 'good' of good consequences is identifiable with happiness. A deontological theory is one which asserts that at least some actions are right or wrong,
and we have a duty or obligation to perform them or refrain from them, quite
apart from considerations of consequences. Teleological theories thus treat
'good' and 'bad' as the basic ethical concepts, and define others such as 'right'
and 'wrong' in terms of these, whereas deontological theories would treat
'right', 'wrong', 'duty', and 'obligation' as basic, or at least give them equal status with 'good' and 'bad'.

Kant's ethical theory would be one instance of a deontological theory. Many
other philosophers, however, without being committed to Kant's account of
duty and its derivation from the categorical imperative, have wanted to assert
that there are duties which a utilitarian or other teleological theory cannot
explain. A classic statement of this position can be found in W. D. Ross's book
The Right and The Good, published in 1930. Ross offers the following classification of moral duties:

duties of fidelity (keeping promises, telling the truth, paying debts etc.);
duties of reparation (compensating for a harm one has done);
duties of gratitude (repaying a kindness);
duties of justice (distributing goods rightly);
duties of beneficence (improving the condition of others);
duties of self-improvement (improving our own condition in respect of virtue
     or intelligence);
duties of non-maleficence (not injuring others).

The last three could be regarded as very broadly utilitarian or at least
teleological in character, but the others are not, and carrying them out may
sometimes require us to produce less overall good than we could otherwise
have done. Therefore, if there really are such duties, they pose an obvious
problem for utilitarianism.

Ross argues the point effectively with respect to the example of promising,
and the example is a good one. Now we can agree that keeping a promise will
normally have at least some good consequences and breaking it will have bad
consequences, for if I keep it, the person to whom I made it will be pleased,
and if I break it, he or she will be annoyed. We can also agree that in some cases
the results of keeping a promise would be so bad, or of breaking it would be so
good, that I ought to break it. If, for example, I have promised to meet you for
a drink and, when I am about to set out, my child is taken ill and I have to rush
her to hospital, it would generally be agreed that I am right to break my
promise. Certainly, then, consequences are relevant to the keeping or breaking

of promises. There is, however, another factor which is equally relevant to what I ought to do in such cases, namely *the fact that I have promised*; and this, according to Ross and others, is what utilitarians lose sight of when they assume that the rightness or wrongness of promise-keeping is simply a matter of consequences. According to Ross, I have a duty to keep a promise, just as such, simply because I have promised. This duty may be reinforced by potential consequences. It may be outweighed by consequences. It is, however, a duty in its own right, and utilitarianism cannot explain this.

Ross asks us to imagine an example. He presents it in highly abstract terms, and I will therefore concretize it. Suppose that I have arranged to visit a friend on my bicycle, and have promised my daughter that I will take her with me on the child-seat of the bicycle. As I am about to leave, my son says that he wants to go with me. I cannot take them both. Now suppose that my son and my daughter would equally enjoy going with me, and would be equally disappointed if they cannot go (and suppose that this is the case, even when we take into account the added disappointment which my daughter will feel as a result of having had her expectations roused). Or suppose that my son will even enjoy it very slightly more than my daughter would. The utilitarian will have to say that if my son would enjoy it even more, I ought to take him; and that if they would both enjoy it equally, it would be equally right for me to take either my son or my daughter. To say this, however, is to deny all significance to what is, in fact, the crucial difference between the two alternatives, the fact that I have made a promise to my daughter, but not to my son. In virtue of that fact it is clear that, even though the consequences might be just as good in either case, I ought to take my daughter. This shows that there is a duty to keep one's promises, quite apart from utilitarian considerations.[1]

Similar examples could be constructed to illustrate other duties. Take the case of justice. Ross understands justice as the duty of distributing rewards in proportion to merit. Others have understood it as requiring, at least to some degree, an *equal* distribution of goods. Suppose that we are comparing two modes of social and political organization, instantiated in society A and society B. Suppose that the overall level of general well-being (measured, perhaps, as the sum total of economic wealth) is slightly higher in A than in B. Suppose, however, that in A there are massive inequalities, such that a fortunate few enjoy unparalleled luxury, while a significant number of others live in abject poverty, whereas in B goods are distributed much more equally, and everyone enjoys a good life. It would surely have to be said that in comparison with B the organization of A is unjust and to that extent wrong, even though the sum of well-being in A is higher. Now there may be more to be said. Some might argue, for example, that the promotion of equality is possible only at the cost of coercion and the destruction of liberty, and that it would therefore be wrong to try to replace the mode of organization of A with that of B. Other arguments might be advanced for the same conclusion. What can hardly be denied, however, is that in assessing the rights and wrongs of the two societies, considerations of justice are relevant, and that they are distinct from, and may conflict with, considerations of maximizing utility.

What is common to the two examples, that of promise-keeping and that of justice? What they both bring out is that utilitarianism, focusing exclusively on the overall maximization of benefits, attaches no ethical significance to *who gets the benefits*, because it attaches no significance to the nature of the *relations* between the persons involved. Ross again puts this well. Any form of utilitarianism, he says,

> seems to simplify unduly our relations to our fellows. It says, in effect, that the only morally significant relation in which my neighbours stand to me is that of being possible beneficiaries by my action. They do stand in this relation to me, and this relation is morally significant. But they may also stand to me in the relation of promisee to promiser, of creditor to debtor, of wife to husband, of child to parent, of friend to friend, of fellow countryman to fellow countryman, and the like; and each of these relations is the foundation of a *prima facie* duty, which is more or less incumbent on me according to the circumstances of the case.[2]

Unfortunately Ross does not take this any further. What it calls for is a developed account of social relations and their ethical significance. Ross does not provide one, and without it we shall not be able to form a clear idea of what is valid in the deontological approach to ethics. In the next chapter we shall look at an attempt to provide such an account.

Before moving on, we should note one way in which Mill himself attempts to accommodate the idea of moral duties which appear to have a deontological character. This is by acknowledging the place of *moral rules* within a utilitarian morality. To act rightly we need to be guided by traditional rules such as that we ought to keep our promises, to tell the truth, and so on. We cannot calculate the consequences of every single action from scratch. If we tried to do so we should never get round to acting at all. Moral rules encapsulate the accumulated experience of many generations about which kinds of actions will have good or bad consequences. If we look at the role of rules in moral behaviour, we may think that they represent deontological duties independent of consequences. In doing so, however, we should be forgetting that, though in particular cases we act simply by following the rules, what lies behind the rules is a long history of experience of the consequences. We speak the truth because the rule tells us to do so. The rule itself, however, is one which we should adopt not simply for its own sake, but because it reminds us that the practice of truth-telling is of great utility, essential for the effective functioning of human society. Mill speaks of moral rules as 'landmarks and direction-posts', as 'corollaries', as 'secondary principles' derivative from the fundamental principle of utility.

It will be apparent that Mill's is a two-tier theory of moral decision-making, of a kind which we have previously encountered. The first tier of moral deliberation is that of deciding what to do by consulting the rules; the second is that of assessing the rules themselves by looking at their consequences. In the chapter on Hume I referred to the distinction between two versions of utilitarianism, *act-utilitarianism* and *rule-utilitarianism*. Mill's discussion of rules has given rise to a debate about which of these two camps he should be assigned to.[3] As we have seen, a version of utilitarianism which recognizes the importance of rules does not necessarily amount to a separate theory, 'rule-utilitarianism', radically distinct from act-utilitarianism. The utilitarian's conception of rules may be the idea of what have been called 'rules of thumb'. This is the idea that rules are convenient guidelines, and that the reasons for being guided by them on particular occasions are themselves act-utilitarian reasons: following the rule saves time, is a safeguard against bias and special pleading, and is therefore the best bet for producing the best consequences. Much of what Mill says about rules tends to suggest that he is working with the 'rule of thumb' conception.

We also noted in the chapter on Hume that there is another utilitarian account of rules, distinct from act-utilitarianism and deserving the distinct label 'rule-utilitarianism'. This has sometimes been called 'generalized rule-utilitarianism'. It is the theory that we should be guided by a moral rule because it is the one which, *if generally followed*, would produce the best consequences. This seems to provide a real contrast with act-utilitarianism. It implies that in particular cases one may have to act in a way which will *not* have the best consequences on this occasion; but that one should nevertheless follow the rule because *in general* this course of action has the best consequences. There is one point at which Mill appears to espouse this position. He says:

> In the case of abstinences indeed—of things which people forebear to do from moral considerations, though the consequences in the particular case might be beneficial—it would be unworthy of an intelligent agent not to be consciously aware that the action is of a class which, if practised generally, would be generally injurious, and that this is the ground of the obligation to abstain from it. (II.19)

This however is an isolated remark of Mill's, and much of what he says about rules seems to fit more readily the act-utilitarian, 'rule-of-thumb' conception.

It is a matter for debate whether Mill is an act-utilitarian or a rule-utilitarian, and perhaps the answer is that he does not clearly distinguish between the two positions. The more important question is whether his account of rules enables him adequately to meet his deontological critics. Up to a point it does. He can account for the intuitive plausibility of deontological ethics, and can explain why we feel obliged to keep a promise or to tell the truth without calculating the consequences of this particular action on this particular occasion. Mill fails, however, to get to grips with the more fundamental objection. As I have suggested, he fails to do justice to the way in which moral obligations may be rooted in specific social relations.

The 'Proof'

So far we have been considering objections to utilitarianism from the point of view of generally accepted moral beliefs. Mill, like other utilitarians, thinks it incumbent on him to meet these objections, and to show that such beliefs are, in their main essentials, consistent with utilitarianism. There is, however, a shorter way which he could have taken with them. Mill thinks that he can also provide an independent defence of utilitarianism, an argument from first principles which does not require any appeal to accepted moral beliefs. There-fore, if those beliefs then turn out to be incompatible with utilitarianism in certain respects, it is open to Mill to respond: so much the worse for conventional morality—it must be mistaken on these points, since we have independently demonstrated that utilitarianism is correct.

The attempted demonstration has three stages (although they are not presented by Mill in this order):

1. If everyone desires happiness for its own sake, then happiness is desirable as an end in itself.
2. Nothing else separate and distinct from happiness is desired as an end in itself.
3. If happiness is the only thing desirable as an end in itself, then the general happiness is the proper end of conduct.

The passage which gives us the essence of stage (1) is this:

> The only proof capable of being given that an object is visible, is that people actu-ally see it. The only proof that a sound is audible, is that people hear it: and so of the other sources of our experience. In like manner, I apprehend, the sole evidence it is possible to produce that anything is desirable, is that people do actually desire it ... No reason can be given why the general happiness is desirable, except that each per-son, so far as he believes it to be attainable, desires his own happiness. This, how-ever, being a fact, we have not only all the proof which the case admits of, but all which it is possible to require, that happiness is a good ... (IV.3)

Mill's argument in this passage has been attacked, most notably by G. E. Moore in his 1903 book *Principia Ethica*, on the grounds that something's being *desired* does not entail that it is *desirable*. From the mere statement of psychological fact that people *do actually desire* happiness for its own sake, one cannot, it is said, deduce the evaluative conclusion that happiness is desir-able, i.e. that it *ought* to be desired. It is logically possible that people in fact desire something which they ought *not* to desire, something which is not really desirable. The argument is not, it is claimed, a valid proof.

Mill's defenders hasten to point out his quite explicit assertion that he is not offering a proof 'in the ordinary and popular meaning of the term'. 'Questions of ultimate ends', he says, 'are not amenable to direct proof' (I.5). He is not claiming that if people desire happiness, this *logically entails* that it is desirable.

What then is he claiming? If he is not offering a proof in the normal sense, what is he offering? Here is his answer.

> Questions of ultimate ends do not admit of proof, in the ordinary acceptation of the term. To be incapable of proof by reasoning is common to all first principles; to the first premises of our knowledge as well as those of our conduct. But the former, being matters of fact, may be the subject of a direct appeal to the faculties which judge of fact—namely, our senses, and our internal consciousness. Can an appeal be made to the same faculties on questions of practical ends? Or by what other faculty is cognisance taken of them? (IV.1)

It is clear from this passage that Mill's argument does not appeal to a general logical relation between words ending in '-ed', and words ending in '-ble'. That is not the point of the analogy with 'visible' and 'audible'. It would not suit his purposes, for example, to claim that the only proof that Manchester United are beatable is that they have been beaten. The appeal, rather, is to a specific view about the ultimate grounds of knowledge. This view is an *empiricist* one, the view that all valid claims to knowledge must ultimately be based on experience. Our knowledge of the external world is based on the experience of the senses—and this is the point of Mill's remark that we know that things are visible because we see them, and we know that things are audible because we hear them. Mill would also claim that our knowledge of our own mental states is based on the experience of introspection, our 'internal consciousness'. In these cases, then, the experience which is the grounds of our knowledge is provided by the faculties of sight, hearing, and the other senses, and by the faculty of internal consciousness. Mill then asks: what of our knowledge of values, of the ends of conduct? What kind of experience provides the grounds of this knowledge? What psychological faculty is the source of this experience? His answer is: the faculty of desire.

Now the experience of desire does not furnish any conclusive proof, any more than do the experiences of sight or hearing. If I want to convince you that the Post Office Tower is visible from Hampstead Heath, and I therefore take you to Hampstead Heath and let you see the Tower, this does not *prove* that it is visible. The senses are fallible, and the experience may be the result of some complex optical illusion. There are ways of checking on this, and these will involve further appeal to the evidence of the senses. If, after all possible checks have been made, you still insist that the Tower is not visible and that your experience must be some kind of illusion, I cannot prove you wrong. Nevertheless the fact remains that one normally convinces people that something is visible by appealing to their experience of seeing it, and if this experience consistently supports the claim, it provides the best evidence one could possible have. Similarly if one wants to convince people that something is desirable as an end in itself, the appropriate way of doing this is to point out to them that, as a matter of experience, they do in fact desire it. This will not, strictly speaking, prove that it is desirable, but it will provide 'all the proof which the case admits of, and all which it is possible to require'.

So far, so good. The first stage of Mill's argument is not fallacious in the way that it has sometimes been thought to be. Mill now has to show that people do in fact desire happiness for its own sake, and furthermore that nothing other than happiness is in fact desired for its own sake, for this is how he must make good the utilitarian claim that the production of happiness is the *sole* test of right and wrong. It is clear that people desire a host of different things. It is also clear that many of the things which people want are wanted, not for their own sake, but for the sake of something else. If I want some petrol, I want it not for its own sake, but so that I can drive my car; driving my car is something which I want not for its own sake, but so that I can get to work, and getting to work is in turn not something which I want for its own sake. Here we have a typical sequence of means and ends, each intermediate end being in turn a means to a further end. What Mill has to show is that every such sequence of means and ends eventually comes to a halt at happiness. He has to show that happiness is the one thing which is wanted purely for its own sake, and that everything else which people want is ultimately wanted for the sake of happiness. Can he show this?

It would seem not. He says:

> Now it is palpable that they do desire things which, in common language, are decidedly distinguished from happiness. They desire, for example, virtue, and the absence of vice, no less really than pleasure and the absence of pain. The desire of virtue is not as universal, but it is as authentic a fact, as the desire of happiness. (II.4)

The example takes us back to Mill's concession to Kantian ethics, and his revision of Bentham so as to allow that people can and should aim at disinterested devotion to moral duty for its own sake. The recognition of this possibility now poses problems for Mill's claim that happiness is the only thing desired for its own sake. He goes on to identify other apparent counter-examples. People like music for its own sake, they aim at health for its own sake, and, less admirably perhaps, they desire things such as money and power and fame for their own sake. We could construct other counter-examples of the same kind. How is Mill to deal with them? He does so as follows:

> The ingredients of happiness are very various, and each of them is desirable in itself; . . . besides being means, they are a part of the end. Virtue, according to the utilitarian doctrine, is not naturally and originally part of the end, but it is capable of becoming so; and in those who love it disinterestedly it has become so, and is desired and cherished, not as a means to happiness, but as a part of their happiness. (IV.5)

Here the crucial phrases are 'ingredient of happiness' and 'part of happiness'. Mill's way of dealing with the counter-examples is then to say that these other things such as virtue and health are indeed, or can come to be, desired for their own sake, but that this is quite consistent with the assertion that they are desired as parts or ingredients of happiness. Of any such thing we can say that

> In being desired for its own sake it is, however, desired as *part* of happiness . . . The desire of it is not a different thing from the desire of happiness, any more than the love of music, or the desire of health. They are included in happiness. They are some of the elements of which the desire of happiness is made up. Happiness is not an abstract idea, but a concrete whole; and these are some of its parts. (IV.6)

There is a positive merit in this formulation, but there is also a danger. As to the merit, we have encountered it previously in connection with Mill's discussion of higher pleasures. We saw there the need to move away from Bentham's purely additive and instrumental conception—the idea that happiness is simply a sum of homogeneous units of pleasurable experience, and that anything else of value is related to happiness simply as a means to the production of such units. To give an adequate account of happiness, we have to look at the character of a human life as a whole, and to consider what overall kind of life human beings experience as most deeply and fully satisfying. The vocabulary of 'parts' or 'ingredients' of happiness, as distinct from that of means and ends, is a move in this direction, though perhaps still conceding too much to the additive conception.

Such a vocabulary has its value, then, when used as part of an attempt to work out an adequate and substantial moral psychology. The danger arises when Mill uses it in the present context, as part of an attempt to prove that happiness is the only thing desired for its own sake. The danger is that any apparent counter-examples will *automatically* be redescribed by Mill in the language of 'ingredients of happiness'. Of anything which appears to be desired for its own sake Mill can simply say, 'That just shows that it is a part of happiness'. In other words, 'being desired for its own sake' would be regarded as *meaning* 'being desired as a part of happiness'. The claim that happiness is the sole end, and that everything else that people desire is desired as a means to, or as a part of happiness, would then have become an empty truism. 'Happiness' would simply have been redefined as 'satisfaction of desire', and the assertion, 'People desire happiness', would amount to no more than 'People desire the satisfaction of their desires'.

This might not matter if the third stage of Mill's argument could be accepted. That stage is supposed to provide the transition from the agent's own happiness to the general happiness. All that the previous two stages can have shown is that each person necessarily desires his or her own happiness, and desires nothing else, except as a means to or part of this, and that therefore each person's own happiness is desirable for that person, and is a rational end for that person to aim at. What now has to be shown is that it is equally rational and desirable for each person to aim at the happiness of everyone else. And even if the first two stages have established only that each person's satisfaction is a rational end for that person, still, if some argument could then be found to show that it is equally rational for each person to aim at the satisfaction of everyone, a substantial ethical theory would have been validated. This is, in fact, the form in which some contemporary utilitarians have re-stated the theory. They have replaced the concept of 'happiness' with something like 'preference-satisfaction'. They have adopted a version of utilitarianism which does not aspire to a theory of value, but simply a theory of distribution. It does not offer any substantial answer to the question, what kinds of things are valuable or desirable. It simply recognizes that people have preferences, whatever they may be, and argues that any human agent ought to aim at maximizing the satisfaction of preferences, whether they are one's own or other people's. If this is how Mill is to be reformulated, everything depends on the third stage of the argument.

Unfortunately that stage is the weakest of all. Indeed, it can hardly be said to exist. All that Mill gives us is half a sentence, the continuation of a passage I have previously quoted.

> No reason can be given why the general happiness is desirable, except that each person, so far as he believes it to be attainable, desires his own happiness. This, however, being a fact, we have not only all the proof which the case admits of, but all which it is possible to require, that happiness is a good: that each person's happiness is a good to that person, and the general happiness, therefore, a good to the aggregate of all persons. (IV.3)

If the last half-sentence contains any argument at all, that argument would presumably have to be:

(a) Each person desires his or her own happiness.
(b) Therefore each person ought to aim at his or her own happiness.
(c) Therefore everyone ought to aim at the happiness of everyone.

The move from (b) to (c) is, however, entirely fallacious. It is no more valid than would be the argument that, if each husband ought to love his own wife, every husband ought to love everyone else's wife.

In Chapter V, Mill makes one other perfunctory attempt to fill the gap. He says that the Principle of Utility is 'a mere form of words without rational significance, unless one person's happiness . . . is counted for exactly as much as another's' (V.36). He adds, in a footnote, that 'equal amounts of happiness are equally desirable, whether felt by the same or by different persons . . . for what is the principle of utility, if it be not that "happiness" and "desirable" are synonymous terms?' In so far as there is any argument here, it would have to be some kind of universalizability argument: if I apply the word 'desirable' to my happiness, and you apply the word 'desirable' to your happiness, then I must apply the word 'desirable' to your happiness, for the word 'desirable' must be used consistently, with the same meaning on each occasion of its use. This, however, is just another attempt to squeeze too much out of the requirement of consistency or universalizability. All that can be said is that, if I regard it as rational (or linguistically appropriate) for me to apply the word 'desirable' to my happiness, I must regard it as equally rational (or linguistically appropriate) for you to apply the word 'desirable' to your happiness. That is not what Mill wants.

Ironically, the materials for a more satisfactory argument are available to Mill in his own Chapter III. He there suggests that utilitarian morality has 'a natural basis of sentiment', and that this natural basis is 'the social feelings of mankind, the desire to be in unity with our fellow-creatures'. The social state is 'natural, necessary and habitual' for human beings. All human beings grow to maturity within a social environment, and in this way they 'grow up unable to conceive as possible to them a state of total disregard of other people's interests'. Through innumerable experiences of co-operating with others, people come to identify with the interests and feelings of others, and to think in terms of collective rather than individual interests (III.9–10). All of this is offered by Mill not as a *justification* of the altruistic aspect of utilitarianism, but simply as a psychological *explanation* of how it is possible. Nevertheless, properly employed, this account of the social character of human experience would have enabled Mill to show not just that such behaviour is possible, but that it is rationally justifiable. That is a claim which I shall try to substantiate in due course.

As an ethics of altruism, then, Mill's theory fails just as Kant's did. He sets out to provide a completely universalistic morality. Each of us is to treat every other person's happiness and suffering as having just the same importance as our own; in Bentham's words, 'everybody to count for one, nobody for more than one'. It turns out, however, that Mill can provide no satisfactory account of why anyone ought to act in this way.

The Two Strands in Mill's Utilitarianism

We have found a pervasive tension between two strands in utilitarianism. On the one hand, there is what can be called the 'mathematical' strand, which derives from Bentham. Happiness is treated as an unproblematic concept, whether it be composed of Benthamite states of pleasurable sensation or the preference-satisfactions of latter-day utilitarianism. The individual's happiness is arrived at simply by adding together these units. And the general happiness which is supposed to be the aim of all conduct is treated as equally unproblematic; it is simply a matter of adding up the happiness of all the individuals. I have argued that this strand is inadequate on both counts. The concept of happiness can and should be given more than this superficial treatment; and the universalistic altruism of the theory lacks any satisfactory justification.

Mill is torn between this and what I will call the 'Platonic–Aristotelian' strand. The consistent development of this strand would involve treating happiness as an essentially qualitative notion. Happiness would then be a matter of the overall character of a person's life, such as would satisfy his or her most deeply felt needs. In order to identify the form such a life would take, we would have to look at what is distinctive about human beings, and what constitutes a fully human life. In the manner of Plato and Aristotle, this enriched conception of the agent's own happiness would then provide the overall framework within which relations to others would be located. An adequate account of these social relations, in all their complexity, would make it possible to do justice to the moral duties of deontological ethics. In the next chapter we shall look at a theory which tries to do all of this.

Notes

1. My formulation of Ross's example is indebted also to Russell Grice's version of it in his book *The Grounds of Moral Judgments* (Cambridge, 1967), 57–63.
2. W. D. Ross, *The Right and the Good* (London, 1930), 19.
3. For some contributions to this debate and some typical defences and criticisms of rule-utilitarianism see J. O. Urmson, 'The Interpretation of the Moral Philosophy of J. S. Mill', J. D. Mabbott, 'Interpretations of Mill's "Utilitarianism"', John Rawls, 'Two Concepts of Rules', and J. J. C. Smart, 'Extreme and Restricted Utilitarianism', in Philippa Foot (ed.), *Theories of Ethics* (Oxford, 1967).

8
Hegelian Ethics
Self-Realization

Reading: F. H. Bradley, *Ethical Studies* (first published 1876)

The chapters to which I shall refer are:

Essay II: Why Should I Be Moral?;
Essay III: Pleasure for Pleasure's Sake;
Essay IV: Duty for Duty's Sake;
Essay V: My Station and its Duties;
Concluding Remarks.

My discussion will be overwhelmingly concentrated on 'My Station and its Duties', which can be found reprinted in various anthologies of moral philosophy. My references will be to paragraph numbers. The essay has 74 paragraphs, excluding the Note at the end. Paragraph 67 is the incomplete sentence beginning '(1) Within the sphere . . .', and paragraph 68 begins '(a) It is impossible . . .'. I shall also give a few references to Essay II 'Why Should I Be Moral?', which has 69 paragraphs (again excluding the Note). Readers who wish to follow up the original Hegelian sources of Bradley's ethical theory will find references in the footnotes.

Bradley and Hegel

Ideally, I should like this chapter to deal directly with the ethical philosophy of Hegel, the nineteenth-century German philosopher whose ideas on the history of philosophy I mentioned in Chapter 1. Hegel's ethics seems to me to be by far the most interesting theory to go beyond the deficiencies of Kantianism and utilitarianism in the direction of an ethics of social relations. (Hegel wrote before Mill, but was acquainted with Bentham's work.) Hegel's philosophy is, however, notoriously difficult—not, perhaps, as utterly forbidding as it is sometimes made out to be, but still a formidable task for the beginner.

There is, however, a solution readily available, for one of Hegel's foremost British interpreters, F. H. Bradley, is eminently readable (if sometimes over-rhetorical), and meets the needs of this chapter perfectly. Bradley was one of the group of philosophers known as the British Idealists, centred mainly at Oxford, who were responsible for introducing Hegel's philosophy into this country in the latter part of the nineteenth century. They drew on Hegel and his German idealist predecessors (including Kant), principally to counter the then-dominant tradition represented by Mill, not only in ethics but in all areas of philosophy.

It is a matter for argument whether Bradley's presentation of Hegelian ethics is a faithful reflection of the original. Bradley himself is not an orthodox Hegelian, and *Ethical Studies* is not an exegesis of Hegel, but an important work in its own right. The general methodology of the book is Hegelian, however, and the chapter entitled 'My Station and its Duties' is a sympathetic exposition of a broadly Hegelian position, buttressed with extended quotations from Hegel.[1] Bradley's own judgement on it is that 'the theory which we have just exhibited (more or less in our own way) . . . seems to us a great advance on anything we have had before, and indeed in the main to be satisfactory' (V.64). He adds, however, that 'if put forth as that beyond which we do not need to go, as the end in itself, it is open to very serious objections', and he proceeds to state these. It is not clear whether in doing so he thinks that he is criticizing Hegel, that is, whether he thinks that Hegel would regard the ethics of 'my station and its duties' as 'that beyond which we do not need to go'. Certainly, the direction in which Bradley himself goes beyond it, into the religious faith of the Concluding Remarks, is not Hegel's. I shall, then, treat *Ethical Studies* as a work in its own right, not concerning myself too much with the question of its fidelity to Hegel, but recognizing that its underlying inspiration is Hegelian.

Some initial remarks are nevertheless needed about the Hegelian influence on Bradley's method. I said something about this in Chapter 1, where I mentioned Hegel's idea of philosophical development taking place through the negation of limited and partial positions, and the retention of them in their negated forms as elements within a whole. This philosophical method is called by Hegel 'dialectical', and it is the method of Bradley's *Ethical Studies*. In Hegelian fashion that work exhibits a sequence of different conceptions of morality, each of which arises out of the negation of the previous conception. Each ethical position, when examined, is found to contain contradictions within it, and the resolution of these requires a progress to a new and higher position. The initial movement is from the hedonistic utilitarianism of 'pleasure for pleasure's sake' to the Kantian morality of 'duty for duty's sake', and from that to the social morality of 'my station and its duties'. This is subsequently incorporated within a rather hazily defined 'ideal morality', an examination of which reveals contradictions in the very idea of morality as such, and requires us to go beyond morality to religion. The most characteristically Hegelian part of this sequence is the first three stages, for it is a feature of Hegel's dialectic that particular positions come to be seen as defective in so far as they are *one-sided*. The typical movement is this: the first position is found to be one-sided, the second position corrects this only by being one-sided in the opposite direction, and a third position then incorporates the two opposites into a higher unity which retains what is valid in each. Since the second position is the negation of the first, the third can be described as 'the negation of the negation', and Hegel uses this phrase to indicate that, in negating the second position, we do not regress to our original starting-point, but rise to a higher position which is a unity of opposites.

That is the movement in *Ethical Studies* from 'pleasure for pleasure's sake' to 'duty for duty's sake' to 'my station and its duties'. I shall not go into the details of the critiques of utilitarianism and Kantian ethics, for this would be to repeat much of my previous two chapters (which themselves owe a good deal to Bradley). I can, however, indicate schematically how they exhibit the above pattern. Bradley's chapter 'Why Should I be Moral?' identifies 'self-realization' as the central concept of ethics, and the fundamental aim of morality. The task for ethics is then to determine what self-realization consists in, and Mill and Kant each offer one-sided answers to this question, Mill identifying self-realization with the attainment of pleasure, and Kant identifying it with the achievement of a good will through the performance of duty. These answers are one-sided in the following respects: Mill emphasizes the aspect of the *particular* to the exclusion of the universal, whereas Kant emphasizes the aspect of the *universal* to the exclusion of the particular; and Mill emphasizes the aspect of *content* to the exclusion of form, whereas Kant emphasizes the aspect of *form* to the exclusion of content. Each of them fails to do justice to the unity of particular and universal, and to the unity of form and content.

Let me try to explain. Utilitarianism, in equating the good life with the maximization of pleasure, thereby identifies it with a mere series of isolated particulars, a mere succession of states of feeling, the only object being to achieve as many of these as possible. They are mere particulars, not standing in any significant relation to one another, and thus there is lacking any conception of a universal, which unites all these particular states of pleasurable feeling into a coherent whole. They are simply added up. They are therefore a mere content without form, for when added together they are not seen as falling into any significant overall shape or pattern. They are a mere accumulation. Kant, on the other hand, stresses the aspects of universality and form, but in such a way that they become a mere empty universality, and a mere empty form, divorced from any way of becoming particular and concrete. Kantian morality simply prescribes conformity to the idea of universal law, it proposes a purely formal test of right and wrong. But as we have seen, absolutely any action can be universalized, and therefore in order to derive from the universalizability test concrete results, Kant has to smuggle in a content from outside, and to bring in considerations of utility and of consequences which he had previously insisted on excluding.

Bradley, then, is looking for a conception of morality which unites these two poles, and he claims to find it (at least partially) in the morality of 'my station and its duties'. This is the Hegelian morality which stresses the *social* character of the individual, and finds the content of moral life in the actions which derive from particular social relations and functions.[2] Such a morality, according to Bradley, synthesizes particular and universal, content and form, in the concept of the *concrete universal*. This is a difficult idea, but it seems to mean something like the following. (a) The self to be realized is a concrete universal in the sense that it is a whole, an organized totality. It is not, like the Kantian self, an empty form and universality, but a self which expresses itself as a whole in each of its particular acts and experiences. Conversely, these individual acts and experiences are not isolated occurrences, but get their significance from their place in the context of an organized life. (b) The self to be realized is 'universal' in a second sense. It is a unity with other selves. The self which I am to realize is a social self—not the self which I am as an isolated particular, but the self which I am through my relations to other selves, the self which I share with others, as a social being. The relation of society to the individuals here mirrors that of the overall self to the particular actions. Just as the self is not simply the sum of individual actions, nor yet something divorced from them, but is their organized unity, so also society is not just the sum of individuals, but is actively and fully present in each of them; it is constitutive of the individuals, so that they cannot exist without society, but neither can it exist except through them. And this presence of the society in the individual is the concrete universal.

The Ethics of Social Relations

To support his Hegelian morality, then, Bradley has to vindicate the concept of the individual as essentially a social being. This he attempts in paragraphs 5 to 19 of 'My Station and its Duties', where he offers two main lines of defence. These we can refer to as the biological argument (13–15), and the cultural argument (16).

The biological argument is, in essence, that the individual is a social being because he or she is the product of genetic inheritance, and is therefore born as a member of a certain family and a certain race. This is a weak argument and will not, I think, take Bradley very far. Partly I have in mind the fact that the case for the inheritability of mental characteristics remains to this day extremely controversial (witness the disputes about IQ and inheritance, or about Chomskyan linguistics). More importantly, however, even if it could be demonstrated that genetic inheritance plays a very large determining role, this would still not show that human beings are *social* in any very strong sense. This relation between social influences and the individual would be a purely *causal* one. It would show only that the individual was a product of these social influences, and would be quite compatible with the assertion that, once one is born, one can exist essentially as an individual having no ties with and owing nothing to society. It need have no ethical implications.

Such implications properly emerge only when the biological argument itself shades into the cultural argument. It is initially a biological fact that the human child is born into and nurtured by some kind of family, which itself exists within some wider social group. What this also means, however, is that the mental growth and development of the individual is essentially a social process. One comes to understand who one is, as an individual, by coming to understand the relations in which one stands to other people, and the responsibilities which these carry with them, and by acquiring the habits and customs of one's community, through which these relations are understood. Bradley emphasizes especially, and rightly, the importance of language in this connection. Language is necessarily a social acquisition, and in acquiring it one is acquiring not just a set of words, but a set of ideas and conceptions, a way of thinking which is built into the language itself. This set of ideas is not something which one can take or leave at will. One can exist as a thinking, rational individual only by acquiring the language of a community, and then one necessarily apprehends the world through the concepts of that language.

Bradley claims, then, that the identity of the individual is constituted by his or her relations to others. This claim undergoes a crucial transition in paragraph 19. Bradley says:

> To know what a man is (as we have seen) you must not take him in isolation. He is one of a people, he was born in a family, he lives in a certain society, in a certain state. What he has to do depends on what his place is, what his function is, and that all comes from his station in the organism. . . . There are such facts as the family, then in a middle position a man's own profession and society, and, over all, the larger community of the state.

Here the notion of 'relations of community' has already undergone a drastic curtailment. It has immediately been equated with the notion of one's social *function*, and that is something much more specific. According to Bradley the most important of these functions are the roles which one occupies in one's family, in one's profession, and as a citizen of the state. He is here echoing Hegel's division of ethical life into the family, civil society (Hegel's term for the sphere of work and economic life), and the state.[3] Hegel's position is itself a limited one; my relations to others are certainly not exhausted by the facts of my being a father, a university lecturer, and an Englishman. Nevertheless Hegel does, at any rate in his philosophical treatment of ethical life, provide an extended discussion of family relations and work relations. The same cannot be said of Bradley. He continues:

> Leaving out of sight the question of a society wider than the state, we must say that a man's life with its moral duties is in the main filled up by his station in that system of wholes which the state is . . .

Without explanation, the family and civil society have dropped out of sight, and Bradley has decided to focus entirely on the state. This focus dominates the rest of the chapter, in which morality is more or less equated with patriotic duty to one's country. This duty is eulogized by Bradley in tones of nationalistic fervour.

> The non-theoretical person . . . sees in the hour of need what are called 'rights' laughed at, 'freedom,' the liberty to do what one pleases, tramped on, the claims of the individual trodden under foot, and theories burst like cobwebs. And he sees, as of old, the heart of a nation rise high and beat in the breast of each one of her citizens till her safety and her honour are dearer to each than life, till to those who live her shame and sorrow, if such is allotted, outweigh their loss, and death seems a little thing to those who go for her to their common and nameless grave. (V.32.)

This concentration on duties to the state is not justified by Bradley's original argument. I believe that the argument does, however, succeed in showing the ethical importance of the social relations which serve to define the individual, and this is something which can be accepted much more plausibly if we reject Bradley's own narrowing of focus. If we look now at a much wider range of social relations, we can bring out more effectively their importance for ethics.

Let us begin at the opposite extreme from Bradley and the state, with very small-scale and short-term relations between people. Consider the problem of the ethics of promising, which has already been so prominent in the last two chapters. We saw that it is difficult to give a purely utilitarian account of the obligation to keep a promise. Utilitarianism, because it concentrates entirely on future good to be achieved, cannot do justice to the way in which a fact about the past, the fact that one has promised, is itself a reason for acting in a certain way; nor can it do justice to the fact that the obligation to keep a promise is an obligation to a specific individual, not an obligation to humanity in general. On the other hand, it is not enough for the deontological moralist simply to assert that we have a duty to keep promises. We want to know *why this should matter*, why such a duty has the ethical significance which it does have. That is a question which utilitarianism purports to answer, though unsuccessfully, but it is not answered by the baldly uninformative and dogmatic assertion that promise-keeping is a duty.

As we saw in the last chapter, Ross gives us an important clue when he points out that utilitarianism 'seems to simplify unduly our relations to our fellows'. Suppose we now ask: what is the nature of the relationship which is involved in the act of making a promise? The answer must surely be that a promise typically creates or presupposes a relationship of *trust*, of *reliance*. This is the crucial fact, whose importance is missed both by the utilitarian account and by most deontological accounts. What is wrong with breaking a promise is that it is a violation of a relationship of trust. We can see this more clearly if we notice that there is nothing vital about the actual *word* 'promise'. If I simply *tell* someone that I will do something and thereby get him to trust me, my breaking that trust is just as much of a wrong, whether or not I actually said, 'I promise'. We could perhaps agree with the utilitarian that to violate a relationship of trust is to harm the other person, and that this is what makes it wrong. What the utilitarian fails to grasp, however, is the quite specific and unique nature of the harm. We can only understand what makes it a harm if we first understand the relationship of trust, and understand what it is to have one's trust betrayed.

Here, then, is a very simple but very important social relation into which people can enter, and which is by its very nature an ethically significant relation. Other similar examples involving small-scale, short-term social relations would be telling the truth, and paying a debt. In these cases too, the relationship of trust is crucial.

Moving now to equally small-scale but more long-term social relations, consider such examples as friendship, or sexual relations, or parent-child relations. Here again the point is that each such relationship carries a specific ethical significance. Loyalty to one's friends, for example, is part of what it is to be a friend. I stand by my friend just because he or she is my friend, and if I did not do so I would not be a true friend. Someone who did not understand this would have failed to understand what is involved in the relation of friendship, and the kind of affection it involves. Similarly, a parent's devotion to a child is part of what is involved in a particular kind of affection, the close and intimate sharing of a life, the particular kind of responsibility which follows from the child's vulnerability, the identification with the child which stems from bringing it up and sharing in its process of growth. Here again, to understand the relationship is to understand its ethical significance. Something like this could also be said of sexual relations. In this case there may be additional complications, but if we can give any real sense to the notion of sexual fidelity, it must be by seeing it as part of what is involved in the intimacy of a sexual relationship.

Notice that, in dealing with these kinds of relations, we are dealing with particular kinds of emotion, and that the character of the relationship is in part a matter of the kind of emotion it involves, the kind of affection or love which is felt for a friend or child or beloved. This does not mean, however, that the loyalty, or care, or fidelity required by the relationship is to be seen simply as the immediate and spontaneous expression of the emotion one happens to be feeling at the time. I may feel infuriated with my friend, or exasperated with my child, and yet recognize that the underlying relationship—my emotional commitment if you like, but not just my transitory feelings—demands of me a certain kind of concern.

Consider now a more large-scale example. Take the case of work relations. Here there is room for considerable complexity. To understand, for example, the ethical notion of 'loyalty to one's colleagues', we have to look at the kinds of relations in which one may stand to those colleagues. One may be sharing with them in a common enterprise, where all participate jointly in the overcoming of common problems. The requirement of loyalty will then be neither a mere instrumental recognition that one's own interests depend on the satisfaction of other people's interests, nor an abstract demand of altruistic duty, but rather the expression of one's identification with the common task and with those who share it. All of this presupposes, however, that the work really is a co-operative enterprise. If one works within a context which is structured entirely in terms of individual career advancement, for example, and if one's colleagues are primarily interested in getting one's job for themselves or using one for their own advancement, then the notion of loyalty will be a hollow mockery. Similarly, if one is working for a wage, one may perhaps also recognize a loyalty to one's employer(s), but to the degree that the relationship is in reality exploitative, such loyalty will be misplaced. Loyalty to one's colleagues or workmates may then actually take the form of solidarity in opposition to one's employers (and one can see how this could be extended to the ethical notion of class solidarity, the solidarity of an exploited class in opposition to its exploiters). The general point here is that the kinds of ethical requirements or loyalties which can be rationally justified, will depend on the kinds of relations in which one stands to others.

With this last example we are coming closer to Bradley's own examples. Bradley, we have seen, focuses entirely on institutionalized relationships, and on the duties which attach to institutionalized social roles. I want to suggest that if we are to understand and justify the moral force which these institutionalized relations have, we must see them as built upon pre-institutionalized relations, loyalties, and commitments. The notion of institutionalized family duties, for example, can be given a rational foundation only in so far as these duties can be seen as a formalization of the pre-institutionalized commitments and loyalties involved in parent-child relations and sexual relations. Similarly, one can provide a rational justification for regarding oneself as bound by the institutionalized duties of one's work or profession only in so far as those duties are grounded in authentically co-operative relations with those with whom, or for whom, one works. Along these lines we might eventually find a rational foundation for Bradley's dominant preoccupation, the idea of duty to one's country. This, however, will require more than simply the assertion that one is a member of a certain nation, and is therefore bound by the duties of that role. We should have to look at the ways in which a sense of commitment to one's country might arise out of various components: an attachment to a certain place, the place where one was born and brought up and which may therefore have very special associations; one's being immersed within a national culture, a language, and a set of literary, artistic, and intellectual traditions which form one's whole way of thinking and feeling about the world; the network of relations and loyalties to innumerable individuals and groups, with all of whom one shares a common nationality. Upon such a foundation the idea of duties to one's country might make rational sense, but the presentation of such duties is often a counterfeit, and without such a foundation it is bound to be.

Bradley's ethics of social relations needs to be revised in this way if it is to be plausible and acceptable. It requires this radical extension of the kinds of social relations to be considered. When thus enlarged, however, it becomes a theory of tremendous importance, and we can begin to appreciate that importance if we think back to the problems which we found in Kant and Mill. The basic problem which they shared was that of providing a rational justification for disinterested altruism. What we learn from their failure (and from the failure of their innumerable successors) is that such a justification cannot be provided by an appeal to purely formal rationality or logic. Kant, we saw, tries to show that obligations to respect the rights or promote the interests of others can be derived from the formal requirement of universalizability. This cannot be done. So long as the universalizability principle is grounded in purely formal rationality, it can legitimately be interpreted as a principle of consistency, and as a principle of the impersonality of reasons, but not as a principle of impartiality. Again, we saw that Mill starts with a notion of the individual desiring his or her own happiness, and supposes that mere logic can show that we all ought to desire one another's happiness. He too is unsuccessful. The transition from individual happiness to the general happiness cannot be made, so long as we start from the idea of the isolated individual. Disinterested concern for others can be exhibited as rational only when we look at the real ties which do in fact bind human beings to one another. That is to say, we have to start not, like Mill, with the asocial individual, but like Bradley, with the idea of the individual as a social being involved in relations which carry with them commitments to others. We can bridge the moral gap between self and others only when we understand the self as a social self. Once we appreciate this, we can provide a refutation of egoism which consists not in adding on something external to self-interest, but in showing that the kinds of things which matter to human beings are not just desires and interests. Relations with others play just as vital a part in human life as the pursuit of interests and the satisfaction of desires, and they are not reducible to the latter.

What we are doing here is not arguing from egoism to altruism, but revealing the inadequacy of the dichotomy between egoism and altruism. Take the case of loyalty to a friend. If I give up my time and effort to help a friend in need, I am not doing it out of long-term self-interest. If I am a true friend my thought is not, 'Maybe he will do the same for me some day.' It would be equally inappropriate, however, to suppose that I am therefore sacrificing myself to something external. The friendship is an integral part of my life. Along with all my other commitments and loyalties to other individuals, and to various human groups, causes, and institutions, it defines my identity and gives my life its meaning. As Bradley has it, my self 'is penetrated, infected,

characterized by the existence of others, its content implies in every fibre relations of community' (V.16). And this is not to say that when I act on the basis
of such loyalties I do it in order to retain my sense of identity, or in order to
give meaning to my life. Rather it is to say: the fact that these relations to
others are a part of my own identity, and part of what gives meaning to my
life, finds its natural expression in my willingness to devote myself to these
concerns.

Bradley's Self-Criticisms

This enlarged reading of Bradley can in part help to answer his own self-
criticisms at the end of 'My Station and its Duties'. Bradley is aware that the
Hegelian position has its problems and its limits. His criticisms revolve
around two main points: (i) that there are aspects of the moral life which do
not derive from one's membership of any social community (paragraphs
70–2); and (ii) 'that the community in which he is a member may be in a confused or rotten condition' (69 and 71).

(i)   As examples of activity which has a moral aspect but which 'does not fall
wholly within any community', Bradley cites artistic and intellectual activity
(72). 'The production of truth and beauty', he says, '(together with what is
called "culture") may be recognised as a duty; and it will be very hard to
reduce it in all cases to a duty of any station that I can see.' Now, what *is* true is
that people do not engage in such activities primarily in their capacity as citizens of the state (or, if they do, then they are mere propagandists); and the
duties which such activities involve are not duties to the state. What makes
Bradley's self-criticism seem plausible and necessary, then, is his narrow preoccupation with the state. If we consider a wider range of social relations, it
certainly is the case that we engage in intellectual and cultural activities as
social beings. Artistic work, for example, necessarily involves a relationship to
an artistic tradition. Even the most iconoclastic artist must, if his or her iconoclastic response is to be a meaningful and intelligible one, make some use of
an inherited style and an inherited artistic vocabulary. The artist does not
work within a vacuum; he or she works within an artistic community, even if
no one actually sees his or her pictures, or reads his or her novels. The same is
true of the intellectual or scientific worker. The problems he or she works on
are problems posed by an existing tradition of scientific or intellectual work.
They are the problems created by the science at this stage of its development,
and any solution will, by its very nature, have the character of being a contribution to the intellectual or scientific community (again, whether or not it is
actually recognized as such).

A more problematic case which Bradley mentions is 'what may be called
cosmopolitan morality' (71). Bradley is rather cryptic here, but presumably

part of what is involved is the idea of duties to people who are not members of one's own community. Now, in part, the recognition of social relations other than those of the state can help to meet this point too. There are innumerable human beings with whom we do not share membership of the same nation-state, but to whom we may stand in other relations which carry responsibilities with them. We may, perhaps, share with them membership of an intellectual or scientific community which transcends national boundaries; or we may be fellow-participants with them in a political movement which has an international character; or we may be linked with them by direct or indirect economic relations. It may still be felt, however, that this does not take us far enough—that it still leaves unrecognized the moral responsibilities which we have to people to whom we stand in no specific relation at all, responsibilities which we have to them *simply as human beings*. This idea is to be found in the Kantian principle of respect for persons. It is to be found in Mill's insistence that the happiness or suffering of any human being, just because it is human happiness or suffering, cannot be morally indifferent to us. I have been arguing that the Hegelian ethics of social relations is more successful than Kantian and utilitarian ethics in justifying concern for others. If, however, the Hegelian position, because it focuses on social relations, has to stop short of the universal humanitarianism of Kant and Mill, that may be felt to be too severe a limitation. We shall have to consider, in due course, whether the ethics of social relations can be so extended as to incorporate the idea of one's moral responsibility to all other human beings. I shall come back to this question in Chapter 12.

(ii) Bradley's second self-criticism is that the existing moral world is not as it should be. The actual communities in which people happen to find themselves are likely to be defective in one way or another; and then it will not be the case that in such a community the individual can find self-realization simply by carrying out the tasks which fall to his lot, and thereby live a morally good life.

This is undoubtedly true. If, for example, I had lived in Nazi Germany, it is unlikely that I could have lived either a fulfilling or a morally decent life by faithfully carrying out all the duties allotted to me. As before, the point can be partly, but only partly, met by pointing to social relations other than those of the state. My resistance to carrying out the duties imposed on me by a corrupt political state may in part stem from other social relations in which I am involved, for example, my solidarity with other social groups or movements. But though my duties to the state may conflict with the requirements of other social relations, that is only part of the answer. Other sets of social relations, besides those of the state, may also be defective or corrupt. And if that is so, we seem to need some standpoint, independent of the social relations themselves, from which they can be assessed.

Where then do we go from here? Bradley moves into the realm of religion. He asserts, in his Concluding Remarks, that since the moral world is inevitably imperfect, the conflict between the ideal and the real remains an inescapable contradiction in morality. Only in religion, in a condition of oneness with God, are we able to realize a self which is also the ideal self. That at any rate is the claim of religion, and specifically of the Christian religion. Bradley offers no grounds for thinking it to be true. As he explicitly acknowledges, he is simply reiterating what the religious consciousness asserts about itself. Its claim to reconcile what cannot be reconciled in the moral and social world has simply to be taken on faith.

I want to propose a different route out of the difficulty. Bradley's guiding concept has been that of self-realization. Utilitarian and Kantian ethical theories offered an inadequate interpretation of this, because they worked with inadequate notions of the self. 'My Station and its Duties' seemed at first more satisfactory, because it involved an organic and social conception of the self. It turns out, however, that in so far as any existing social community is defective, it will fail to make for the self-realization of its members. Now this suggests that confronted with the imperfection of the social world, we might, instead of abandoning it for the world of religion, ask instead what social relations would have to be like, in order to make genuine self-realization possible. The concept of self-realization would then serve us as the standpoint from which to assess different kinds of social relations. We therefore need to look more closely at that concept.

Self-Realization

In Essay II, 'Why Should I Be Moral?', Bradley sets out an extremely abstract argument in defence of the view that self-realization is the ultimate end of moral activity. The argument has a certain similarity to Mill's attempted 'proof' of utilitarianism, in that it appeals to a very general theory of human action. Put very schematically the argument is this:

1. All action aims at realizing desire.
2. 'In desire, what is desired must in all cases be self.'
3. Therefore all action is an attempt at self-realization.

This argument is set out in paragraphs 26 to 32 of Essay II. Proposition (i) may seem plausible, but (ii) looks much more problematic. What could Bradley mean by the claim that all desire is for self? He provides some slight elaboration:

> all objects or ends have been associated with our satisfaction, or (more correctly) have been felt in and as ourselves, or we have felt ourselves therein; and the only reason why they move us now is that when they are presented to our minds as motives we do now feel ourselves asserted or affirmed in them. The essence of desire for an

> object would thus be the feeling of our affirmation in the idea of something not our-
> self, felt against the feeling of ourself as, without the object, void and negated; and it
> is the tension of this relation which produces motion. (II.31)

This is still very vague, and sounds quite compatible with the idea that any satisfaction whatever would count as 'feeling oneself affirmed in something', and
would therefore count as self-realization. Bradley seems aware of its incom-
pleteness, for he continues: 'Is the conclusion that, in trying to realize, we try to
realize some state of ourself, all that we are driving at? No, the self we try to
realize is for us a whole, it is not a mere collection of states' (33).

This idea that full satisfaction is achieved only when the self is affirmed *as a
whole* was referred to earlier in connection with Bradley's criticism of utilitarianism, and I shall return to it again. Bradley adds a second requirement.
Genuine self-realization requires that the self be affirmed not only as a whole,
but as an infinite whole. Bradley is here drawing on Hegel's distinction between
a true infinity and a false infinity. The false infinite is the popular conception
of the infinite, as the constant repetition of the finite. It is the infinite as the
unending series, or the indefinitely extended straight line. According to Hegel
(and Bradley) this kind of infinite is 'false' because it forms no real contrast to
the finite, it simply repeats the finite. We might ask what is wrong with that:
why should 'infinite' involve any stronger contrast with 'finite'? But Hegel, I
think, has in mind the honorific connotations of 'infinite', especially as a
description of God. God is not 'infinite' in the sense of being like the finite but
indefinitely more so. What then is the true infinite? It is that which is unlim-
ited, unbounded, because it incorporates everything else within itself. It does
not stand over against something else which would thereby limit it. An example would be the infinite character of consciousness. In some sense, perhaps,
there is a contrast between consciousness and its objects, but these objects do
not limit it, they exist within consciousness, as the content of consciousness,
and in that sense consciousness is infinite. By definition, consciousness could
never come up against something external which was outside of consciousness and could limit it (for if it were external to consciousness, consciousness
could never encounter it). Now, it is in this sense that Bradley thinks that the
self to be realized must be an infinite self. It must leave nothing outside it. In
particular, it must not leave other selves outside it, for then it would be finite,
limited by its opposition to every other self. Here we see, adumbrated in very
schematic terms, the subsequent thesis of 'My Station and its Duties', that full
self-realization is possible only for the social self.

This, then, is Bradley's abstract argument. It is intended to provide the basis
for the subsequent chapters, which are to be read as successive attempts to
explain how this self-realization could more concretely be achieved. Although,
then, the subsequent chapters make the thesis less abstract, they still depend
upon the abstract argument to explain why we should be interested in self-
realization in the first place. And the trouble with that abstract argument is

that, like all such arguments, it is so general as to admit of innumerable interpretations, and it then trades on that ambiguity. Self-realization, argued for in
this way, is so general that it sounds as though it *must* be the aim of all our
activity, for what other aim could there be? But, because it is all-embracing, it
can then give us no definite guidance as to how we ought to act, and any
attempt to make it more specific will inevitably be arbitrary and contentious.
This problem is reflected in some of the standard objections to the ethics of
self-realization, as we shall now see.

Probably the most common interpretation of self-realization is the idea of
realizing one's potentialities. It is in this sense that the concept has achieved
popularity outside the confines of philosophy. If I am told, however, that I
ought to aim at realizing my potentialities, this simply poses the question:
which potentialities? I have the capacity to engage in all sorts of different
activities, many of which would conflict with one another, and indeed whatever activity I engage in will necessarily realize some potentiality or other.
When people talk of 'realizing one's potentialities', they usually have in mind
talents and capacities of a kind appropriate to some useful or socially
approved career—realizing one's potentialities for being a musician, or an
architect, or a gymnast, or whatever. What grounds are there, however, for fas-
tening upon those particular potentialities? The nimble-fingered person who
decides to go in for the life of a pick-pocket rather than a concert pianist is just
as certainly realizing his potentialities. I may have a remarkable talent for
deception, or for practising subtle kinds of cruelty—am I to realize such
potentialities? The assumption that certain kinds of potentialities rather than
others are the ones to realize can, in the absence of further justification, only
appear as arbitrary.

A common suggestion, aimed at meeting this difficulty, is that we ought to
realize our *distinctively human* potentialities and our distinctively human
selves. This of course takes us back to Aristotle, who is an important source for
the idea of self-realization. It also takes us back to familiar difficulties. There is
first the problem of determining what these distinctively human potentialities
are. The exercise of rationality or creativity is distinctively human, but so is
cooking, or waging nuclear war; why should not the latter activities count as
'self-realization' in the required sense? Now this problem is not intractable.
We can argue that among the many uniquely human activities, some are more
basic than others, and perhaps something like 'rationality' is fundamental to
all of them. But even if we solve this problem there remains the question
which we came up against when discussing Aristotle. Why do what is distinctively human? What is so great about being human? If a certain activity is
unique to human beings, why is that any reason for engaging in it? (Mill, we
have seen, has another answer to the question, which I shall come back to in a
moment.)

For Bradley the self which we are to realize is not so much the distinctively
human self, but rather the *social self*. I have, in this chapter, tried to indicate the

merits of this emphasis. The fact is that the specific relations in which we stand to others are a vitally important aspect of our lives, and the recognition of this is essential for ethics. When, however, Bradley tries to elevate the idea of 'realizing the social self' into a comprehensive ideal, it combines the defects of both the previous interpretations. What is the social self? Bradley claims to have shown that the self is permeated through and through by its social character, and that all our ideas and sentiments come to us from society; but in that case everything we do will be 'realizing the social self', and the injunction to realize it (like the injunction to realize our potentialities) will exclude nothing. If, on the other hand, Bradley does want to work with a distinction between the social self and the non-social self, this raises the question: Why realize the social self rather than the non-social? The requirement is as arbitrary and unsupported as the requirement to realize the distinctively human self.

These are standard objections to the ethics of self-realization, and they are cogent ones. They seem to indicate that the concept of self-realization cannot by itself function as the one underlying principle of ethics. By itself it cannot tell us how to act, even when made more concrete. If it is to be of value it will have to be integrated with other ethical concepts. I suggest that at this point we abandon the abstract approach, that is, abandon the attempt at a general a priori defence of self-realization as a comprehensive ideal. It will be more helpful if we ask instead: What are the important particular emphases conveyed by the concept? What are the important features of the good human life to which it draws attention? I want to indicate three things which it especially picks out.

1. **The need for coherence** Recall how Bradley contrasts self-realization with the Benthamite ideal of 'pleasure for pleasure's sake'. He sees that a life may be filled with innumerable particular pleasures, without these pleasurable experiences ever cohering into a self. Of course they belong to a self in the sense that they are all states of one and the same continuing person, but if the particular pleasures do not have any meaningful relation to one another, they will not give any satisfying overall character to one's life—one will not, in Bradley's phrase, find oneself affirmed in them. This failure of coherence need not be confined to the pursuit of pleasures. In much the same way, one's life may be one in which innumerable particular ambitions are achieved (career ambitions, domestic ambitions, the acquisition of consumer goods), and yet one may have a sense that these various achievements do not hang together, that one's life lacks any overall shape or meaning. Such examples give us a negative contrast with self-realization as coherence. What more positively can we say about it? What can make a human life into a coherent unity? It may be, perhaps, that one's life is given a shape by some dominating aim or object. This may be an involvement in a certain kind of work; or a commitment to a religious or political ideal; or the focus of one's life may be some relationship or set of relationships with other people, family relationships perhaps, or sexual

relationships. To give unity to one's life, such a dominating concern will not be all-embracing, but it may be the centre around which everything else organizes itself, so that one may be able to say of it, 'This is what ultimately matters to me', and other independent interests may be integrated into one's life by being brought into relation to this central concern. Bradley puts it like this:

> If we turn to life we see that no man has disconnected particular ends; . . . each situation is seen (consciously or unconsciously) as part of a broader situation. . . . I am not saying that it has occurred to everyone to ask himself whether he aims at a whole, and what that is. . . . Nor further do I assert that the life of every man does form a whole; that in some men there are not coordinated ends which are incompatible and incapable of subordination into a system. What I am saying is that if the life of the normal man be inspected and the ends he has in view (as exhibited in his acts) be considered, they will, roughly speaking, be embraced in one main end or whole of ends. . . . You will find that his notion of perfect happiness or ideal life is not something straggling, as it were, and discontinuous, but is brought before the mind as a unity, and, if imagined more in detail, is a system where particulars subserve one whole. (II.36–7)

Bradley may be too sanguine about the extent to which people are able to achieve this, but he is right that they need to achieve it.

2. The need for identity The concept of self-realization takes up and develops the Kantian idea of persons as ends in themselves. It recognizes that human beings need to have a sense of existing as persons in their own right, with a life of their own and with aims and ideas of their own. There are two important pre-conditions of this sense of identity. The first of these is the *need for recognition*. This is a major theme in Hegel's philosophy—the idea that the individual's consciousness of himself depends upon its being confirmed by others.[4] It is through other people's responses to me, not necessarily positive or supportive responses, but at any rate reactions which take me seriously, that I have a sense of myself as an agent, as a distinct individual, as one whose actions make a difference in the world. This is a further element in the Hegelian stress on the social nature of the individual, and the theme is hinted at in Bradley's long quotation from Hegel (V.35–7). More recently writers on schizophrenia such as R. D. Laing have shown from empirical studies how the constant invalidating or ignoring of a person's actions and utterances, especially within the family, can quite literally produce a loss of any coherent sense of who one is, or of being a person, to the point of mental breakdown.

A second and closely-linked pre-condition of a sense of identity is the *need for self-expression through work*. This too is a point made by Hegel, and it is taken up and developed more extensively by Marx in his discussion of alienated labour. I shall refer again briefly in the next chapter to Marx's idea that it is through their work on the world that human beings give objective expression to their own identity, in a public and visible form.

3. The need for activity Closely connected with the previous point is the idea that human beings cannot derive full satisfaction from a life of purely passive enjoyment. Bradley says:

> Is a *harmonious* life all that we want in practice? Certainly not. . . . It is no human ideal to lead 'the life of an oyster.' We have no right first to find out just what we happen to be and to have, and then to contract our wants to that limit. (II.44)

Bradley is at one with Mill here. It is the striving for achievement, in activity which makes full use of our faculties, that makes life genuinely rewarding. Normally, other things being equal, as we acquire skills and talents we shall enjoy using them and want to use them—one can see this in the young child learning to crawl, to walk, to talk, and so on. This is the important insight to be retained from the idea of 'realizing one's potentialities'. As we saw earlier, that phrase does not tell us which potentialities to realize. What it does rightly emphasize, however, is that we need to realize *some* of our potentialities, and a substantial set of them at that. Certain kinds of life will make it impossible for us to do this; the life on the assembly line, working at screwing nuts on bolts, or the life of the full-time housewife washing dishes and changing nappies, is therefore likely to be intrinsically frustrating.

The use of the term 'frustrating' is crucial here. In the case of this, and of all the needs which the concept of self-realization points to, I want to suggest that they are genuine needs only because they are, ultimately, *felt* as needs. In this respect I am assimilating the ethics of self-realization to the ethics of Mill, who, it will be remembered, says that the higher pleasures are higher because, in the light of a full and complete experience of them, human beings will prefer them, and be more fully satisfied by them. I contrasted Mill's approach with the Aristotelian essentialist argument, that happiness as rationality is to be sought just because it is distinctively and essentially human. I am now suggesting that it is Mill's approach rather than Aristotle's that we should follow in looking for a viable element in the ethics of self-realization.

Now to say that needs, if they are to count as genuine needs, must be *felt* needs does not mean that they must be blatant and obvious. I do not necessarily mean that self-realization (or the various needs which make it up) is valuable only in so far as it is consciously and explicitly desired. In talking of 'felt needs' we need to recognize the existence of different levels of awareness, and the concealed ways in which needs can be experienced. In many cases, for example, people may think that they have everything they want, they may genuinely believe that they are content and happy, and yet may still feel a vague sense of malaise or frustration which they perhaps cannot explain. We need to recognize too the possibilities of self-deception in this area. People's awareness of their frustration may be manifested precisely by the ways in which they hide it from themselves. An example might be the phenomenon of 'keeping up with the Joneses', living for an endless succession of consumer goods, each of which is pursued as the one thing needed to make one's life complete. The immersion in the pursuit of the next commodity, and the fact that the acquisition of it is immediately succeeded by the emergence of a new desire, may function as a mechanism by which people avoid having to confront the overall nature of their life and its pointlessness. So in speaking of 'felt needs', we should have to draw on a subtle and sophisticated psychological account. The fact remains that self-realization in its various forms can justifiably be regarded as a need only because, at some level or other, it is experienced as a need, and because the achieving of it is experienced as satisfaction.

This way of treating the concept of self-realization brings it closer to that of happiness. Bradley himself is not averse to making this connection. At the end of 'Pleasure for Pleasure's Sake' he says: 'We agree that happiness is the end; and therefore we say pleasure is not the end.' Similarly, at the end of the additional Note to that chapter, he allows that 'if "happiness" means well-being or perfection of life, then I am content to say that, with Plato and Aristotle, I hold happiness to be the end.' Mill likewise is concerned to bridge the gap between 'happiness' and 'self-realization' from the other side. Each concept has something to be said for it. Talking of 'happiness' stresses more firmly that the ultimate test of desirability is the appeal to experience. Talking of 'self-realization' emphasizes more clearly that the accumulation of superficial satisfactions may leave one's life incomplete. The danger with either concept is that it suggests too easily the idea of a single ultimate end, and the assumption that all human activity can be measured on a single scale, according to the degree to which it contributes to that end. There is no one commodity, happiness, which satisfies all human needs. Felt needs may be experienced as a feeling of unhappiness; but human beings also experience boredom, frustrations, malaise, anxiety, insecurity, loneliness, emptiness, alienation, and meaninglessness. Possibly we could describe all these as different *forms* of unhappiness; that way of putting it would be appropriate in some cases, less so in others. But they are not all *synonyms* for a single state, unhappiness, varying only in intensity. They are experiences which point to a multiplicity of human needs. The concept of 'happiness' or that of 'self-realization' may equally serve as a *shorthand* to refer to the range of these needs, but neither concept should become a *substitute* for the recognition of their multiplicity.

Finally, having allowed something of a *rapprochement* between the concepts of 'happiness' and 'self-realization', we should remind ourselves of the two crucial ways in which Bradley's conception of self-realization differs from the utilitarian conception of happiness.

(a) Traditional utilitarianism employs an additive, cumulative conception of happiness. Whether one's life is happy is determined by putting together individual units of happiness, adding up experiences of pleasure and subtracting pains. Mill, we saw, breaks only tentatively with this conception. Bradley breaks with it decisively. The Hegelian vocabulary of 'organic unities' provides a clear alternative to the Benthamite vocabulary of addition and subtraction, and indicates effectively that self-realization has to do with the character of one's life as a whole.

(b) The two conceptions differ in where they locate relations to others. The utilitarian approach is to extend the concept of happiness, from the individual to the general happiness. The utilitarian starts with the idea that it is rational for the agent to pursue his/her own happiness, and then adds on, *externally*, the requirement that the agent must also aim at everyone else's happiness. For Bradley, commitments to others are *internal* to self-realization, because they are internal to the self.

I have argued that this recognition of the social nature of the self constitutes Bradley's advance on Hume, Kant, and Mill, enabling him to provide a more satisfactory account of altruistic concern for others. His 'social-relations' approach then leaves us with the question: can we justify not only specific concerns stemming from specific relations to others, but also a generalized humanitarianism—a concern for the needs of all human beings?

Notes

1. The substantial quotation constituting paragraphs 35–37 of 'My Station and its Duties' comes from the section 'The Actualization of Rational Self-Consciousness through its own Activity', in Hegel's *Phenomenology of Spirit* (trans. A. V. Miller, Oxford, 1977), 212–14 (paras. 349–51).

2. Hegel refers to this conception of social ethics as 'Sittlichkeit' (stressing the etymological link with 'Sitte', customs) and contrasts it with individualistic morality which he calls 'Moralität'. The idea of 'Sittlichkeit' is set out in Hegel's *Philosophy of Right* (trans. T. M. Knox, Oxford, 1952), paras. 142–57. For a clear introductory exposition of Hegel's social philosophy see Peter Singer, *Hegel* (Oxford, 1983), ch. 3.

3. Hegel's *Philosophy of Right* deals with the family in paras. 158–81, civil society in paras. 182–256, and the state in paras. 257–360.

4. Hegel's discussion of the need for recognition and self-expression through work can be found in the section 'Independence and Dependence of Self-Consciousness: Lordship and Bondage' (often referred to as the 'Master and Slave' section) in his *Phenomenology of Spirit* (paras. 178–96 in Miller's translation), and in the corresponding section 'Self-Consciousness Recognitive' in his *Philosophy of Mind* (trans. William Wallace and A. V. Miller, Oxford, 1971), paras. 430–5.

9
Nietzsche
Beyond Morality

Reading: Friedrich Nietzsche, *On the Genealogy of Morals* (first published 1887)

There are four translations available: by Francis Golffing (New York, 1956), by Walter Kaufmann and R. J. Hollingdale (New York, 1967), by Carol Diethe (Cambridge, 1994), and by Douglas Smith (Oxford, 1996). That by Golffing is the most readable, but is a rather free translation and to that extent is not wholly reliable. My quotations will be from the Kaufmann and Hollingdale translation. The work is divided into a Preface and three Essays, and to numbered sections within each of these parts. I shall concentrate almost entirely on the Preface and the First and Second Essays. (The Third Essay ranges much more widely than moral philosophy, discussing the influence of what Nietzsche calls 'ascetic ideals' on artists, philosophers, priests, scholars, and scientists.) References will be given as: P = Preface, I = First Essay, and II = Second Essay, followed by the section number.

   Towards the end of the chapter I shall also discuss briefly the accounts of morality offered by Karl Marx and by Sigmund Freud. References to relevant reading are provided in the Notes.

Nietzsche's philosophical work is roughly contemporary with that of Bradley (though condensed within a shorter period of time), and he is conscious of writing in the wake of the tradition represented by Kant and Hegel. His first published work, *The Birth of Tragedy* (1872), was written from the standpoint of Kantian metaphysics as developed by Schopenhauer. The publication of *Human, All Too Human* in 1878 marked a decisive break with the tradition of German philosophy, and in that work he declares an alternative allegiance to the tradition of French thought, as represented especially by the *Maxims* of the seventeenth-century writer La Rochefoucauld, a collection of aphorisms uncovering the hidden motives of 'virtuous' conduct. From 1878 onwards he increasingly emphasizes what he sees as the uniqueness and originality of his writing, and he becomes less and less inclined to locate himself within any philosophical tradition at all. He presents himself as a totally new voice in philosophy, in reaction against all past philosophies. Nevertheless, he can usefully be seen as reacting particularly against the Kantian and post-Kantian tradition, from which he therefore takes his bearings.

His philosophical style, too, is quite unlike that of any of the other writers we have been considering so far. Most of his works from *Human, All Too Human* onward consist of collections of aphorisms (on the model of La Rochefoucauld) and of short essays, usually only a paragraph or two in length. *The Genealogy of Morals*, on which I shall concentrate in this chapter, is the closest to a conventional philosophical work, with more continuity; but even so, it is stylistically diverse and exhibits abrupt changes of direction. Some of the sections develop arguments of a recognizable philosophical kind, but these are mixed with passages which sometimes appear to be offering no more than unargued rhetoric, and it is not clear whether that would be a fair judgement on them or whether Nietzsche has a distinctive conception of philosophical method to which we should adjust. Inconsistencies are frequently apparent, and it is difficult to know what to make of these. Since his style is often deliberately ironic, one does not know whether apparently conflicting remarks are intended to be taken with equal seriousness. Moreover, it is an avowed feature of his theory of knowledge that there is no one privileged point of view from which to understand the world, and that the closest one can get to 'objectivity' is the accumulation of diverse perspectives; so the appearance of contradiction can always be explained as the conjunction of complementary points of view.

The situation is further complicated by the relation between his different works. Some commentators claim that at least his later writings all contribute to a relatively coherent philosophical system; others maintain that his thought was constantly developing and changing, and that it is therefore dangerous to use one of his works in order to interpret another. The works from *Human, All Too Human* onwards all seem to me to be successive contributions to a single philosophical project, but in keeping with my overall approach in this book I shall confine myself to the engagement with one particular piece of writing, *The Genealogy of Morals*, and make only occasional use of Nietzsche's other writings.

Genealogy and Critique

Our first task, in view of the idiosyncrasies of Nietzsche's method, is to try to determine exactly what he takes himself to be doing in *The Genealogy of Morals*, but in order to do so I need to begin with a point which features more prominently in some of his other works. Unlike most of the writers I have discussed so far, Nietzsche does not set out to defend a substantive moral theory. He rejects the idea that there are objective values, and he rejects the idea that we can employ reason to justify moral truths. The following passage from *Twilight of the Idols* exemplifies his approach to the philosophical study of morality.

> One knows my demand of philosophers that they place themselves *beyond* good
> and evil—that they have the illusion of moral judgement *beneath* them. This
> demand follows from an insight first formulated by me: that *there are no moral facts*
> *whatever*. Moral judgement has this in common with religious judgement that it
> believes in realities which do not exist. . . . To this extent moral judgement is
> never to be taken literally: as such it never contains anything but nonsense. But as
> *semeiotics* it remains of incalculable value: it reveals, to the informed man at least,
> the most precious realities of cultures and inner worlds which did not know enough
> to 'understand' themselves. Morality is mere sign language, mere symptomatology.[1]

Of the philosophers whom we have considered previously, Hume is the one to
whom Nietzsche comes closest in this passage, but the recognition that there
are 'no moral facts' is something which Hume accepts with equanimity; our
moral judgements may be the product of sentiment rather than reason, but
they are left undisturbed by this philosophical conclusion, and we can go on
making such judgements much as we did before. Nietzsche's reaction is altogether more iconoclastic. If there are no moral facts, our philosophical
approach to morality must be fundamentally altered. Instead of looking to
justify moral beliefs, we must treat morality as a phenomenon to be explained
and interpreted. We have to investigate the historical and psychological origins of different moralities, and to ask what such investigations tell us about
the historical cultures and psychological states which have produced particular moralities.

This is why Nietzsche offers us a 'genealogy' of morals. To uncover the
genealogy of someone or something is to trace their historical ancestry, and
Nietzsche indicates in the Preface that his task is to trace the historical origins
of our moral ideas (P.3–4). As a way of throwing light on the nature of morality, this enterprise links him with a Hegelian approach (in contrast to that of
someone like Kant). Morality is not a timeless product of a priori reason; it is
a social phenomenon, which changes over time with the historical development of human societies. But whereas Hegel sees this process as one of historical progress, guided by reason, Nietzsche sees his historical perspective as
revealing the contingency of all moral beliefs.

As we shall see shortly, Nietzsche proceeds to offer an account which we can
read, at one level, as a straightforwardly social history of moral ideas. However, the Preface soon offers a different characterization of Nietzsche's enterprise. In Section 5, referring to his previous writings which have addressed the
historical question, he says: 'Even then my real concern was something much
more important than hypothesis-mongering, whether my own or other people's, on the origin of morality (or more precisely: the latter concerned me
solely for the sake of a goal to which it was only one means among many).
What was at stake was the *value* of morality.' This second enterprise, then,
apparently more fundamental than the historical one, is what he calls elsewhere 'a revaluation of values'. At first it is presented as the evaluation of a spe-

cific set of values, those which he brings under the heading of 'the ethics of pity' (exemplified by Schopenhauer's ethical theory). 'What was especially at stake was the value of the "unegoistic", the instincts of pity, self-abnegation, self-sacrifice' (P.5). From the standpoint of my own earlier chapters, we can see him as addressing what I have identified as the distinctive contrast between 'the Ancients' and 'the Moderns'—the idea that morality has especially to do with the requirement of altruism, and the question of why altruistic actions should be valued. However, Nietzsche goes on to suggest that his concerns are wider than this—not just the evaluation of the morality of pity and altruism, but the evaluation of 'all morality' (P.6). 'We need,' he says, 'a *critique* of moral values, *the value of these values themselves must first be called in question.*' (P.6)

I take the phrase 'a critique of moral values' to be the definitive description of what Nietzsche is attempting in *The Genealogy of Morals*, and I hope that my subsequent discussion will bear this out. The description is problematic, however, and raises two problems in particular. First, how comprehensive is this critique intended to be? It is a critique of 'moral' values—presumably a sub-set of values in general, and we therefore need to know what distinguishes moral values from other kinds of value. But how small is the sub-set? Nietzsche has said that it is wider than just those values associated with 'the morality of pity'. So, in so far as he is concerned with specifically moral values, morality cannot be defined simply by the focus on altruistic values. It must be wider than that. But the wider its scope is drawn, the more pressing becomes a second problem. What is the standpoint from which the critique of moral values is to be undertaken? If moral values are to be evaluated, this evaluation will presumably have to appeal to some other values. What are these? Are there non-moral values, in the light of which we can evaluate moral values? Is that enterprise a legitimate one? And if the scope of 'moral values' should after all turn out to be so wide that the critique is in fact intended as a critique of *all* values (as Nietzsche sometimes seems to suggest), then how can there be any standpoint at all from which such a critique could be undertaken?

These are central questions to bear in mind as we review and analyse Nietzsche's critique of moral values in *The Genealogy of Morals*. I add one other preliminary comment. Here, as elsewhere, Nietzsche is fond of presenting himself as a pioneer, as a thinker who is doing something quite unprecedented. We need not accept that self-image. It should be apparent that Nietzsche's enterprise brings us full circle in this book; the questions he is raising, and his reasons for raising them, are strongly reminiscent of the Sophists.[2] Like them, he recognizes that moralities have a history, that they vary from society to society; and, like them, he questions whether we should accept the morality which is dominant in our own society or, indeed, any morality at all. He has his predecessors, then, and they are not just the Sophists; there have been other such critical voices. What can perhaps be said on Nietzsche's behalf is that he is one of the most radical and uncompromising, and probably the most complex, of those voices. At any rate, when we read Nietzsche, morality is again up for judgement.

Historical Genealogy

We have seen that, in the Preface, before introducing the idea of a critique of moral values, Nietzsche describes his task as that of providing a 'genealogy', in the sense of an account of the historical origins of moral ideas. The opening sections of Essay 1 encourage us to take this description at face value, and doing so will help to make Nietzsche's thoughts initially accessible before we start adding the complexities. He presents us with two contrasting moralities, 'noble morality' and 'slave morality', and a historical transition from the one to the other. For noble morality the core pair of moral concepts is the opposition between 'good' and 'bad', for slave morality it is the opposition between 'good' and 'evil', and it is the contrast between these two pairs that provides the First Essay with its title. The historical genealogy is then formulated as an account of how slave morality comes to displace noble morality.

Nietzsche hints at various historical exemplars for 'noble morality'— ancient Greek, Roman, and Celtic. Though he does not mention Homer by name, a classic literary illustration would be the heroic values espoused by the aristocratic warrior-kings in the *Iliad*. According to Nietzsche, the characteristic feature of the 'good'/'bad' opposition is that the positive term 'good' carries the primary weight. The value it expresses is the positive self-affirmation of the noble class. 'Good' just means 'noble', possessing the distinctive qualities of the nobles, such as courage, physical and mental strength, and pride.[3] 'Bad' is the secondary concept, designating those who are inferior and who lack the noble qualities. They are not blamed for being bad, they are just constitutionally inferior. This vocabulary amounts to a 'morality' in so far as it encapsulates a coherent set of positive and negative values which govern the way of life of a certain kind of society.

Nietzsche follows his account of noble morality (I.2–5) with what he calls 'the priestly mode of valuation' (I.6–7), and, though his divisions are not entirely clear, he appears to envisage this as a transitional stage between noble morality and slave morality, a system of values which predominates in a class which is a priestly rather than a warrior aristocracy. These values are ascetic values, which repudiate physical and sensory pleasures and turn their adherents 'away from action' (I.6) towards the cultivation of the inner, spiritual life. Though Nietzsche again sees this system of values as a broad type with various instantiations, and refers briefly to Hinduism and Buddhism to illustrate features of it, he says that the classic example of priestly values is Judaism. It is Judaism which brings out most clearly the contrast with noble morality, by placing a positive value not on power and success and worldly happiness, but on *suffering*, thereby preparing the way for 'the slave revolt in morality' (I.7). Judaism gives birth to Christian ethics.

This brings us to Nietzsche's account of slave morality (I.8–10), exemplified by Christianity. It is not confined to those who are literally slaves, but it is the distinctive morality of the common people, the poor and lowly, those who are driven by the 'herd instinct', and that is why it values humility rather than pride, meekness rather than strength, suffering rather than success. The Beatitudes in Jesus's Sermon on the Mount would be a classic text of slave morality.[4] It brings to the forefront of moral concern the preoccupation with the egoism–altruism dichotomy (I.2)—the movement of thought which I have previously linked with the transition from 'the Ancients' to 'the Moderns'. It would be too simple to equate noble morality with egoism and slave morality with altruism. The adherents of noble morality can act altruistically, but theirs is the altruism of spontaneous generosity; from a position of strength they can exhibit 'consideration, self-control, delicacy, loyalty, pride and friendship' (I.11), especially towards their own kind. Slave morality, however, makes a special virtue out of *self-denying* and *self-sacrificing* altruism. The subordination of one's own interests and desires is given a positive value. Moreover, this positive valuation is not the core value. The morality of 'good'/'evil', in contrast to that of 'good'/'bad', puts the primary emphasis on the negative concept 'evil' (I.10, 11). Its fundamental value judgement is the moral condemnation of those who act immorally by selfishly pursuing their own self-interest.

So far, then, we have a recognizable historical thesis, and a recognizable historical sequence. The noble morality dominant in the ancient world gives way to the priestly values of Judaism and then to the slave morality of Christian ethics. The values of noble morality are said to be not entirely dead; 'There was . . . in the Renaissance an uncanny and glittering reawakening of the classical ideal, of the noble mode of evaluating all things', and the last embodiment of that ideal is said by Nietzsche to have been Napoleon (I.16). But the slave morality of Christian ethics predominates in the modern world, and historically it is to be seen as a reaction against the noble morality of the ancient world.

I have said that this is a recognizable historical sequence. It is, however, a highly schematic one and, as such, unconvincing. The broad typology cannot do justice to the complexities of actual historical developments—for example, to the intricacies of moral debate and disagreement within the ancient world, not just on the part of the philosophers but at the level of popular moral consciousness. The Homeric heroes may, for instance, illustrate noble morality, but where do the very different moral values explored by Greek tragic drama fit into Nietzsche's scheme? Likewise that scheme seems to have no room for the moral values which emerge with the more settled life of the Greek polis, values which represent a transition from heroic values, but one which is by no means the same as the transition from noble morality to slave morality. There is no room in the scheme for the moral conflicts which we find within the ancient world, represented, for instance, by the accounts which the Greek historians give us of debates in the Athenian assembly.[5]

Even more importantly, Nietzsche's schematic history by itself provides no *explanation* of why moral ideas have developed in this way. Nietzsche has more to say on this score. He does have an account of the nature of the process which explains how and why the changes have taken place. It is a *psychological* explanation, couched in terms of the *motives* of those who have introduced new values, and I shall look at it in a moment. But it sits uneasily with his historical account. Taken in that context, it looks like a 'conspiracy' theory of a kind which is highly implausible as an explanation of large-scale historical changes, and above all of changes in ideas. The historical account is undeniably important for Nietzsche, particularly because it reveals the diversity of moral systems and thus helps to free us from the idea of a single 'morality' given for all time. But though he needs to draw on the historical account to make this point, I do not think that he has, in the end, a properly worked out historical thesis. I want to suggest that his psychological genealogy—his account of the psychological origins of moral ideas—is more convincing and valuable than his historical genealogy. He reveals the psychological reasons which make particular moral values attractive to people, and the psychological needs and purposes which they serve. And, as we shall see, it is the revelation of the psychological motives underlying certain moral values that leads into his critique of those values.

Psychological Genealogy

The key concept for Nietzsche's psychological genealogy is that of resentment, for which he uses the French word *ressentiment* (I.10). It is this which explains why the negative evaluation of people and actions as morally evil is the primary value for slave ethics. That evaluation is a way of getting back at the adherents of noble morality who value themselves as 'good' in virtue of their strength, power, courage, and success. Slave morality is thus motivated by vindictiveness. It is a *reactive attitude*, a reaction against the success of others, in contrast to the attitude of those whose evaluations are an active expression of their pleasure in their own success. The triumph of slave ethics is sealed when it becomes the dominant social morality and is accepted by the masters themselves. The herd is thereby able to take its revenge on its superiors, humiliating and abasing the once-proud nobles who gloried in their superiority. The point is again couched in historical terms, but for Nietzsche it is the explanation of the enduring psychological appeal of slave morality.

There is a further dimension to the psychological genealogy, which emerges more clearly in Essay 2 and which I shall discuss shortly; but we are already in a position to see why this genealogy also furnishes a critique. Immediately after introducing the idea of a 'critique of moral values' in the Preface, Nietzsche adds, 'for that there is needed a knowledge of the conditions and circumstances in which they grew, under which they evolved and changed (morality as consequence, as symptom, as mask, as tartufferie, as illness, as misunderstanding . . .)' (P.6). The psychological analysis is thus intended to reveal moral values as a *symptom* of an underlying condition, and to provide a diagnosis of the *illness* of which they are a symptom. (The implicit appeal here to the positive value of health is something on which I shall comment later.) More illuminating still is the idea of moral values as a *mask*, and thus of the psychological genealogy as an *unmasking*. The obvious way in which this furnishes a critique is that it reveals a morality to be deceptive and dishonest. The values of Christian ethics are not what they seem. Their surface appearance is a distortion and concealment of their true nature. 'While the noble man lives in trust and openness with himself . . . , the man of *ressentiment* is neither upright nor naive nor honest and straightforward with himself. His soul *squints*; his spirit loves hiding places, secret paths and back doors' (I.10). Note the implication that the adherents of slave morality conceal their true motives and feelings not only from others but also from themselves.

This, then, is how Nietzsche's psychological unmasking of Christian ethics leads to his critical judgement. Such a morality is dishonest. Its dishonesty also points to a further ground for criticism. Such a morality is not merely different from what it purports to be; it is actually the direct opposite of what it purports to be. It extols the virtues of love, kindness, and sympathy, but is in fact an expression of 'an imaginary revenge', of 'submerged hatred, the vengefulness of the impotent' (I.10). It therefore stands condemned in its own terms.

Nietzsche's psychological genealogy of moral phenomena is extended and deepened in Essay 2, and at this point I should say something about the content and structure of that essay. It deals with a number of different themes: promising, responsibility, conscience, punishment, guilt, bad conscience, and religion. These apparently disparate themes are confusingly intertwined, and it is not clear how they are related either to one another or to the themes of Essay 1. The difficulty is increased because Nietzsche again seems to take an ambivalent attitude to the phenomena he discusses. I am not convinced that he has a consistent story to tell in Essay 2, but before proceeding further I shall try to disentangle the various themes and to clarify their sequence.

The essay begins abruptly and disconcertingly with the question of how it is that human beings are able to make *promises*. It is at first puzzling why Nietzsche poses this question and why he sees it as a problem, but the deeper theme which emerges is that of *responsibility*. Nietzsche's concern is to explain how it is that human beings have become capable of taking responsibility for their actions, and of exercising that responsibility over an extended period of time. The link with promising is that the latter involves being true to one's word, and thus assuming responsibility for what one will do in the future and being able to exercise that responsibility. Nietzsche again sees this as, in part, a historical question—or rather, a problem of pre-history. Behind it there appears to lie a commitment to evolutionary theory, and thus the problem is that of how the human species can have evolved from an animal governed by instincts and immediate responses to a being capable of exercising this long-term responsibility for its behaviour. Nietzsche wants to emphasize the tremendous difficulty of this transition, which can have been made possible only over an immense period of time, 'the greater part of the existence of the human race', by the imposition of 'the social straitjacket' on animal instincts (II.2). This brings us to the links with two of his other themes. The end-product of this process, the consciousness of the ability to take responsibility for one's actions, 'this power over oneself and over fate', is what 'sovereign man' calls 'his *conscience*' (II.2). The process itself has involved, above all, the practice of *punishment*; this huge transformation has been made possible only by means of the harshest and cruellest punishments to tame and control man's instincts—and here Nietzsche dwells with disconcerting relish on the horrific cruelty of penal codes and punishments even in relatively recent historical times (II.3).

At II.4 we come to one of the most confusing transitions in the essay. Nietzsche introduces another concept, that of '*bad conscience*'. To make sense of this, we must recognize the distinction he is making between 'conscience', the positive feeling of pride in one's responsibility for one's actions, and 'bad conscience', the negative feeling of *guilt*. Having linked 'punishment' with 'conscience'—the former being the historical means by which the latter has been produced—he now wants to question the supposed link between 'punishment' and 'bad conscience'. Modern ideas of punishment suppose it to rest on the idea of guilt: people are punished because they deserve it, that is, because they are guilty. Nietzsche sees this as a relatively recent idea. He thinks that the practice of punishment has much more primitive psychological roots. It is rooted in feelings of anger and vengeance, in the desire to hurt those who have hurt us. And to understand this, we have to recognize the fact that human beings take a positive pleasure in the infliction of pain; only on this basis can we explain why hurting those who have hurt us provides us with some kind of compensation. These are the psychological origins of the practice of punishment. Only over a long period of time have these primitive desires for vengeance come to be modified and tempered by the idea of *justice*—the idea that punishment has its limits and must be standardized so that it matches the crime. The link between ideas of 'punishment' and 'justice' is therefore relatively recent. It is this account of the historical development of punishment that occupies Nietzsche in sections 4 to 15.

In sections 16 to 18 he returns to the phenomenon of 'bad conscience', the negative consciousness of guilt, and it is here that the links with Essay 1 begin to emerge. Nietzsche finds the origin of 'bad conscience' in the *internalization*

of the instincts. He sees this as a response to the imposing of social constraints, the historical process which he has been describing in his account of
'conscience' and 'punishment'. In sections 17 and 18 he identifies two successive
historical transformations. The first is the imposition of social constraints by
'a conqueror and master race which, organized for war and with the ability to
organize, unhesitatingly lays its terrible claws upon a populace perhaps
tremendously superior in numbers but still formless and nomad' (II.17). These
'conquerors' are presumably to be identified with, or are perhaps the ancestors
of, the 'masters' who feature in Essay 1 as the originators of noble morality. The
second historical transformation is then the response by those who find themselves mastered and dominated—presumably the 'slaves' of Essay 1. Denied
the satisfaction of directing their instincts at the external world, they turn
these same instincts in upon themselves. Prevented from inflicting suffering
on others, they derive a compensatory pleasure from the infliction of suffering
on themselves, since this is now the only way in which they can satisfy their
need for a sense of power. Nietzsche describes this as a 'delight in imposing a
form upon oneself', the 'uncanny, dreadfully joyous labor of a soul voluntarily
at odds with itself that makes itself suffer out of joy in making suffer' (II.18).
What emerges here is, in fact, a second psychological explanation of the origin
of altruistic ideals, the values of 'selflessness, self-denial, self-sacrifice' (II.18).
In Essay 1 these were explained in terms of resentment, the satisfaction of getting back at and humiliating the masters. Here the complementary aspect is
that they also provide the satisfaction of imposing on oneself the power which
one cannot impose on others. The common theme of both explanations is that
altruistic ideals are a compensation for impotence. This second explanation
therefore reinforces the critical judgement emerging from the first explanation; altruistic ideals are dishonest, deceptive, the opposite of what they purport to be.

Finally, in II.19–23, we discover one further dimension of altruistic ideals,
the religious dimension. Man's self-denial is taken to its ultimate conclusion
with the positing of a god before whom he can abase himself; 'this man of the
bad conscience has seized upon the presupposition of religion so as to drive
his self-torture to its most gruesome pitch of severity and rigor. Guilt before
God: this thought becomes an instrument of torture to him' (II.22). Thus religious belief is fitted into Nietzsche's psychological account of altruistic values,
and is a further aspect of the illusion and self-deception involved in those
ideals.

Psychological Critique

So much by way of a preliminary account of how Nietzsche's psychological
genealogy leads into his critique of moral values. At this point I want to raise
two questions about his enterprise as so far described. I have suggested that

the 'genealogy' offered in Essay 1 is more plausible as a psychological than a historical one. To suggest that Christ or the early Christians, even unconsciously, devised a morality of altruistic love for one's neighbour in order to effect the historical transformation which Nietzsche describes, to subvert the power of a ruling aristocracy by a historical act of vengeance, is hardly credible. If Nietzsche has a plausible thesis, it can only be that the emergence of Christian ethics represents the triumph of vindictiveness because it is, by its very nature, a resentful and vindictive morality. This is indeed what Nietzsche appears to maintain. His psychological analysis appears intended to apply not just to the original devisers of Christian morality, but to its subsequent and present-day adherents. Likewise, the account in Essay 2, though presented in historical terms, commits him to a psychological claim about the very nature of a morality of self-denial. These features explain the enduring appeal of such a morality; it fulfils the psychological need of enabling the weak and inferior to enjoy compensatory feelings of power. At that level, I suggest, Nietzsche has a plausible thesis; but we should then press the question: even if the thesis is intelligible, is it actually true? What reasons are there for accepting it?

We can recognize, I suppose, that the psychological phenomenon described by Nietzsche does indeed exist. Undoubtedly there are people whose purportedly altruistic devotion to the interests of others is fuelled by a positive desire to impose suffering and hardship on themselves, and this desire in turn appears deliberately designed to induce feelings of guilt in others. 'Don't worry about me,' says the martyr, 'I'm not important, I'll stay at home and look after Granny, you go off and enjoy yourselves'—and off we go, compelled by her words to try to reassure ourselves that actually there is no reason why we *should* feel guilty. That is a simple case; the strategies of self-abasement as a means of guilt-inducement can be highly complex, and we know that this happens, because we can recognize it in ourselves and in others. Nietzsche, however, is committed to a stronger claim: not just that purportedly altruistic behaviour *can* take this form, but that a morality of altruism *essentially* has this character, that the 'ethics of pity' can never be taken at face value. I have noted that Nietzsche is not committed to denying the possibility of altruistic concern. Noble morality, as he describes it, leaves room for acts of spontaneous generosity. What he does maintain is that as a morality, as a general way of life, the morality of pity is always motivated by resentment.

He therefore has the task of defending this very general claim about human nature and, as with all such generalizations, it is not at all clear how it can be defended. The very experiences which acquaint us with the more limited psychological phenomenon must count against Nietzsche's general thesis, for we experience these limited cases as ones in which someone's altruistic concern is not genuine, implying thereby that we are also acquainted with the genuine article. If that is so, then why should there not be a morality which sets the highest value on genuine altruism? The onus is on Nietzsche to show that this

is impossible, and that the appearance of such a morality will always be deceptive, because its adherents will *always* be motivated by vindictive feelings. It is
difficult to see how he or anyone could amass a body of psychological evidence sufficient to sustain this general claim.

What Nietzsche would appeal to, I suspect, is not any such body of empirical evidence, but a metaphysical view of human action. His claim would be not
just that altruistic morality as a matter of fact always turns out not to be genuine, but that it *could not* be genuine. What is doing the work here, I suspect, is
Nietzsche's doctrine of the 'will to power'. This concept, which plays a prominent role in some of his writings, appears only occasionally in *The Genealogy
of Morals*[6]—and the work is, I venture to suggest, all the better for that. The
doctrine of the will to power appears intended as a thesis about the very
nature of human action—'all action is will to power'. Sometimes, indeed, it
seems to be an even wider, cosmological thesis—'everything in the universe is
will to power'. As a cosmological thesis it is too murky to be worth our attention here, but something needs to be said about it as a view of human action.
Some misinterpretations can be excluded. Nietzsche is not necessarily talking
about political or social power; he is not saying that all human action is motivated by the desire to dominate others (a misinterpretation which assisted the
appropriation of his philosophy by the Nazis). He is talking about power in a
wider sense, and the claim seems to amount to something like this: that all
action is an attempt to impose one's will on the world, to fashion and shape the
world so that it bears the imprint of one's own agency. The relevance of this
claim to Nietzsche's critique of altruistic morality is, then, that pure self-denial
is impossible, that it always conceals some form of self-assertion. In II.18 he
says that the satisfaction of 'a soul . . . that makes itself suffer out of joy in
making suffer' is the expression of 'the *instinct for freedom* (in my language:
the will to power)'. On the other side, the spontaneous generosity of the
nobles is likewise a secondary phenomenon, an expression of their confidence
in their own power. These are the reasons why altruism cannot be a, or the,
fundamental value.

I have suggested that Nietzsche might see this metaphysical thesis as obvi-
ating the need to appeal to empirical evidence in support of his psychological
claims about Christian ethics. I doubt whether it can succeed. It is no better
grounded than any empirical generalization about human actions. Like all
such monistic, philosophical views of human agency, it suffers from a fatal
ambiguity. As a substantive thesis it is hopelessly simplistic, reducing all the
variety and complexity of human motivation to just one kind of motive. On
the face of it we can refute it with innumerable counter-examples. In order to
accommodate the counter-examples, the proponent of the thesis may interpret it more broadly, but it then starts to become vacuous. If it is to encompass
the range of undeniably real human motives, it has to be interpreted so widely
as to amount to no more than some such claim as 'all human action is a form

of acting on the world'. So, to be both interesting and plausible, the thesis must trade on its ambiguity as between a narrow and a wide interpretation; and that ambiguity is its undoing. (Note that this objection is parallel to the objection to the similarly all-embracing, hedonistic theory of human action—that all actions are motivated by the desire for pleasure. See the discussion of this thesis in connection with Mill, p. 105 above.)

I conclude that if Nietzsche is to sustain his claim that the ethics of altruism masks attitudes of resentment and vindictiveness, and is essentially a compensation for experiences of impotence and frustration, he needs to deploy a richer, less simplistic and more plausible background psychological theory in defence of it. I turn now to the second question which I said I would raise about his psychological genealogy. I have suggested that the genealogy in turn grounds his critique of the ethics of altruism. But how exactly does it do so? My suggestions so far are that the 'unmasking' of the ethics of altruism furnishes a negative judgement on it in so far as it shows it to be dishonest, and in so far as it shows it to be condemned in its own terms. These are powerful *ad hominem* criticisms—but they are only *ad hominem*. They create difficulties for anyone who wants to endorse altruistic ethics as an honest and open morality, but anyone who, on the contrary, embraces deviousness and deception would be unperturbed by it. Nietzsche, however, has appeared to promise more than just *ad hominem* critical judgements. He has promised a 'critique of moral values'; and this suggests an assessment, from a vantage-point outside noble morality and slave morality and any other specific morality, of the strengths and weaknesses of the different sets of values. How, if at all, can Nietzsche provide this? Where can he find such a vantage-point?

Evaluative Critique

We should first note that Nietzsche's critical position is more complex and more ambivalent than it might at first appear. An initial reading of Essay 1 might suggest that he is setting up the contrast between noble morality and slave morality in order to portray noble morality as good and slave morality as bad, and that this is the sum total of his critical assessment. However, matters are not so simple. His attitude to slave morality, in particular, is more nuanced. Consider passages such as the following. After introducing the priestly system of values, he says:

> but it is only fair to add that it was on the soil of this *essentially dangerous* form of human existence, the priestly form, that man first became an *interesting animal*, that only here did the human soul in a higher sense acquire *depth* and become *evil*—and these are the two basic respects in which man has hitherto been superior to other beasts! (I.6)

And of the transition from priestly values to slave morality he says:

from the trunk of that tree of vengefulness and hatred, Jewish hatred—the profoundest and sublimest kind of hatred, capable of creating ideals and reversing
values, the like of which has never existed on earth before—there grew something
equally incomparable, a *new love*, the profoundest and sublimest kind of love . . .
(I.8)

There is a certain amount of deliberate irony in these passages, but there is
also, I think, a genuinely positive evaluation of both priestly values and slave
morality in so far as they represent creative achievements. Any radically new
departure in values would, by the same token, represent a feat of creative originality. Nietzsche is inclined to describe these as aesthetic achievements;
human nature, with its drives and instincts, is the raw material which the
moral innovator as artist shapes and fashions, imposing on it a significant
form. This view of the creation of ideals as artistic creation becomes most
explicit in Essay 2, where, for example, he says of the emergence of the ideals of
selflessness, self-denial, and self-sacrifice:

this artists' cruelty, this delight in imposing a form upon oneself as a hard, recalci-
trant, suffering material . . . also brought to light an abundance of strange new
beauty and affirmation, and perhaps beauty itself . . . (II.18)

A simple dichotomy between 'good' noble morality and 'bad' slave morality
would therefore be an oversimplification of Nietzsche's position.

This, however, merely complicates our original question. In addition to
noble morality and slave morality we now have another set of values, aesthetic
ones such as creativity and originality, on the basis of which we can make our
evaluations. In a sense, these aesthetic values provide a standpoint outside
noble morality and slave morality, one from which those two moralities can be
assessed. Perhaps this is an appropriate vantage-point for Nietzsche's critique
of moral values. But why? It is simply another system of values, and we have no
reason as yet for supposing that it provides a privileged standpoint, or that
there is any such privileged standpoint from which a critique of moral values
can be conducted.

It may be that Nietzsche would be content to deny that possibility. This
would be in keeping with the general theory of knowledge which he espouses
elsewhere, and which I have already mentioned briefly—the theory which he
and others have called 'perspectivism'. According to this theory, there is no
such thing as a privileged standpoint from which to achieve purely objective
knowledge and understanding. All thought, all knowledge, is an active process
of ordering and organizing our experience, and therefore all knowing is
knowing from a particular 'perspective', from which we shape our experience
in accordance with particular emotions and interests. The search for a privileged, objective standpoint, independent of all interests, is illusory. This might
suggest that the most we can hope for is to recognize the diversity of perspectives available to us, and accumulate a multiplicity of these instead of

being trapped within a single perspective which we assume to be the only 'true' one.[7]

Perhaps, then, this is all that Nietzsche is attempting with his critique of moral values. Perhaps he is content simply to point out to us that there are various different moralities and systems of values, and to release us from the limited perspective of a single morality which we assume to be the only true one. We can see the morality of altruism in a new light when we look at it from the standpoint of noble morality, and vice versa, and we can also look at both moralities from the additional standpoint of aesthetic values. Does Nietzsche rest content with this?

Perhaps, to be consistent, he should do so; but on reading *The Genealogy of Morals* it is difficult to resist the impression that he wants more. Certain values are invoked in a way which strongly suggests that Nietzsche does, after all, want to give them a privileged status. One of these is the value of 'health', which is alluded to in the Preface (e.g. section 6) and in Essay 1 (e.g. sections 6 and 11) and emerges more clearly in Essay 2 (e.g. sections 16, 19, and 24). The appeal to the idea of 'health' as a psychological criterion of a good human life is something which we have encountered previously, particularly with Plato. Plato equated health with the harmonious functioning of the components of an organic system, and he took the human self and personality, like the human body, to be such a system. Nietzsche's conception of 'health' is different. It is not spelt out with any precision, but he appears to equate health with *energy* and *activity* in contrast to passivity. These ideas, indeed, seem to function in their own right as Nietzsche's evaluative court of appeal, and I doubt whether the idea of 'health' adds anything significant to them. The appeal to the values of energy and activity underpins, in particular, the criticism of slave morality as a morality of resentment, *reactive* rather than the expression of spontaneous activity. It is illustrated by the following passage:

> The 'well-born' *felt* themselves to be the 'happy'; they did not have to establish their happiness artificially by examining their enemies, or to persuade themselves, *deceive* themselves, that they were happy (as all men of *ressentiment* are in the habit of doing); and they likewise knew, as rounded men replete with energy and therefore *necessarily* active, that happiness should not be sundered from action—being active was with them necessarily a part of happiness . . .—all very much the opposite of 'happiness' at the level of the impotent, the oppressed, and those in whom poisonous and inimical feelings are festering, with whom it appears as essentially narcotic, drug, rest, peace, 'sabbath', slackening of tension and relaxing of limbs, in short *passively*. (I.10)

The values of energy and activity are the ones to which Nietzsche most consistently appeals in order to establish the superiority of one morality over another.

Is there any reason which Nietzsche can provide to justify giving these values a special status? Again I suspect that the metaphysical doctrine of 'the will to power' is doing the work here. Nietzsche takes the values of energy and activity to be most in accordance with the essential nature of human beings (and perhaps of all life and all natural processes). Once again, however, his position reveals the limitations of the concept of 'the will to power'. He is committed to claiming that the will to power, as a universal phenomenon, is covertly the force behind slave morality just as much as noble morality. It explains the need felt by the meek and lowly to give vent to their bottled-up aggressiveness in disguised forms, and thereby to experience after all the satisfaction of imposing their will on the world. If noble morality and slave morality are equally manifestations of the will to power, however, then that concept cannot furnish a criterion by which to judge between the different moralities. I conclude that Nietzsche needs a more developed and more nuanced psychological theory than that of the will to power, if he is to come up with a criterion of value and of a good human life.

Metaphysical Critique

I have so far identified two interlinked dimensions of Nietzsche's 'critique of moral values'. It is a *psychological* critique—a psychological genealogy aimed at unmasking moralities and showing them to be, in their origins, other than what they appear to be. It is also an *evaluative* critique—an appeal to certain values, perhaps with a privileged status, in order to judge the values internal to particular moral systems. I want now to add a third dimension. Nietzsche's critique is also a *metaphysical* critique, intended to undermine certain conceptions of morality by exhibiting the untenable metaphysical presuppositions on which they rest.

This theme is introduced in I.13, and once more it is slave morality which is subject to criticism. As a negative and vindictive morality, slave morality encapsulates an attitude of *blame*. The weak hold the strong and powerful to be *responsible* for oppressing them, and *condemn* them for it. They thereby operate on the assumption, says Nietzsche, that there is 'a neutral substratum behind the strong man, which was *free* to express strength or not to do so'. This assumption, according to Nietzsche, is fallacious; 'There is no such substratum; there is no "being" behind doing, effecting, becoming; "the doer" is merely a fiction added to the deed.'

Nietzsche is here questioning the concept of *moral responsibility* which is an intrinsic feature of at least Christian and post-Christian morality. Essential to moral thinking is the idea that moral judgements typically take the form of judgements of praise and blame of individual moral agents, who are thus held to be responsible for their good and bad actions. This is closely linked with the concept of guilt: those who are responsible for morally bad actions are thereby held to be morally guilty. The questioning of these concepts is, for many philosophers, tied up with the question of 'free will' and 'determinism'. A scientific view of the world, some have argued, carries the implication that human actions, along with all other events, are the inevitable effects of prior causal conditions; and if that is so, then human agents are not in any strong sense free to decide whether or not to perform their actions, and the idea of moral responsibility is therefore an illusion. In other writings Nietzsche endorses this determinist criticism of the idea of free will.[8] Here he adds a further strand to the criticism—a diagnosis of how it is that we come to be deceived by the illusion of free will. The diagnosis is grounded in his general theory of knowledge. He suggests, as we have seen, that all our attempts to know and understand the world are from the perspective of this or that set of practical interests. A fundamental interest is the need to impose order on the flux of experience by positing stable and unchanging entities behind the change. This need is built into our language, with the syntactical structure of subject and verb. The event of a lightning-flash is described by us as the action of a thing: 'the popular mind separates the lightning from its flash and takes the latter for an *action*, for the operation of a subject called lightning' (I.13). In just the same way, our belief in free will and moral responsibility is another example of the myth of 'the subject'. We suppose that behind each human action there is a free and responsible agent who is the author of the deed. Here, too, we simplify and falsify our experience.

There is a problem of consistency in Nietzsche here. We have seen that in Essay 2 he offers an account of how human beings become capable of taking responsibility for their actions. At II.2 he says, 'At the end of this tremendous process . . . we discover that the ripest fruit is the *sovereign individual*, . . . autonomous and supramoral . . . the man who has his own independent, protracted will . . . this emancipated individual . . . this master of a *free* will.' We cannot be certain that Nietzsche intends this as a serious rather than an ironic description; but if he intends it seriously, how can he also say that the idea of responsibility is a myth? We have here a classic example of the difficulty I mentioned earlier, of detecting when Nietzsche is being inconsistent and when he is being ironic.

If we do take seriously the passage which I have just quoted, then our best hope for ascribing to Nietzsche a consistent position is to attribute to him the view that the responsibility of the free agent is not a metaphysical given, but a social product. This would imply that individual responsibility is never an absolute. The extent to which individuals can be held responsible for their actions will itself depend on the social context in which they are acting and the social forces which are acting on them. Human beings can exhibit greater or lesser degrees of responsibility, but they are never the free-floating agents which the myth of 'the subject' presents them as being.

It has to be said that we need here a deeper analysis of the concept of 'responsibility' than anything which Nietzsche offers us. Nevertheless he is right to identify a problem for conventional moral thinking. The latter does indeed seem to presuppose a very strong notion of individual responsibility. The language of moral praise and blame and guilt does tend to abstract individuals from the context in which they act, and to locate the moral value of the action wholly in the individual agent. I shall come back to the question of how coherent or incoherent a notion this is, and whether it renders the very idea of morality suspect.

Beyond Morality?

I have identified three strands in Nietzsche's critique of moral values: his psychological critique, his evaluative critique, and his metaphysical critique. (In a sense, of course, each of them is an evaluative critique, but I have used that label to refer particularly to the critique which rests on an appeal to other values.) It is time to return to my initial question (p. 131): what is this critique a critique *of*? How comprehensive is its scope? We have seen that Nietzsche directs his fire especially against one particular morality, the 'slave morality' which he equates with Christian morality and with the altruistic values of pity, self-denial, and self-sacrifice. However, we have also seen that in speaking of a 'critique of moral values' he implies that morality *as such* is open to criticism. He asks whether perhaps 'precisely morality would be to blame if the *highest power and splendor* actually possible to the type man was never in fact attained? So that precisely morality was the danger of dangers?' (P.6). He envisages the rise of the 'sovereign individual' who is liberated from the morality of custom and is 'autonomous and supramoral (for "autonomous" and "moral" are mutually exclusive)' (II.2). This seems to imply a distinction between moral values and other kinds of values. The former would include the values both of slave morality and of master morality, and their distinguishing feature would seem to be that moral values are embedded in customs and in the way of life of a society, whereas non-moral values are perhaps those of individual artistic creativity and originality, including the creativity of the forgers of new moralities. Finally, there is a third possible interpretation of Nietzsche as a sceptic about *all values*, maintaining that, as human creations, no values can have any objective validity.

Clearly there are grounds for all of these interpretations, and I doubt whether it is possible to attribute to Nietzsche a consistent position. More important are the deeper questions about morality itself, and whether Nietzsche offers us good reasons for thinking that the very idea of morality is suspect. In an attempt to throw more light on these questions, I should like now to look briefly at two other thinkers who can be ranked with Nietzsche as the great 'unmaskers': Marx and Freud. I am not suggesting that Marx, Freud, and Nietzsche share the same views—far from it—but what all three have in common is that they call into question the status of morality by investigating its social and psychological origins. Their accounts of its origins are importantly different, but each offers a genealogy of morals, a genealogy which in turn leads to a critique of morality as traditionally understood.

Marx and Freud

For Marx, morality is an instance of what he calls 'ideology'. It is a product of and a reflection of the underlying economic structure of society. Different kinds of society are distinguished by their economic structure, which is constituted by the relations of production, the relations of ownership and control of the means of production. These relations divide a society into economic classes with conflicting interests—in the ancient world the classes of slave-owners and slaves, in the feudal world the classes of feudal lords and serfs, and in modern capitalist societies the bourgeois class, which owns the means of production, and the proletariat or working class, which makes its living from wage labour. Morality serves as a mask for class interests. Different classes with their conflicting interests give those interests an illusory generality by articulating them as impersonal moral values. Though each class, whether dominant or subordinate, will have its own distinctive values, the ruling ideas in any society will be those of the ruling class, and will serve to legitimate existing society and its class structure. In particular, the dominant moral ideas function to divert exploited classes from the pursuit of their own interests by requiring a concern for a spurious 'general interest'. This, for Marx, is the role of an 'altruistic' morality which calls on people to obey the law, to work hard, to moderate their demands, to respect other people's property, all in the name of a 'common good' which is really the good of the dominant class.

There is an obvious comparison to be made here with Nietzsche's distinction between noble morality and slave morality as the moralities of two opposed social classes. I think it is fair to say, however, that Marx takes much more seriously the task of examining actual historical societies and the details of their class structure; he has a properly worked-out theory of history within which his theory of ideology and of morality is located.[9] I think that we can also easily recognize historical examples of moral ideas functioning as class ideology. Think of Aristotle's relegation of women and slaves to an inferior status, incapable of living a fully human life—ideas which uncritically reflect the prejudices of a male, slave-owning citizen class. Think of Hume's automatic limiting of justice to the protection of private property, reflecting the narrow interests of a landowning aristocracy. Marx and Engels explicitly comment on utilitarianism, in its crude Benthamite formulation, as an example of bourgeois ideology:

> The apparent stupidity of merging all the manifold relationships of people in the one relation of usefulness, this apparently metaphysical abstraction arises from the fact that, in modern bourgeois society, all relations are subordinated in practice to the one abstract monetary-commercial relation.[10]

Moral ideas function as ideology not only at the level of philosophical theory; more importantly, they do so at the level of popular moral consciousness. For example, in the *Communist Manifesto*, Marx and Engels dismiss individualistic ideas of personal freedom as mere reflections of bourgeois interests in free trade and the free market. Such examples seem to me successfully to illustrate the claim that moral ideas *can*, and *sometimes do*, function as ideology. We have, however, the same ambiguity in Marx as in Nietzsche. How extensive is his critique? Is it a critique of particular moral values (implying that there can also be non-ideological moral values), or is it the claim that *all* morality is, *as such*, ideological and has an illusory status?

Before getting to grips with this question let us turn to the case of Freud. We have already considered briefly, in the Plato chapter, Freud's view of mental health and illness, and his division of the self into *ego*, *id*, and *super-ego*. The term 'super-ego' is employed by Freud to refer to the phenomenon of moral conscience, especially in its negative aspect as forbidding certain kinds of actions and producing in us a feeling of guilt when we perform these actions. The super-ego is, according to Freud, the internalization of external authority. It is formed in the young child from the commands and wishes of his or her parents, whom the child obeys out of a fear of forfeiting their love. As the child comes to identify with the parents, their wishes come to be felt as commands issuing from within the child's own self, and conflicting with his or her own inclinations. The aggressiveness with which the super-ego combats these inclinations is fuelled by the hostility which the child feels as a result of these frustrations, and which, since its outward expression is blocked, is turned inward against the inclinations themselves. The gnawing or agonizing sense of guilt which one feels when contemplating or committing morally forbidden actions is thus an anxiety traceable to one's ambivalent childhood feelings of love and hostility towards one's parents.

Morality, then, is part of the mechanism of repression, serving to control the drives and instincts of the id and forcing unacceptable ideas into the unconscious. The similarity with Nietzsche is obvious. For both morality is, at least potentially, a *pathological* phenomenon, a compensatory response to the frustration of desires, which may produce a psychological equilibrium but may also fuel ongoing psychological disturbances. As with Marx, morality has an illusory status; it is not what it seems. Freud is less inclined than Nietzsche and Marx to present his account of morality as a critical theory. He does not think that we can dispense with the super-ego and the mechanisms of repression. Radical Freudians may have thought that we can, but for Freud the harsh super-ego is part of the necessary machinery of social control and self-control. Freud is a cultural pessimist who thinks that our natural aggressive instincts, if they were not repressed, would make social life impossible.[11] Nevertheless, he also stresses the harmful effects of excessive repression, particularly of sexual desires, and sees this as the cause of mental illness. Repression

is possible only to a certain degree; when it is carried further, the mental conflict between the instincts and the repressing forces continues at an unconscious level, and the repressed instincts find other outlets, especially in the
form of the symptoms of nervous illness which serve as substitute satisfactions. These symptoms may be seriously incapacitating. In the case of the nervous illness known as hysteria they may take the form of the paralysis of a
limb, or loss of speech, or severe physical pain. In other kinds of illness, such
as obsessional neurosis, the symptoms may be psychologically rather than
physically paralysing, involving obsessions and anxieties which dominate and
distort the person's emotional life, rendering him or her quite incapable of
functioning effectively in everyday life. Freud's practice of psychoanalysis, the
starting-point for his theorizing, was his technique for dealing with mental illness by bring the repressed desires into consciousness and thus enabling the
sufferer to deal with them at the level of rational understanding and control.

Freud, then, emphasizes the danger of excess repression, but he thinks that
the morality of the super-ego remains necessary. It is a necessary *illusion*, in so
far as the apparently impersonal authority of the moral conscience has a very
specific and personal psychological basis in one's love–hate relationship with
one's parents.

These, then, in brief summary, are the Marxist and Freudian theories which
have had such an influence, more so than Nietzsche, on modern sceptical attitudes concerning morality. Let us now return to the question of how comprehensive such critical scepticism can plausibly be. Whatever ambiguities there
may be in their avowed position, I do not believe that either Marx or Freud
could coherently maintain that *all values* are ideological, or are the internal-
ized reflection of parent–child emotional relationships. This is because their
positions both depend on a foundation of values, which must underpin their
criticisms of class oppression and of excess repression respectively, and to
which they must at least implicitly ascribe some rational status. I want to suggest that those values are most plausibly expressed in the vocabulary of *needs*
which we began to explore in the previous chapter.

Needs

Marx sometimes appears to endorse, and has often been taken to endorse, a
crudely economistic picture of human needs, in which oppression involves
simply the frustration of people's material needs. However, especially in his
early writings, he has, in fact, a much richer theory of needs. He inherits from
Hegel a 'self-realization' perspective, and he further develops Hegel's idea that
it is through working on the world that one realizes one's potentialities and
affirms one's identity both as an individual and as a human being. Work is the
objective manifestation of one's distinctively human creativity and imagina-
tion. In his early essay, 'Alienated Labour', Marx analyzes the way in which, for

the wage labourer in a capitalist economy, the need for meaningful work is thwarted. Because the worker works for another, not for himself, he is estranged from the products of his labour, from the potentially fulfilling activity of work itself, and from his own humanity.

> What, then, constitutes the alienation of labour? First, the fact that labour is *external* to the worker, i.e., it does not belong to his essential being; that in his work, therefore, he does not affirm himself but denies himself, does not feel content but unhappy, does not develop freely his mental and physical energy but mortifies his body and ruins his mind. The worker therefore only feels himself outside his work, and in his work feels outside himself. He is at home when he is not working, and when he is working he is not at home. His labour is therefore not voluntary, but coerced; it is *forced labour*. It is therefore not the satisfaction of a need; it is merely a *means* to satisfy needs external to it. . . . As a result, therefore, man (the worker) no longer feels himself to be freely active in any but his animal functions—eating, drinking, procreating, or at most in his dwelling and in dressing-up, etc.; and in his human functions he no longer feels himself to be anything but an animal. What is animal becomes human and what is human becomes animal.[12]

These ideas of the early Marx about the need for meaningful work, and the frustration of that need in a capitalist economy, continue to inform his economic analyses and his account of exploitation in his later writings, as the following passage illustrates:

> Within the capitalist system all methods for raising the social productiveness of labour are brought about at the cost of the individual labourer; all means for the development of production transform themselves into means of domination over, and exploitation of, the producers; they mutilate the labourer into a fragment of a man, degrade him to the level of an appendage of a machine, destroy every remnant of charm in his work and turn it into a hated toil; they estrange him from the intellectual potentialities of the labour process . . .[13]

For Freud, the harmful effects of excessive repression are, of course, the result of the frustration of sexual needs. He is not committed to a simplistic claim that sexual abstinence always causes mental illness. Such a claim would be easily refuted by the plentiful examples of individuals who lead fulfilling lives of total celibacy. Freud recognizes that the strength of the sexual instinct varies significantly between one individual and another. He recognizes that individuals vary in their capacity for sublimation (channelling sexual energy into other activities, cultural, intellectual, or spiritual). His general thesis is therefore stated with caution. 'A certain amount of direct sexual satisfaction,' he asserts, 'seems to be indispensable for most organizations, and a deficiency in this amount, which varies from individual to individual, is visited by phenomena which, on account of their detrimental effects on functioning and their subjective quality of unpleasure, must be regarded as an illness.'[14]

Just as Marx sometimes seems to invite a crude economistic reading of his view of human psychology, so Freud sometimes seems to invite a 'pansexualist' reading of his view of human motivation. Though he explicitly disavows such a position, his vocabulary does also at times encourage a crude picture of sexual fulfilment as a matter simply of physiological discharge and the release of physical tension. His case studies, however, make it apparent that this is not the real picture. The fundamental need, frustration of which leads to suffering and a diminished quality of life, and sometimes to mental illness, is the need for sexual relationships which are both physically and emotionally fulfilling.

Marx and Freud, then, both appeal to a certain view of human needs in their critique of the repressive role of a narrow conception of morality. I want to suggest that we can make the best sense of Nietzsche if we try to fit him into this kind of framework. There is no doubt, as we have seen, that he intends his theory of 'will to power' as a monistic theory of human motivation, but as such it is no more successful than crude and simplistic Marxist or Freudian claims that all motivation is economic or sexual. I believe that we can, however, usefully reinterpret the idea of 'will to power' as pointing to a basic human need—the need to make one's mark on the world, to obtain a sense of one's own agency and to make use of one's creative powers and energies. Nietzsche's own values of activity, energy, creativity, and health reflect these needs. The fundamental character of such needs is evidenced by the psychologically distorting effects of their frustration, which Nietzsche describes: the vengeful and vindictive moral condemnation of those who are more successful and more powerful, or the masochistic turning against one's own desires in a morality of self-denial. These insights in Nietzsche can contribute to the account of human needs which we began to develop in the last chapter.

'The Morality System'

Where does this leave the concept of 'morality'? If the theories of Nietzsche, Marx, and Freud all involve a commitment to certain values—values which I have suggested can be, at least in part, usefully formulated in terms of the concept of needs—and if these values are to coexist with a critique of morality, then it looks as though we (or at any rate they) require a distinction between *moral* and *non-moral* values. Can such a distinction be made, and is it worth making? In the end the question of whether or not we call certain values 'moral' values comes down to a matter of verbal preference. Nevertheless it is, I think, worth identifying a particular narrow conception of morality which is often equated with 'morality' as such, and is vulnerable to the sorts of criticisms derivable from Nietzsche, Marx, and Freud. Following Bernard Williams, we might refer to it as the 'peculiar institution' of 'the morality system'.[15] I suggest that this problematic conception of morality can be distinguished by three important features.

The first of these is what I want to call morality's 'alienated' character. We have seen that Marx uses the term 'alienation' to describe the way in which the products and the activity of wage labour come to be experienced as external to and foreign to the worker. Marx also uses the term more widely to refer to the fact that social institutions and practices, which are the product of human activity, take on a life of their own and come to dominate the human beings who have created them. The narrow conception of morality is, in this sense, an alienated phenomenon. It is experienced by human beings as a set of external demands to which they must conform. It is what Kant illuminatingly calls the 'moral law', the 'categorical imperative' which has to be obeyed. Nietzsche and Freud plausibly reveal the psychological mechanisms which explain this phenomenon. We might contrast it with Hume's picture of moral values rooted in the natural human feeling of sympathy, or with Aristotle's picture of moral virtues rooted in the conditions of the agent's own happiness and flourishing. Hume and Aristotle provide two widely differing contrasts with alienated morality, and it is an open question what a satisfactory non-alienated conception of 'morality' or 'ethics' might look like, but at this point I want simply to suggest that it is worth trying to develop such a conception.

The second feature of the narrow conception of morality is its self-denying character. Marx explains this in terms of subservience to a spurious 'general interest', which is really the interests of the dominant class. Nietzsche explains it in terms of the need for psychological compensation on the part of an oppressed class. The two definitions are not mutually exclusive; they both focus on the idea that morality serves to rationalize and legitimate social institutions which sacrifice the interests of a subordinate class. We have seen that Nietzsche does not regard self-denying morality as the only morality. Nevertheless, he recognizes that the very idea of 'morality' has increasingly come to be identified with this morality of self-denial, and this is as true in our day as it was in his. 'Morality' is typically thought of as a set of negative constraints which require one to forgo one's own interests for the sake of others. The alternative is not, as Nietzsche and occasionally Marx seem to imply, a reversion to an egoistic conception. Any realistic ethical theory is going to recognize that it may sometimes be right to give other people's interests priority over one's own, and, more fundamentally, that attitudes of concern and respect for other human beings must be at the heart of an adequate ethics. I have suggested that the ethics of altruism is the distinctive ethical stance of 'the Moderns' in contrast to 'the Ancients'. What we now need to explore is the possibility of an ethical position which transcends the rigid dichotomy between egoism and altruism—which goes beyond the Kantian idea that actions, even altruistic actions, performed because one finds such actions satisfying and fulfilling, are thereby precluded from having any moral worth. Again, it remains to be seen what such a position might look like.

The third distinctive feature of the narrow conception of morality is its individualistic character. 'Moral' judgements tend to be narrowly focused on the moral status of the individual agent—on his or her moral merit and, even more strongly, on the negative idea of his or her moral guilt. This preoccupation rests on an untenably strong notion of individual responsibility. It involves a failure to recognize that the behaviour of individuals takes place in a social context, and that value judgements need to be focused as much on the social institutions which lead individuals to act in certain ways. It fails to do justice to the fact that individuals act as they do in response to social and psychological pressures, and that if we want them to act differently we may do better not to address moral imperatives to them, but to try to change the circumstances which give rise to their behaviour. We have seen that the inadequacy of the preoccupation with individual guilt and responsibility is sometimes (and sometimes by Nietzsche) put in the language of determinism, as the claim that, given the social and psychological conditions, it is inevitable that individuals will act as they do and that it is therefore pointless to blame them for it. However, I do not think that the criticism of narrowly individualistic morality depends on the truth of determinism. The point may be more appropriately put, as it is by Williams, in terms of the idea of 'luck'. The morality system ignores the fact of luck. It ignores the fact that it is a matter of luck that some individuals, more than others, happen to find themselves in circumstances where they are able to act morally well. The morality system aspires to a total voluntariness which is, as Williams says, illusory.[16]

This, then, is the conception of morality which has a strong hold on the popular consciousness and which tends to be equated with 'morality' as such. I have intimated that Kant is the philosopher whose moral theory most closely reflects this conception (though it would be nonsense to regard Kant's moral theory simply as an uncritical ideological reflection of it). Drawing on Nietzsche, and on Marx and Freud, we have good reason to be suspicious of this narrow conception. We have reason to try to work towards a more adequate 'non-moralistic' conception of morality—understanding the term 'morality' now in a broader sense, as a comprehensive set of values, as a way of thinking about how we should live. This broader conception of morality would have to be a non-alienated one, not in the sense of advocating a pure spontaneity, but as rooting moral requirements in natural human dispositions and responses. It would have to transcend the rigid dichotomy of egoism and altruism, aiming for a synthesis of the 'ancients' and the 'moderns'—and I have previously suggested that the starting-point for this would have to be the Hegelian recognition of the social character of the individual. It would have to transcend the narrow focus on individual agency, recognizing, for instance, that social institutions and practices which systematically frustrate fundamental human needs and lead people to act 'immorally' are themselves equally 'immoral'. In Part III I shall come back to the possibilities for articulating such a broader conception.

Finally, however, we have to remind ourselves that there remains in Nietzsche a more all-embracing moral scepticism. This wider scepticism derives from his general theory of knowledge, his 'perspectivism', which appears to deny the very possibility of objective knowledge and to suggest that all claims to knowledge, including moral knowledge, reflect some pre-existing non-rational practical stance or other. There are reminders in Nietzsche of the relativism which I have previously associated with the Sophists. His emphasis on the historical diversity of value-systems stems from a rejection of the very idea of moral knowledge and moral facts even in a broad sense. This kind of scepticism, in a more sober guise, has been a theme of much contemporary moral philosophy, as we shall see in the next chapter.

Notes

1. *Twilight of the Idols*, Section 1 of 'The "Improvers" of Mankind', in Friedrich Nietzsche, *Twilight of the Idols and The Anti-Christ*, trans. R. J. Hollingdale (Harmondsworth, 1990), 66.
2. The most striking similarity is between Nietzsche's ideas and those of Callicles, a possibly fictitious character portrayed in Plato's *Gorgias* as an ambitious young Athenian politician strongly influenced by the Sophists.
3. In Homer the Greek word 'agathos' is indeed translatable both as 'good' and as 'noble'.
4. Matthew 5: 1–12. Cf. above, p. 48.
5. For a more nuanced account of this history which nevertheless owes something to Nietzsche, see Alasdair MacIntyre, *After Virtue* (London, 1981).
6. The most explicit passages are in II.12, II.18, III.7, and III.18. Fuller discussions in other works by Nietzsche include *Thus Spoke Zarathustra*, trans. R. J. Hollingdale (Harmondsworth, 1961), and in *The Portable Nietzsche*, ed. and trans. Walter Kaufmann (New York, 1954), the sections 'On the Thousand and One Goals' in Part 1 and 'On Self-overcoming' in Part 2; *Beyond Good and Evil*, trans. R. J. Hollingdale (Harmondsworth, 1973), e.g. sections 13, 19, 23, 36, 51, 230 and 259; and the notes collected posthumously under the title *The Will to Power*, trans. W. Kaufmann and R. J. Hollingdale (New York, 1968).
7. The best statement of this in *The Genealogy of Morals* comes in III.12: 'All seeing is essentially perspective, and so is all knowing. The more emotions we allow to speak in a given matter, the more different eyes we can put on in order to view a given spectacle, the more complete will be our conception of it, the greater our "objectivity". But to eliminate the will, to suspend the emotions altogether, provided it could be done—surely this would be to castrate the intellect, would it not?' A useful text for further exploration of Nietzsche's perspectivist theory of knowledge is *Beyond Good and Evil*, e.g. Part I and Section 34.
8. See e.g. *Human, All Too Human*, trans. Marion Faber and Stephen Lehmann (Harmondsworth, 1994) sections 39, 99, 102, 106 and 107, and the section 'The Four Great Errors' in *The Twilight of the Idols*, trans. R. J. Hollingdale (Harmondsworth, 1969), and in *The Portable Nietzsche*, ed. and trans. Walter Kaufmann (New York, 1954).
9. The most interesting text in which Marx (and his collaborator, Friedrich Engels) set out this theory of history is Part I of *The German Ideology*, written in 1845–6 but not published until 1932, long after Marx's death. A classic brief statement of the theory is Marx's Preface to his 1859 *Contribution to the Critique of Political*

Economy. The best philosophical examination of the theory is G. A. Cohen, *Karl Marx's Theory of History: A Defence* (Oxford, 1978). On the particular topic of Marxism and morality I should like to acknowledge the stimulus of the work of my colleagues, Tony Skillen (see e.g. his *Ruling Illusions,* Hassocks, 1977) and Sean Sayers (see e.g. his 'Analytical Marxism and Morality', in Robert Ware and Kai Nielsen (eds.), *Analysing Marxism,* Calgary, 1989).

10. Marx and Engels, *The German Ideology,* in David McLellan (ed.), *Karl Marx: Selected Writings* (Oxford, 1977), 185.

11. This view is put clearly in Freud's *Civilization and its Discontents* (in *The Pelican Freud Library,* xii: *Civilization, Society and Religion,* Harmondsworth, 1985; first pub. 1930), chs. 5–7. Chapter 7 provides a convenient account of Freud's theory of the super-ego.

12. Karl Marx, *Economic and Philosophical Manuscripts of 1844,* trans. Martin Milligan, in Robert C. Tucker (ed.), *The Marx-Engels Reader* (2nd edn., New York, 1978), 74.

13. Karl Marx, *Capital,* Volume I, trans. S. Moore and E. Aveling (London, 1970), ch. 25, Section 4.

14. Sigmund Freud, ' "Civilized" Sexual Morality and Modern Nervous Illness', in *The Pelican Freud Library,* xii: *Civilization, Society and Religion* (Harmondsworth, 1985), 40.

15. Bernard Williams, *Ethics and the Limits of Philosophy* (London, 1985), ch. 10. See also Skillen's work, referred to in n. 9 above.

16. Ibid. 194–6.

Contemporary Themes

10
Facts and Values

Reading: As explained below, the remaining three chapters will not be built around classic texts. Relevant reading will be referred to in the course of the chapters. A useful collection to accompany all three chapters is James Rachels (ed.), *Ethical Theory*, 1. *The Question of Objectivity* and 2. *Theories About How We Should Live* (Oxford, 1998). The first volume is particularly relevant to the present chapter.

In Part III I shall be discussing a body of work which represents one continuation of the tradition explored in the previous chapters. My approach will, however, be different. I shall not be focusing on a single major figure in each chapter. The work I shall be dealing with is that of twentieth-century academic writers working in university philosophy departments. Whether any of them will in due course be seen to have the stature of an Aristotle or a Kant is a question which still awaits the verdict of history. Some of the work is rather technical, and for that reason too I shall concentrate more on providing an exposition of a number of different contributions, rather than responding to a few major texts. I shall nevertheless try to show how this work does indeed continue the themes of the classic tradition and how it has made important contributions to them, even though the contributions are more narrowly academic.

Though less selective in one sense, the tradition I shall be presenting is selective in another, quite different sense. It is the tradition of what can best be called 'English-language philosophy'. Academic philosophers in the English-speaking countries, in particular Britain and Ireland, North America, and Australasia have constituted a relatively cohesive intellectual community with a shared philosophical style—the style of 'analytical philosophy' in the broad sense of that label. There has been a great deal more common ground and dialogue between philosophers within that tradition than there has been between it and philosophical work in, for example, other European countries such as France and Germany. This work is, therefore, just *one* continuation of the classic tradition. There are others, equally deserving of attention—but to have dealt with them would have meant writing a different book.

The Naturalistic Fallacy

I referred at the beginning of this book to the distinction between substantive or normative ethics on the one hand, and meta-ethics on the other. The former is the investigation of questions about what constitutes a good life, what kinds of actions are right or wrong, and how we ought to live. The latter is the investigation of logical, linguistic, or epistemological questions about what we are doing when we try to answer questions of the first kind, and about whether our conclusions can have a rational basis, can be 'true' or 'false', or can count as 'knowledge'. My previous chapters have been largely concerned with the substantive ethical theories of the philosophers I have been considering, but in the process I have also been looking at their meta-ethical implications. That concern began with the Sophists, who, we saw, were inclined to point to the diversity of customs and conventions of different societies and to conclude from this that there could be no 'true' or 'correct' moral beliefs. In the same vein we have seen Hume claim that our moral judgements are the product not of reason or understanding but of sentiment, and we have seen Nietzsche assert with a more radical urgency that 'there are no moral facts whatever'. In contrast to that kind of position, the tendency of this book so far has been towards a form of ethical *naturalism*—the view that we *can* properly seek to establish true moral conclusions, and that these can be derived from facts about human nature, about human psychology and social life. I saw this as the important legacy of Plato and Aristotle, and from the writers subsequently discussed I have derived what I take to be contributions to a viable ethical naturalism, even if their explicit meta-ethical position was not a naturalistic one.

This whole ethical tendency receives a fundamental challenge from one of the most influential works of twentieth-century moral philosophy, *Principia Ethica*, written by the Cambridge philosopher G. E. Moore and published in 1903. According to Moore, any attempt to defend a version of ethical naturalism is liable to be guilty of what he calls 'the naturalistic fallacy'. That phrase, and the accusation which it embodies, have set the terms of much subsequent meta-ethical discussion, which I shall survey in this chapter.

Why does Moore think that naturalism rests on a fallacy? To understand this we need to look at his positive meta-ethical theory. He takes the central concern of ethics to be the attempt to answer the question 'What is good?' He is especially concerned, however, with one particular use of the word 'good', to denote what he calls 'intrinsic value', the goodness of things which are good as ends in themselves. Some things are good as means to some further end. Virtuous actions, for instance, are good as means, and that is to say that they tend to bring about what is good in itself. Similarly a 'right' action can, according to Moore, be defined as one which will produce the greatest possible amount of what is good in itself. These concepts, then, are dependent on the central concept of something's being 'good' in the sense of possessing intrinsic value. Now

Moore's most important claim about 'good' when used in this sense is that *it cannot be defined*. It is, he says, a simple and unanalysable property. We know it when we encounter it, but we cannot analyse it in terms of anything more fundamental. He compares it to the property 'yellow', which is likewise simple and unanalysable. We can come to understand what 'yellow' is by being directly acquainted with the property, but there is no definition by which we can convey, to someone who has never seen the colour, what 'yellow' is. 'Good' and 'yellow', then, are alike in this respect, but they differ in that, whereas yellow is a simple *natural* property, good is a simple *non-natural* property. By a 'natural' property he means an empirical property, one which can be 'an object of experience'. Natural properties are those which are the subject-matter of the natural sciences and of psychology.[1] Good is not a natural property. It is a simple and indefinable non-natural property.

Why is the indefinability of 'good' so important? Because, Moore thinks, a great many moral philosophers have attempted to establish substantive moral conclusions by appealing to a definition of good. They have claimed to show what things are good, and hence what actions are right and how we ought to live, by deriving such conclusions from a claim about what 'good' means. In doing so they have been guilty of the naturalistic fallacy. Moore calls it the *naturalistic* fallacy because he thinks it has been committed particularly by those who have built an ethical theory on a definition of 'good' which equates it with some *natural* property. A classic example is hedonism. Moral theories such as utilitarianism have asserted that right actions are those which will produce the greatest amount of pleasure, and they have typically defended this view, according to Moore, by claiming that 'good' just *means* 'pleasurable'. Now it may perhaps be true, Moore says, that pleasure is good, or that certain kinds of pleasure are good, but whether or not it is true, it cannot be true simply by definition. Good is one thing, and pleasure is another, and if we consider carefully these two properties we can recognize that they are distinct. No-one, therefore, can establish the truth of hedonistic utilitarianism by appealing to a claim about the definition of 'good' which simply equates it with the empirical property of being pleasurable. (We have seen in Chapter 7 that Moore specifically criticizes Mill for defending utilitarianism in a similar way, equating 'good' with the distinct and separate property of being 'desired'.)

Another typical example of the naturalistic fallacy is provided, Moore thinks, by defences of evolutionary ethics. Writers like Herbert Spencer had tried to use evolutionary theory to establish ethical conclusions. They had tried to show that certain modes of conduct, such as co-operation or mutual aid, are characteristic of the more evolved species, those species which are 'higher' in the evolutionary scale, and that such modes of conduct are therefore ethically desirable. Moore objects that arguments of this form fail to recognize 'what a very different thing is being "more evolved" from being "higher" or "better"' (section 31). If 'more evolved' simply means 'coming later in the evolutionary process', this is a natural property, and it can be established empirically what kinds of conduct are 'more evolved'. But from the fact that something is 'more evolved' in this sense, it by no means follows that it is 'higher' in the sense of 'better', and those who think that it does follow appear to be making the fallacious assumption that 'good' just *means* 'more evolved'.

Moore thinks that essentially the same mistake is committed by those theories which equate good with some non-natural, supersensible property. Someone who attempted to defend a 'divine command' theory of ethics by claiming that 'good' just *means* 'willed by God' would be guilty of the same fallacy. But he calls it the *naturalistic* fallacy because he thinks it is most often committed by the defenders of one or another version of ethical naturalism. The fallaciousness of any such defence of naturalism can, according to Moore, be shown by what subsequent commentators have dubbed the 'open question' argument. Whatever the natural property which is taken to be the basis of a naturalistic ethics, whether it be the promotion of happiness, or the satisfaction of human needs, or anything else, we can always meaningfully ask 'Is it *good* to promote happiness, or to satisfy human needs, or whatever?' And since this is always an open question, it follows that the answer cannot be true by definition. Moore and many subsequent philosophers have regarded this as a decisive objection to all the standard forms of ethical naturalism.

It is important to recognize that Moore's criticism of naturalism is not like that of Hume or Nietzsche. They assert that there are no moral facts. Moore thinks that there *are* moral facts. As we have seen, he thinks that we can establish what kinds of actions are right by looking at the empirical facts about the causal consequences of actions. Right actions are those which will produce the greatest possible amount of good (and in this respect Moore's substantive moral theory is a kind of utilitarianism, or at any rate consequentialism). But this still leaves us with the task of establishing what kinds of consequences are intrinsically good, and Moore thinks that, though these too are facts which can be established, they are not facts about the natural world. They are not facts which can be established empirically, either by direct observation, or by analysing 'good' in terms of some other natural property which can be empirically observed. How, then, does Moore think that moral truths can be ascertained? What we have to determine is whether certain states of affairs do or do not possess the simple, unanalysable, non-natural property 'good'. Moore claims, however, that once the nature of this question is made clear, the answer is self-evident.

> By far the most valuable things, which we know or can imagine, are certain states of consciousness, which may be roughly described as the pleasures of human inter-course and the enjoyment of beautiful objects. No one, probably, who has asked himself the question, has ever doubted that personal affection and the appreciation of what is beautiful in Art or Nature, are good in themselves. . . . (section 113)

If we are agreed on this, however, we can return to our previous question 'What actions are right?'. The correct answer will be that right actions are those which most effectively bring about the pleasures of personal affection and the enjoyment of beautiful things.

What is most striking here is Moore's suggestion that the basic judgements of value are simply *self-evident* (section 86). According to Moore, we just *know* that they are true. This aspect of Moore's ethical theory has sometimes been described as 'Intuitionist', and Moore does himself use the word 'intuition' to refer to our supposed direct awareness of the goodness of things which are good in themselves. Moore emphasizes, however, that he is not an 'Intuitionist' in the sense in which this term has regularly been used. His theory differs from what had previously been called 'Intuitionism' in two important respects. First, it is not our beliefs about what actions are right, but only our beliefs about what things are good in themselves, that Moore wants to call 'intuitions'. Second, Moore emphasizes that in calling these latter beliefs 'intuitions' he does not wish to imply that there is some special way in which we can know them to be true. He means only, he says, that we can know them to be true, and that we cannot give any further reasons why they are true. An 'intuition', for Moore, is not some special form of cognition which guarantees the truth of what one claims to know. It is simply a belief which one knows to be true, but for which one has no reasons.

That, however, is precisely the problem for Moore. How can one know such things? We may agree with him that there are some truths for which no further reasons can be given; indeed, there must be, for the giving of reasons cannot go on *ad infinitum*, it must come to an end at some point. When one gets to that point, however, one must be able to say *something* about *how* one knows these things, and Moore's problem is that he can say nothing at all. So if someone were to disagree with one of those basic value judgements which Moore takes to be self-evident—for example, that the enjoyment of artistic beauty is good in itself—it would seem that Moore's only response could be, 'I think that you are mistaken, because what is self-evident to me is different from what is self-evident to you.'

The implausibility of Moore's talk of 'self-evidence' becomes especially apparent if we compare him with another philosopher who has also been called an 'intuitionist', W. D. Ross. In his book *The Right and the Good*, published in 1930, Ross criticizes utilitarianism for reasons which we encountered in Chapter 7, and he applies his criticism also to the utilitarian aspect of Moore's substantive ethical theory. It is not the case, he says, that the only thing which makes right acts right is their tendency to produce as much good as possible. Certain kinds of action are right or wrong in themselves, quite apart from their good or bad consequences. As we have seen, Ross identifies these kinds of action by providing a list of what he calls 'prima facie duties' ('prima facie' because they may sometimes conflict with one another, and one duty may then have to be overridden by the other). These are duties of fidelity such as the duty to keep a promise, duties of reparation, duties of gratitude, duties of justice, duties of beneficence, duties of self-improvement, and duties of non-maleficence.

Ross's substantive moral theory, then, is importantly different from Moore's. His meta-ethical theory, however, is similar to Moore's, in that he thinks that the fundamental moral truths are self-evident. It appears, there-fore, that what is self-evident to Ross is not self-evident to Moore, and vice versa. Ross says:

> That an act, *qua* fulfilling a promise or *qua* effecting a just distribution of good, or *qua* returning services rendered or *qua* promoting the good of others, or *qua* pro-moting the virtue or insight of the agent, is *prima facie* right, is self-evident; not in the sense that it is evident from the beginning of our lives, or as soon as we attend to the proposition for the first time, but in the sense that when we have reached suffi-cient mental maturity and have given sufficient attention to the proposition it is evi-dent without any need of proof, or of evidence beyond itself.[2]

This use of the term 'self-evident' is essentially the same as Moore's, but the judgements which they take to be self-evident are very different. Ross is quite explicit about this:

> If we are told, for instance, that we should give up our view that there is a special obligatoriness attaching to the keeping of promises because it is self-evident that the only duty is to produce as much good as possible, we have to ask ourselves whether we really, when we reflect, *are* convinced that this is self-evident, and whether we really *can* get rid of the view that promise-keeping has a bindingness independent of productiveness of maximum good. In my own experience I find that I cannot, in spite of a very genuine attempt to do so.[3]

Clearly Ross's experience must be different from Moore's, for what is self-evidently true for one of them is self-evidently false for the other. This must surely cast doubt on the very idea of 'self-evidence'. Philosophers who claim that fundamental value-judgements are self-evident are not necessarily com-mitted to claiming that their truth is always apparent to everyone. Moore and Ross both acknowledge that people can be mistaken about these things, and that disagreement is therefore possible. It does, however, seem remarkable that these two philosophers themselves, whose moral awareness is presumably as great as anyone's, should form exactly opposite judgements about matters which are supposed to be self-evident. Moreover, since the truths which are supposed to be self-evident are, by definition, ones for which no reason can be given, there can be no way of resolving the disagreement or of showing which of the views in question is really the apprehension of a self-evident truth. It is not surprising, then, that other philosophers have concluded that these funda-mental value-judgements are not really the expression of self-evident truths at all; they are merely the expression of personal preferences, of feelings and emotions, of individual likes and dislikes.

Subjectivism and Emotivism

One of the first to draw this conclusion was Bertrand Russell, perhaps the most famous British philosopher of the twentieth century. Although he was very active in public life as an advocate of particular moral and political views (for instance on sexual morality, and on the question of nuclear disarmament), little of his extensive philosophical writing was directly concerned with ethics. He did, however, give some attention to these matters. He was a friend and colleague of Moore at Cambridge, and in his earliest writing on ethics he fully accepted Moore's position. By 1914, however, he had decided that Moore's view of the self-evidence of fundamental value judgements could not be sustained. Assertions that certain things were 'good in themselves' were not really expressions of self-evident truths; they did not express any knowledge at all, since the terms 'good' and 'evil' did not refer to any objective features of the universe. During the First World War Russell campaigned actively against the British government's war policies, and was imprisoned for his opposition to the war; but in his polemical writings on the subject he admitted that, philosophically, he had to regard his moral criticism of the war, like his opponents' support for the war, as in the end 'the outcome of feeling rather than of thought'.[4]

Russell's fullest exposition of this view is the chapter 'Science and Ethics' in his book *Religion and Science*, published in 1935. He still retains the consequentialist element of Moore's theory; moral rules specifying that certain kinds of conduct are right or wrong are 'justified if they promote the existence of what is good on its own account'. But when it comes to judgements about whether this or that is good in itself 'there is no evidence either way; each disputant can only appeal to his own emotions, and employ such rhetorical devices as shall rouse similar emotions in others'.[5] What Moore regards as knowledge of fundamental values, therefore, Russell denies to be knowledge at all:

> Questions as to 'values' lie wholly outside the domain of knowledge. That is to say, when we assert that this or that has 'value', we are giving expression to our own emotions, not to a fact which would still be true if our personal feelings were different.[6]

Russell describes his theory as an assertion of the 'subjectivity' of values. There are no objective values. So-called 'values' are not an independently existing feature of the world. When we ascribe value to something, we are not saying something objective about it, but giving expression to our own states of mind. Russell claims that the chief ground for his theory is the impossibility of finding arguments to prove that something has 'intrinsic value'. If one person says that 'beauty is good in itself' and another person disagrees, there is no way in which either of them can show the other to be mistaken. Now, we have seen that Moore accepted this; it was why he said that such value-judgements are 'self-evident', meaning that we can know them to be true without being able to give any reason why they are true. Russell draws a different conclusion: if we can give no reason why they are true, this shows not that they are 'self-evident', but that they are neither true nor false. They make no statements, and they convey no knowledge.

Russell's theory can accordingly be classified as an example of what have come to be called 'non-cognitivist' theories of ethics. These are theories which maintain that the proper function of ethical utterances is something other than that of conveying knowledge. Russell's version of such a position was subsequently developed into the theory known as 'emotivism'. This theory was first sketched by A. J. Ayer in his 1936 book *Language, Truth and Logic*, and subsequently developed by Charles Stevenson in a number of articles and in his book *Ethics and Language* (1944).[7] What Stevenson emphasized especially was the theory of meaning which he held to be needed for a correct understanding of the nature of moral judgements and other value-judgements. He distinguished between *descriptive* and *emotive* meaning. Factual utterances have descriptive meaning; they make statements about the world, they convey beliefs which can be true or false and which, if true, can constitute knowledge. Ethical utterances, in contrast, have emotive meaning; they do not make statements or convey beliefs or knowledge, and cannot be true or false, but their meaning consists in their capacity to express and arouse feelings. It is important to notice also that many utterances have both descriptive and emotive meaning. If I say of someone, for example, 'She is a brave woman', I am in part making a statement of fact. I am saying that she tends to behave in certain kinds of ways, facing danger and not yielding to fear, and empirical evidence can establish whether this statement is true or false. I am, however, also doing something more than stating a fact. My use of the word 'brave' would normally be taken to express my feeling of approval or admiration for her behaviour and would be intended to elicit the same feeling from others. Someone who accepted my factual description of her but did not share my feeling of approval would be likely to use some other word, referring to her perhaps not as 'brave' but as 'rash' or 'stubborn'. Words like 'brave' thus have both descriptive and emotive meaning.

Stevenson emphasizes the connection between the *meaning* of language and its *use*. The emotive meaning of a word is defined by Stevenson as its tendency to express and evoke certain feelings or emotions or attitudes and thereby be suited for 'dynamic' use. 'Meaning' is thus not the *same* as 'use'. A word will be put to a particular use on a particular occasion, and this will vary. The sentence 'Stealing is wrong' when addressed to a child who has emptied her sister's money box may, on that particular occasion, express strong feelings and be firmly intended to elicit an emotional response, but on another occasion it may be used much less dynamically, for instance if two people are dispassionately drawing up a list of moral principles and are in full agreement with one another. Use varies, then, whereas meaning is more constant, but the meaning is what underlies the use. It is a word's *tendency* to have a certain effect, even if it does not do so on every occasion of its use.

Stevenson refers to this tendency as the 'magnetism' of emotive language, which enables it to be employed as a social 'instrument' to 'influence' people. Words can carry 'a subtle kind of suggestion' which can be used to 'modify' people's attitudes.[8] Stevenson sometimes seems to imply that ethical discourse is essentially manipulative, a kind of propaganda technique, and this, as we shall see, has been one of the principal grounds for criticism of the emotivist theory.

Corresponding to the distinction between two kinds of meaning, Stevenson offers an account of disputes about values by distinguishing between two kinds of disagreement. There is 'disagreement in belief', but there is also 'disagreement in attitude'.[9] Suppose that, having agreed on the facts, two people nevertheless make different ethical judgements; one says, for instance, 'War is never morally right,' whereas the other says, 'War can sometimes be morally right.' Stevenson says that their disagreement is a disagreement in attitude, not a disagreement in belief. This, he thinks, enables the emotivist theory to meet a criticism which Moore had made of subjectivist theories. Moore argued that if ethical utterances were simply statements about the speaker's feelings and attitudes, then the two disputants would be saying 'I approve of some wars' and 'I disapprove of all wars', and it would then follow that there was no real disagreement between them, since each utterance could be a true description of the speaker's state of mind. Moore concluded that the subjectivist account makes moral disagreement impossible. Stevenson says that this objection would indeed be valid if the claim were that ethical utterances are used to *describe* feelings and attitudes. If, however, we pay due regard to emotive meaning, we can see that there is a perfectly proper sense in which they disagree: they have divergent attitudes, and each is trying to redirect the other's feelings. Their disagreement is not a disagreement *about* attitudes, but a disagreement *in* attitudes. It is thus possible for there to be meaningful disagreement in ethics, and the emotivist theory cannot be criticized on the grounds that it excludes this possibility.

The emotivist theory enjoyed considerable popularity in the 1940s and early 1950s, partly because it seemed to coincide with more general tendencies in the philosophy of language. Wittgenstein's later philosophy was beginning to exert its influence, and a particularly relevant feature of it was his criticism of the idea that words have meaning by standing for objects. We have the idea, Wittgenstein says, that the meaning of a word is the object for which the word stands, but in fact this idea is a very misleading one.[10] We could take Moore as a classic example here. He assumes that 'good' must be the name of a certain kind of property. He establishes, rightly, that it is not the name of any empirical or 'natural' property. He therefore concludes that it must be the name of some other kind of property, a supersensible, 'non-natural' property. Under the influence of Wittgenstein, philosophers came to see that the initial assumption here was the source of all the trouble. If we want to understand the meaning of 'good', the way to do so is not to look for some mysterious property which it matches and 'stands for'. We are asking the wrong question. Wittgenstein's alternative suggestion was the following: 'For a *large* class of cases—though not for all—in which we employ the word "meaning", it can be defined thus: the meaning of a word is its use in the language.'[11] This sort of approach had been popularized by others with the slogan 'Don't ask for the meaning, ask for the use', and emotivism seemed to exemplify such an approach, seeking to analyse value-words like 'good' and 'right' not by identifying the supposed properties for which they stand, but by looking at what we *do* with the words.

Though the general approach seemed right, however, the particular account offered by emotivism of the use of value-words seemed, to many philosophers, less satisfactory. It presented ethical discourse as an essentially *non-rational* activity. The emphasis on the expressive use of ethical language seemed to imply that it was some kind of emotional 'letting off steam'—as though a moral discussion were little more than a succession of sighs and grunts and cheers. The emphasis on the use of ethical language to arouse feelings and attitudes seemed to imply that ethical discourse was a manipulative activity, akin to propaganda or advertising, playing on people's emotions in surreptitious ways. What many philosophers were looking for, therefore, was a theory which focused on what we do with ethical language, but which presented ethical discourse as a less manipulative, more rational activity. The most important attempt to develop such a theory was that of R. M. Hare.

Prescriptivism

In his book *The Language of Morals*, published in 1952, Hare takes as his starting-point the link which the emotivists had previously made between ethical language and commands. This is in itself, says Hare, a useful comparison, for the basic overall function of ethical language is to *guide conduct*, to answer the question 'What shall I do?', and in this it obviously plays something of the same role as imperatives, the language of commands. The error of emotivism, according to Hare, lay not in comparing ethical language with the language of imperatives, but in giving a misleading account of both these kinds of language, and he therefore suggests that we can avoid the pitfalls of emotivism if we first look more clearly at how imperatives are used. The important point to stress here is that, though imperatives are obviously action-guiding, this does not mean that their characteristic use is to exercise some kind of causal influence on the behaviour or emotions of the hearer. There is, says Hare, a difference between *getting* someone to do something and *telling* someone to do something. The emotivists implied that the proper use of both moral judgements and imperatives was to *get* someone to do something, and was thus a matter of persuasion and influence, involving the manipulation of people's feelings. Using an imperative, however, is not a case of *getting* someone to do something but of *telling* someone to do something. If I say to you, 'Shut the door,' I am not seeking to persuade you or arouse your feelings or exercise some kind of causal influence on you. I am simply telling you what to do. My use of the imperative is an answer to the question 'What shall I do?'; it is addressed to the hearer as a rational agent, and its use is no less rational than the use of indicative language to tell someone something by stating facts.

In particular, this means that the use of imperatives is governed by logical rules just as the use of indicative statements is. Imperatives can feature in logical inferences. Consider the following:

Take all the boxes to the station.
This is one of the boxes.
∴ Take this to the station.

This is a logically valid syllogism, and no less so for the fact that its major premiss and its conclusion are in the imperative rather than in the indicative mood. It is an example of how an imperative can be logically deduced from a more general imperative together with additional factual information. It shows, therefore, that there can be perfectly good rational arguments involving imperatives, and if moral language is like imperative language in being action-guiding, this will not make it any less rational. One particular rule governing the logic of imperatives is, however, regarded by Hare as being of very great importance. Logically valid arguments can indeed lead to imperative conclusions—*but only if there is also an imperative in the premises.* In the example, the imperative conclusion 'Take this to the station' can be arrived at only because it is a specific application of the more general imperative 'Take all the boxes to the station'. No such imperative conclusion could have been validly reached if all the premises had been indicative statements of fact. The importance of this will become more apparent if we now turn, as Hare does, to the comparison between imperatives and moral language.

Moral language, like the language of imperatives, is a class of prescriptive language. Its primary function is to be action-guiding. Where moral terms differ from simple imperatives is that, as well as being prescriptive, they also have an element of descriptive meaning. Hare uses the phrase 'evaluative term' to refer to those terms which combine both prescriptive and descriptive meaning. These include not only moral terms but also, for example, non-moral uses of the word 'good'. Consider the judgement 'This is a good strawberry'. 'Good', though not being used in a moral sense, is an evaluative term here. Its primary function is prescriptive; it is used to commend, to guide people's choices. To this extent it functions like an imperative, and to say 'This is a good strawberry' is like saying, 'If you want a strawberry, choose this one.' But, as well as having this prescriptive meaning, 'good' also has descriptive meaning. It implies that the strawberry has certain characteristics which *make* it a good strawberry. It does not specify what those characteristics are, but it implies that there are *some* such characteristics. Someone who says 'This is a good strawberry' can, therefore, properly be asked to specify what it is about the strawberry that makes it a good one. Suppose I were to say, 'It is a good strawberry because it is sweet and juicy.' This logically commits me to saying that any other strawberry which is like it in the relevant aspects, namely in being sweet and juicy, is also a good strawberry. If I were to say of two strawberries that one is and the other is not a good strawberry, but could not specify any good-making characteristic which is possessed by the one and not the other, then I would be misusing the word 'good' because I would be violating the rules which govern its descriptive meaning. Evaluative terms are like purely descriptive terms in this way. If I say of something that it is 'red', I am thereby committed to saying, of anything else which is like it in the relevant respect, that it too is red. We can put this by saying that evaluative terms, because they have descriptive as well as prescriptive meaning, are, like purely descriptive terms, *universalizable*.

On the other hand, Hare emphasizes that we cannot reduce the meaning of evaluative terms *simply* to their descriptive meaning. 'This is a good strawberry' does not just mean 'This is a sweet and juicy strawberry'. If it did, then we would no longer be able to use the word 'good' for its primary and distinctive purpose, to *commend* strawberries which are sweet and juicy. It is this commendatory purpose that is common to all the applications of the word 'good' to very different sorts of things. Consider the statements 'This is a good strawberry', 'This is a good car', 'This is good weather', 'He is a good person'. Clearly there is no single set of characteristics possessed by good strawberries, good cars, good weather, and good people. We might apply the word 'good' to cars which are safe and reliable and comfortable, to weather which is warm and sunny, and to people who are kind and sensitive. If the meaning of the word were confined to its descriptive meaning, therefore, we should have to say that 'good' has a different meaning when applied to strawberries, to cars, to weather, and to people. There is, however, according to Hare, a common element of meaning in all these different applications of 'good', and that is its prescriptive meaning, its use to commend, to guide choices.

Hare says that, in the case of the most general evaluative terms such as 'good', 'bad', 'right', 'wrong', and 'ought', the prescriptive meaning is primary and the descriptive meaning is secondary. There are also, he says, other evaluative terms whose descriptive meaning is primary and whose prescriptive meaning is secondary. Examples of such terms which are applied to people and to human conduct are words like 'industrious', 'honest', or 'courageous'.

To say that someone is honest is to say that she can normally be relied on to tell the truth, that she does not deceive people, and so on. This is the descriptive meaning of the word, and to that extent there are established criteria for determining whether or not someone should be described as 'honest'. However, in calling someone 'honest' we are usually doing more than just describing her; we are implying that because she possesses this characteristic she is a good person, and we are, therefore, commending her for being honest. Likewise, to call an action 'dishonest' is not only to describe it as having a certain character; it is also a prescription which implies the imperative 'Don't do this'. Again, Hare wants to emphasize the importance of recognizing that the meaning of such words cannot be reduced to their descriptive meaning. We cannot be forced to a moral conclusion by being told, 'She possesses those characteristics which we call "honesty", so she must be an honest and, therefore, a good person.' If 'She is honest' is to entail 'She is good', then the word 'honest' must be used with prescriptive as well as descriptive meaning. In that case we will not agree to call someone 'honest' simply because she possesses the relevant descriptive characteristics; we will do so only if we approve of those characteristics and, therefore, agree in commending someone who possesses them.

It is at this point that the emphasis on the distinction between descriptive and prescriptive meaning links up with Hare's previous claims about the role of imperatives in logical argument. We saw that Hare is committed to two main claims about the logic of imperatives. One is that imperatives can feature in valid logical arguments, just as indicatives do. The other claim is that a logically valid argument can lead to an imperative conclusion only if at least one of the premises is an imperative. Comparable claims can now be made about moral judgements and other kinds of value-judgements. Like imperatives, they can feature as the conclusions of valid logical arguments. Characteristically, they can be deduced from more general value-judgements together with additional factual premises. To continue with the 'strawberry' example, the following would be a valid logical inference.

Sweet and juicy strawberries are good ones.
This strawberry is sweet and juicy.
∴ This is a good strawberry.

And an example of a valid inference with a specifically moral conclusion would be:

Behaviour which leads to a great amount of human suffering is wrong.
Racial prejudice leads to a great amount of human suffering.
∴ Racial prejudice is wrong.

The possibility of such inferences shows that the making of moral judgements and other value judgements, like the use of imperatives, can be a rational activity. However, such inferences are also governed by the same logical rule as governs imperative inferences. Prescriptive conclusions can only be logically deduced from premises at least one of which is prescriptive. Purely descriptive premises cannot entail prescriptive conclusions. In our examples,

This strawberry is sweet and juicy

cannot by itself entail

This is a good strawberry.

And

Racial prejudice leads to a great amount of human suffering.

cannot by itself entail

Racial prejudice is wrong.

In each case one is logically compelled to accept the evaluative conclusion only if one accepts the evaluative major premiss. This vitally important logical rule is, according to Hare, rooted in the different functions of descriptive and prescriptive language. Value-judgements, like imperatives, are a form of prescriptive language; they are action-guiding, and their function is to tell people what to do. The function of descriptive language, on the other hand, is to state facts, and it, therefore, cannot by itself tell people what to do.

We are now in a position to sum up the role which Hare gives to reason in moral discourse. Because of the possibilities of logical inference leading to moral conclusions, moral discourse can be a rational activity. This is an important corrective to the emotivist picture of moral discourse as a non-rational process of influence and persuasion, intended to arouse people's feelings and emotions. Hare's account also indicates, however, that reason has its limits. A moral judgement may be derived from some more general moral premiss, and that in turn perhaps from some still more general moral premiss; but the process must eventually come to a stop. The ultimate premiss or set of premisses underlying our moral reasoning cannot, for Hare, be descriptive statements, they must themselves be moral premisses, ultimate moral principles. Like the emotivists, Hare is committed to saying that these ultimate moral principles cannot be self-evident truths, nor can they be statements of fact which can be empirically verified. To adopt such a principle is to make what Hare calls a 'decision of principle', and this is something quite different from judging a statement of fact to be true or false. The facts cannot determine what decision we are to make. Herein lies the 'freedom' which Hare refers to in the title of his second book, *Freedom and Reason*:

> If we say that the world is flat, we can in principle be shown certain facts such that, once we have admitted them, we cannot go on saying that the world is flat without being guilty either of self-contradiction or of a misuse of language. . . . Nothing of the sort can be done in morals. . . . It follows that we are free to form

our own moral opinions in a much stronger sense than we are free to form our own opinions as to what the facts are.[12]

The conjunction of this freedom with the aforementioned role for reason is what Hare takes to be distinctive of moral thought.

Despite the differences between them, all the ethical theories which we have considered so far have a common feature. They could all be described as *anti-naturalist* theories. They all maintain that there is a radical dichotomy between value-judgements and statements of fact about the empirical world. For Moore, this dichotomy is formulated as a distinction between two kinds of properties, on the one hand natural properties, and on the other hand the simple, unanalysable, non-natural property, 'good'. Russell, Stevenson, Hare, and others all deny that 'good' and other value-words are appropriately understood as names of certain kinds of properties, or that value-judgements are to be understood as stating some special kind of fact. In that sense, their alternative theories are 'non-cognitivist'. The emotivists formulate the dichotomy as a distinction between descriptive meaning and emotive meaning. Hare formulates it as a distinction between descriptive language and prescriptive language. The formulation which has been most commonly adopted, following Hare, is the distinction between *facts* and *values*. This is not how Moore would put it—he would regard values as a special kind of fact—but Hare thinks that it is the valid point which lies behind Moore's rejection of naturalism.[13] Hare also invokes the famous passage, quoted above in Chapter 5, in which Hume casts doubt on the logical process by which writers on morality pass from a series of 'is'-propositions to an 'ought'-proposition. Hare has been following Hume in maintaining that the impossibility of deducing an 'ought' from an 'is' derives from the *practical* character of moral judgements. Hume, we saw, puts this in psychological terms. Reason, he says, is wholly inactive. Only our sentiments or passions can move us to action. Since moral judgements are intended to lead to action, they must accordingly have their origin in sentiment rather than reason. Hare has translated Hume's claim into the vocabulary of logic rather than psychology. In place of Hume's distinction between 'reason' and 'sentiment' he has offered the distinction between the 'descriptive' and 'prescriptive' functions of language, and the claim that, because moral judgements are prescriptive or action-guiding, they cannot be logically deduced from factual statements about the world. This division between facts and values is, according to Hare, the logical gap which naturalism fails to recognize.

The overall tendency of this book so far has been in the direction of naturalism. I have been suggesting that whatever is of value in the historical tradition of the theories I have discussed can be worked into a broadly naturalistic ethics. That suggestion must now confront the thoroughgoing critique of naturalism mounted by the twentieth-century philosophers reviewed in this chapter.

The Revival of Naturalism: Needs

Ethical naturalism itself experienced something of a revival in the 1950s and 1960s, and I want now to look at two influential articles from that period which helped to revive it. The first of these is an article entitled 'Moral Beliefs' by Philippa Foot, one of Hare's Oxford colleagues, which was published in 1958.[14] Foot there questions Hare's idea that moral judgements have some special 'commendatory' or 'action-guiding' force. The practical significance of moral judgements is, she says, more satisfactorily accounted for not by assimilating them to imperatives but by seeing them as providing *reasons* for acting. The question, then, is whether statements of fact can ever by themselves provide reasons for acting. If they can, then we need no longer maintain, as Hare does, a dichotomy between statements of fact and moral judgements or other value-judgements.

Foot then argues that some statements of fact can provide reasons for acting. Consider, she says, the concept of 'injury'. An injury can be defined in factual terms as any damage to a physical limb or organ which interferes with its performance of its function—which prevents the eyes from being used for seeing, the hands for holding or manipulating, the legs for walking, and so forth. Given this definition, injury is, according to Foot, something which any person has a reason to avoid. In general, she says, a person is given a reason for acting if he or she is shown that the action is necessary for something he or she wants. But if a person wants anything at all, he or she must necessarily need the effective use of limbs and physical organs. Without these, a person cannot act effectively in the world to satisfy his or her wants. Therefore, just in virtue of the facts of the human constitution, injury is something which any human being has a reason to avoid. Foot is claiming, in effect, that there are basic and universal human needs which can be identified objectively. And like Plato, she is taking the case of physical health and physical functioning as a paradigm of objective practical reasoning.

The concept of 'injury' is one whose practical significance derives not from any special kind of linguistic meaning which the concept has, but from the facts of what injury consists in. Can the same be said of moral concepts? Foot suggests that the concepts of the virtues are definitively moral concepts. A morally good person is one who possesses the virtues of prudence, courage, temperance, and justice (a list which appears to derive from Plato). Foot then attempts to show that the concepts of the virtues are reason-giving in essentially the same way as the concept of injury. The virtues are qualities which any human being has a reason to want. This is clear enough in the case of prudence, courage, and temperance, for any human being will need to be able to act with foresight, to resist the temptations of immediate pleasures, and to stand firm against fear and danger. Justice is more problematic. Justice in the wide sense Foot defines as the virtue which covers all our obligations to other people. Therefore it might seem that justice is not something we are bound to want but that, on the contrary, as Plato's Thrasymachus would claim, the person who is inhibited by considerations of justice will be less likely to achieve what he wants. Nevertheless, Foot claims, the facts tell against Thrasymachus. One could live effectively without justice only if one could live quite independently of other people, never needing their help or co-operation, and escaping their detection whenever one wronged them. Since the facts of the human condition are not like this, justice is something which all human beings need to possess in their dealings with their fellows.

Foot's references to Plato should remind us of problems raised in earlier chapters, when we consider Plato's and Aristotle's attempts to link the virtues with happiness. What Foot offers is an *instrumental* vindication of justice in terms of self-interest. It is the kind of justification offered in the *Republic* by Glaucon rather than by Socrates. And the difficulties with this approach are those which I stated in Chapter 4. If one cultivates justice as a means of gaining other people's goodwill and inducing them to reciprocate, it is not really justice (that is, respect for other people's rights and interests as such) that is being cultivated, but only a semblance of justice. Moreover, it is not clear that this kind of argument will justify even that much. If one conceives of one's interests in this way, and then asks what kind of policy towards other people will most effectively maximize those interests, the answer may well be that one should cultivate a reputation for justice, while being prepared to act unjustly towards others when one can get away with it and escape detection.

Foot has subsequently abandoned her position. She no longer thinks that her attempted justification of the virtues, or at any rate of justice, is either possible or necessary. She now says that moral considerations do not, in fact, give reasons to every human being. They constitute reasons for acting only if one already has some commitment to the moral point of view, or to some particular moral value.[15] Though she does not say so, this seems to me to amount to the abandonment of the attempt at formulating an objectivist ethics. In my view, however, there is no need for her, or for us, to abandon that attempt. What we should look for, rather, and what would enable us to escape from her impasse, is a much wider and more thorough theory of human needs. I want now to make some suggestions about how we might develop such a theory.

At one extreme, Foot's example of the need to avoid physical injury is an indisputable need, but of a narrowly biological kind. At the other extreme, her claim that human beings need the virtues involves a much broader notion of needs, but depends on somewhat tenuous claims about social life and human interaction. Between those two extremes there is, I suggest, a range of needs rooted in the facts of human psychology. These represent a broader category of needs than the narrowly physiological need to avoid injury, but their objective status as inescapable needs is more securely grounded than Foot's claims about the virtues. These are the kinds of need which I began to explore in Chapter 8—the need for a shape and a meaning to one's life, the need for a sense of one's own identity, involving the need for recognition and the need for self-expression through meaningful work, and the need for activity which makes full use of our faculties and potentialities. Looking back over other earlier chapters, we can add other examples to this category of needs. We found in Plato and Aristotle the idea that human beings need to achieve the kind of mental harmony which consists in a proper relation between reason and the emotions. I argued that it is Aristotle who offers the better account of this, as a relation in which the emotions are neither repressed by reason, nor simply overcome it, but rather are themselves rational, sensitively attuned to and appropriate to the circumstances. In Kant we encountered the idea (not, indeed, expressed by him in the vocabulary of 'needs') that human beings need to be treated as persons, as rational and autonomous beings capable of choosing for themselves and pursuing their own projects and aspirations. Mill's doctrine of 'higher pleasures' identified the needs of human beings to employ their rational and intellectual faculties. Marx and Nietzsche both help to fill out the idea of the need for creative activity which gives people a sense of putting their stamp on the world and using their energies to the full, and Freud and the psychoanalytic school emphasize the need for physically and emotionally fulfilling sexual relationships.

Given the diversity of human desires and inclinations, what grounds are there for saying that any human being will necessarily need these things? Can we ascribe to these needs an objective status? A basis for doing so which we have encountered frequently in this book is the analogy with physical health. Just as physical needs are prerequisites of physical health, understood as the proper functioning of the various organs of the body, so it can be argued that other kinds of needs, which are not purely physical, are in a comparable sense prerequisites of mental health, understood as that harmony of the personality which enables a person to function effectively. To the extent that people's fundamental needs are unsatisfied, their lives will be empty and frustrated, and their actions are more likely to be irrational, dominated by unconscious motives and compensations, by fantasies, and by compulsive drives. To that extent, they will be less able to function effectively—and to function effectively is something which all human beings need to do, whatever the particular aims and objects to which they may be devoted.

This, then, will be one important basis for the claim that such needs have an objective status. Something more, however, is required. There is surely more to the idea of a good human life than merely being able to function effectively. If a person's needs are satisfied only to the extent that enables him or her to cope, to get by without debilitating mental conflicts, that seems to constitute a bare minimum. A fuller and more adequate picture of the good life would surely have to involve the notion of a life of happiness and fulfilment, a life that is rich, rewarding, and deeply satisfying. What I want now to suggest is that those needs which have to be satisfied in order for one to be able to function effectively are the same needs whose fuller satisfaction makes for a richly happy life. The satisfaction of them up to a certain level enables one to cope; the more complete satisfaction of them produces positive enjoyment. There is no a priori reason why this should be so. It could have been otherwise. It could have been the case that, once our basic needs were satisfied to the point that enabled us to achieve some kind of mental equilibrium, further satisfaction of them produced no added bonus of happiness, and that people's positive enjoyments were found elsewhere. It does, however, seem to be a brute fact of human experience that the two kinds of satisfaction are directly linked. Human beings need their emotional life to be in touch with reality, they need to engage in activities which are not totally mindless and mechanical, they need a basic degree of supportive recognition from other people—and they need these things just in order to stay sane. But it is also the case that the richest enjoyments and satisfactions of human life are to be found in the further meeting of these same needs—in work which uses to the full one's creative capacities, and in the life of the emotions, and the many different kinds of human love and solidarity.

I have said that there is no a priori reason why there should be this continuity between the conditions of effective functioning and those of happiness. We can nevertheless provide a plausible empirical explanation of an evolutionary kind as to why this should be so. Clearly the conditions which make for human survival and effective psychological functioning are more likely to be satisfied if they are also the conditions which make for positive enjoyment. Accordingly, it is not at all surprising that the human species should have developed in such a way that the two coincide.

The notions of happiness and related concepts thus provide a second test of the objectivity of human needs. Notice that this claim is compatible with the undeniable fact of the diversity of aims and objects which human beings pursue. Certainly, not all people find happiness in the same specific kinds of activities, and this has led some philosophers to deny that there can be any objective answer to the question of what constitutes a good life.

> For is there any goal in life at all of which one could say, quite in general, that 'one'—that is, anyone and everyone—should aim at achieving it? . . . The goals appropriate to a 'man of action' are not, surely, to be recommended to the contemplative scholar, the dedicated artist, the religious recluse . . .[16]

Nevertheless, though aptitudes and enthusiasms may differ, there are, I think, certain general psychological features which any activity would have to possess, if it were to occupy a central position in a worthwhile and fulfilling life. The man of action, the contemplative scholar, and the dedicated artist may indeed be engaged in activities which at one level are very different; but in order to find those activities fully satisfying they will need to experience them as activities which are demanding and make full use of their abilities, which offer scope for creativity and initiative, and so on.

I suggested that Foot's project of building a naturalistic ethics on the notion of what all human beings need can be furthered if we develop this more comprehensive picture of human needs. Such an account offers a better prospect of providing an account of the good life. It also offers a better prospect of making the link with what we might think of as distinctively moral considerations. We saw that this was the difficulty on which Foot's project foundered: the question of whether we can show that all human beings need the moral virtues. My enlarged picture of human needs includes an important place for the need for satisfying and fulfilling relationships with others, and may therefore be able to provide a better account of the importance of our obligations to others, and of the altruistic virtues. I shall say a little more in Chapter 12 about the place of all these ideas within a naturalistic ethics.

The Revival of Naturalism: Social Institutions

I turn now to a second article which contributed to the revival of naturalism, John Searle's paper 'How to Derive "Ought" from "Is"'.[17] Whereas Foot attempted to break down the dichotomy of facts and values by attending to facts about human needs, wants, and interests, Searle attempted to do so by focusing on facts about human institutions. Institutional facts, he claimed, do have evaluative implications. Consider the institution of promising. Within that institution it is just a fact that if someone has promised to do something, he or she has undertaken an obligation to do it. That is what promising *is*. Hence we can construct an argument of the following form.

> Jones uttered the words, 'I hereby promise to pay you, Smith, five dollars.'
> ∴ Jones promised to pay Smith five dollars.
> ∴ Jones placed himself under (undertook) an obligation to pay Smith five dollars.
> ∴ Jones is under an obligation to pay Smith five dollars.
> ∴ Jones ought to pay Smith five dollars.

Each of these statements follows from the previous one in conjunction with additional straightforwardly factual premisses (e.g. that no one has released Jones from his obligation). But the initial statement is undeniably factual, and the conclusion is undeniably an 'ought', an evaluative judgement. So it seems that anyone who accepts the factual premisses must accept the evaluative conclusion. The conclusion follows from the premisses because the rule, 'To make a promise is to undertake an obligation', is, according to Searle, a constitutive rule of the institution of promising. It serves to define the institution, and someone who does not recognize the rule cannot understand what promising is. Searle suggests that analogous constitutive rules define the institutions of property, marriage, language, punishment, and so on, and generate ethical principles in the same way.

Searle's opponents, such as Hare, retort that the derivation of 'He ought . . .' from 'He said, "I promise . . ."' will have a very different significance depending on whether one views it from inside or from outside the institution.[18] Someone who simply reports it as an external observer in the manner of a cultural anthropologist, will mean by it only, 'This is what they (the participants in the institution) *call* "promising", this is what they *call* "placing oneself under an obligation".' So long as he speaks from outside the institution, he will not report the 'ought' as a full-blooded 'ought', by which he himself would be bound. The 'ought' applies only to the participants in the institution, and therefore one is bound by it only if one is committed to the institution. According to philosophers such as Hare, one is committed to the institution only if one chooses to be, and the choice is itself an ethical choice; therefore the 'ought' will follow from the 'is' only by way of such an ethical choice, that is, only if one accepts the institution and thereby accepts the substantive ethical principle which is its constitutive rule.

I believe that this objection is valid up to a point. It does indeed make a crucial difference whether one is committed to the institution. The believer in free love, or in sharing all things in common, cannot be shown that they ought to respect monogamous fidelity or property rights by being shown that this is a constitutive rule of the institution of marriage or private property, for it is just this rule and this institution that they question. If they are not committed to the institution it is entirely rational for them to reject the corresponding ethical principle. The question is, then: what is it to be committed to a social institution? Hare and others seem to think that this is simply a matter of individual choice, as though one could stand outside all social institutions, survey them all, and take one's pick. This, as we saw in Chapter 8, is a false picture. Any human individual exists within, and is formed by, a context not only of social institutions but of social relations generally. Thus, though one can in principle criticize any specific social institution, one cannot detach oneself from all social relations in order to make some sort of socially unencumbered autonomous choice. Moreover, one may criticize a particular institution and regard it as ideally needing to be abolished or replaced while nevertheless continuing to participate in that institution, and having a commitment to it in its existing form. One might, for instance, regard the contemporary nuclear family as a radically imperfect institution, but one might nevertheless live within such a family, and one's family relationships might constitute one's own deepest commitments. To understand how and why people come to be committed to institutions, as I suggested in Chapter 8, we have to look at the more basic pre-institutional social relations which underlie them. For example, one's commitment to a particular country as a political institution, perhaps despite deep criticisms of it, may be grounded in one's ties to a place, to a language, to a culture, to a way of life—ties which one cannot just choose. Searle's theory of the ethically constitutive rules of social institutions thus needs to be located within a broader account of social relations and their ethical significance. But Searle is right in this, that the facts about the social relations in which people stand to one another are not ethically neutral. They are, at the same time, facts about the ethical commitments and responsibilities which serve to define those relations, and one cannot understand the social relations without understanding their ethical implications.

Both Foot and Searle point us in directions in which we need to look for the components of a naturalistic ethics. Each, however, is too limited. We have to develop a more comprehensive theory of human needs, and a more comprehensive theory of social relations. The historical tradition can help to provide the materials for such a theory, and for a naturalistic ethics richer in content than those offered by contemporary ethical philosophers. I shall return to this theme in my final chapter. In the meantime I have drawn on the arguments of Foot and Searle sufficiently to show, I hope, that despite the claims of Moore and Hare and others, the naturalistic tenor of this book cannot be dismissed as fallacious.

Notes

1. G. E. Moore, *Principia Ethica* (Cambridge, 1903), sections 25 and 26. (The text is divided into sections, and all subsequent references will be to these rather than to page numbers.)
2. W. D. Ross, *The Right and the Good* (Oxford, 1930), 29.
3. Ibid. 39–40.
4. Bertrand Russell, 'The Ethics of War', in *Prophecy and Dissent, 1914–16* (vol. xiii of *The Collected Papers of Bertrand Russell*, London, 1988), 63.
5. Bertrand Russell, *Religion and Science* (Oxford, 1935), 229.
6. Ibid. 230–1.
7. Charles L. Stevenson, *Ethics and Language* (New Haven, 1944). The articles are collected in Charles Stevenson, *Facts and Values* (New Haven, 1963). The two most important and useful are 'The Emotive Meaning of Ethical Terms' (originally in *Mind*, 46, 1937), and 'The Nature of Ethical Disagreement' (originally in *Sigma*, 1948).
8. *Facts and Values*, 13, 16, 23.
9. See 'The Nature of Ethical Disagreement'.
10. Ludwig Wittgenstein, *Philosophical Investigations* (Oxford, 1953), e.g. paras. 1, 26, 40.
11. Ibid. para. 43.
12. R. M. Hare, *Freedom and Reason* (Oxford, 1963), 2.
13. R. M. Hare, *The Language of Morals* (Oxford, 1952), 30.
14. Philippa Foot, 'Moral Beliefs', in *Proceedings of the Aristotelian Society*, 59 (1958–9). Reprinted in Philippa Foot (ed.), *Theories of Ethics* (Oxford, 1967), and in Philippa Foot (ed.), *Virtues and Vices* (Oxford, 1978).
15. Her self-criticisms can be found in *Theories of Ethics*, 9, and in *Virtues and Vices*, pp. xi–xiv, 130–1, and 161–7.
16. G. J. Warnock, *The Object of Morality* (London, 1971), 90–2.
17. John R. Searle, 'How to Derive "Ought" from "Is" ', in *Philosophical Review*, 73 (1964), repr. in Foot (ed.), *Theories of Ethics*.
18. Cf. R. M. Hare, 'The Promising Game', in Foot (ed.), *Theories of Ethics*.

11

Utilitarianism and its Rivals

Reading: Relevant reading to accompany this chapter can be found in the following collections in the 'Oxford Readings in Philosophy' series:

James Rachels (ed.), *Ethical Theory 2: Theories About How We should Live* (Oxford, 1998)
Samuel Scheffler (ed.), *Consequentialism and its Critics* (Oxford, 1988)
Jeremy Waldron (ed.), *Theories of Rights* (Oxford, 1984)
Roger Crisp and Michael Slote (eds.), *Virtue Ethics* (Oxford, 1997)

In the 1940s and 1950s, non-cognitivism in one or other of its versions was dominant in English-language moral philosophy, and this meant that moral philosophers were largely concerned with questions of meta-ethics—second-order questions about the logic and meaning of moral language. Matters of 'normative' or 'substantive' ethics—questions about what sorts of things are actually good or bad, or what kinds of action are right or wrong—tended to be ignored by philosophers. If there can be no knowledge concerning such matters, then, it was assumed, they cannot be the subject-matter of an intellectual discipline. Philosophers are in no better position than anyone else to say how people ought to live, since this is not a matter about which there can be any true or false statements at all.

In the late 1950s, and increasingly in the 1960s, this began to change. The revival of naturalism, as represented by philosophers like Foot and Searle, contributed to the change. Philosophers generally were beginning to accept that philosophical ethics, as an academic discipline, could have useful things to say about substantive questions of right and wrong. With this renewal of interest in substantive ethics, utilitarianism in particular began to acquire a new plausibility. Non-cognitivism had made people suspicious of ambitious moral theories. Likewise tendencies in the theory of knowledge such as logical positivism, which had been influential in the 1940s and 1950s, had made people suspicious of grandiose metaphysical systems. In this philosophical climate the attraction of utilitarianism was that, compared with other approaches in substantive ethics, it appeared to involve minimal theoretical and metaphysical claims. It presupposed only the recognition that people have desires and interests and inclinations, together with a commitment to take everyone's desires and interests and inclinations into account. The question was, then, what basis there might be for that latter commitment. One possibility, consistent with subjectivist or emotivist approaches, was to interpret it simply as an emotional commitment or attitude which one might or might not adopt, but which many people at any rate would share. Thus J. J. C. Smart, in an influential defence of utilitarianism, combined it with a strict non-cognitivism. Neither utilitarianism nor any other moral system could be proved to be true, he said, since substantive moral positions could not in the strict sense be either true or false. Nevertheless, he claimed that a philosophical defence of utilitarianism could make it acceptable to those who shared the attitude of generalized benevolence.[1]

An alternative possibility was to claim that the commitment to take other people's desires and interests and inclinations into account is a logical commitment built into the language of morality, and this was a position which Hare in particular came to adopt. In his later work, starting with his 1963 book *Freedom and Reason*, he became increasingly committed to the defence of a version of utilitarianism. He claimed that this was consistent with his anti-naturalism, and that his earlier views about the logic of moral reasoning provided the basis for a defence of utilitarianism. I want now to look at that defence, as one influential version of contemporary utilitarianism.

Utilitarianism and Universalizability

We saw that Hare emphasized two features of the logic of moral language: that moral judgements are *prescriptive*, and that they are *universalizable*. The basis for utilitarianism is laid by these two features, Hare thinks, and especially by an understanding of what is involved in the element of universalizability. This may seem surprising, for we have previously seen the idea of universalizability to be a central theme of Kant's moral philosophy, which is often thought to stand in a sharp contrast to utilitarianism, but Hare suggests that one of the advantages of his account is to reveal that the affinities between Kantian and utilitarian positions are closer than has been supposed.

In my discussion of Kant's treatment of universalizability I suggested that we need to distinguish between three senses of that term: universalizability as *consistency*, as *impersonality*, and as *impartiality*. Philosophers who want to derive a substantive moral content from the formal notion of universalizability tend to move from the weak idea of consistency to the increasingly stronger ideas of impersonality and impartiality, and I suggested that those moves are liable to be suspect. This is what Hare does, and in addition he arrives at a particular version of impartiality which is needed for utilitarianism. To see how he does this, we can consider a sequence of examples which he employs in *Freedom and Reason*.[2]

1. **The example of the debtors** This example is adapted from a parable told by Jesus in the Bible. Suppose that A owes money to B, and B owes money to C. B wants to put A in prison in order to force him to pay the money he owes. However, C's relation to B is the same as B's relation to A, so that, according to Hare, if B ought to put A in prison, it follows that C ought to put B in prison. Hare suggests that universalizability then requires B to say to himself: 'I do not want C to put me in prison; therefore, I cannot accept that C ought to put me in prison; therefore, I cannot say that I ought to put A in prison.' He is already invoking not just the weak notion of universalizability as consistency, but the stronger notion of universalizability as impersonality—the idea that something cannot be a reason for *me* to perform a certain action in certain circumstances unless it is also a reason for *anyone* to perform the same action in the same circumstances. Let us, as we did with Kant, allow Hare this, and see where he wants to go next.

2. **The example of the trumpet-player** Suppose that A and B live in rooms next to one another. Suppose that A likes to listen to classical chamber music on his record player, and B wants to practise playing jazz on his trumpet. If, as in the previous example, B were to ask himself, 'If I were in A's position, would I want someone next door to play jazz on the trumpet?', his answer will be 'Yes', for of course B would much prefer to listen to the jazz trumpet rather than listen to classical chamber music. However, according to Hare, what B must ask himself is 'If I were in A's position *with A's likes and dislikes*, would I want someone next door to play jazz on the trumpet?', and of course the answer to that question will be 'No'. Where does this leave B? It might seem to leave him with nothing to say at all. In view of A's likes and dislikes, he cannot say, 'I ought to play the trumpet,' but in view of his own likes and dislikes, he cannot say, 'I ought not to play the trumpet.' What Hare then suggests is this:

> Once he is prepared to give weight to A's interests, as if they were his own, there will arise . . . a complicated problem . . . of deciding what apportionment of the time between trumpeting and silence would be just to the two parties respectively. (113)

In other words, since B is committed to the consideration of his own interests, and since universalizability also commits him to the consideration of A's interests, the two sets of interests must somehow be added together to produce an impartial consideration of the interests of both of them. This represents a further strengthening of the idea of universalizability. Hare is now interpreting it to involve not only a negative commitment to the rejection of egoism, but also a positive commitment to the *impartial consideration of everyone's interests*.

3. **The example of the judge and the criminal** A limitation of the previous examples, says Hare, is that they involve the interests of only two parties. We therefore have to consider the extension of the same form of argument to cases

where the interests of many people are involved. Consider the case of a judge who sentences a criminal to prison. If the criminal were to apply to the judge the same kind of argument as was applied to the creditor and to the trumpet-player in the previous examples, he could say: 'If you think that you ought to sentence me to prison, you must also accept that if you were in my position you ought to be put in prison; but you would not want that; so you cannot say that you ought to send me to prison.' However, Hare suggests, what the judge must consider are not only his own interests and inclinations and the interests and inclinations of the criminal, but also the interests of everyone else who will be affected by his decision. As a judge he has to uphold a system of laws which affects the interests of all members of society. If he does not enforce the law, then 'the interests of at least the great majority of people in the community will be harmed' (117). Taking into account the interests of the majority, there-fore, the judge would say that he ought to sentence the criminal to prison.

The significant addition made by this example is the suggestion that if uni-versalizability commits us to the consideration of everyone's interests, there will then have to be some process of *weighing up* the different sets of interests. Where many people's interests are affected, and there are conflicts between the interests of some people and the interests of others, the *greater* interests (what-ever that means) will have to outweigh the *lesser* interests. This, as Hare says, brings his position very close to a form of utilitarianism.

Classical utilitarianism was formulated in terms of the concept of *happi-ness*. This traditional formulation, we saw, has given rise to difficulties, and in particular to the criticism that people value other things besides happiness. Some contemporary utilitarians have therefore suggested that the theory could be more neutrally formulated in terms not of 'happiness' but of concepts such as 'interests', 'inclinations', 'desires', and 'satisfactions'. This has been called 'preference-utilitarianism'—the theory that what we ought to do is maximize the satisfaction of people's preferences. Such a formulation would leave open the question of what the objects of people's desires and inclinations were, what was in people's interests, and what gave people satisfaction (it might be only happiness or it might be other things). If we formulate utilitari-anism in these broader terms, then Hare thinks that we can establish a 'link between universalizability on the one hand and utilitarian ideas on the other' (123). This link has been illustrated by the examples, and Hare summarizes it as follows:

> It is in the endeavour to find lines of conduct which we can prescribe universally in a given situation that we find ourselves bound to give equal weight to the desires of all parties. . . . But when I have been the round of all the affected parties, and come back, in my own person, to make an impartial moral judgement giving equal weight to the interests of all parties, what can I possibly do except advocate that course which will, taken all in all, least frustrate the desires which I have imagined myself having? But this (it is plausible to go on) is to maximize satisfactions. (123)

This, then, is the route by which Hare thinks that he can arrive at a defence of utilitarianism. The prescriptivity of moral language reflects the fact that we have interests, desires, inclinations to action. The universality of moral language requires us to take into account not only the interests and inclinations which we have from our own perspective, but also the interests and inclinations which we would have when we imagine ourselves in other people's position. A rational moral judgement will therefore be one which amalgamates the interests and inclinations of all the affected parties, and so will be in a broad sense a utilitarian judgement.

We have seen that Hare's case for utilitarianism takes the form of a progressive extension of the idea of universalizability, and I have noted the danger of over-extending it. Hare seems to me to have succumbed to this danger. Suppose we allow Hare the idea of universalizability as impersonality. As I have argued in connection with Kant, this does not yet give us the idea of impartiality. One could quite rationally take the view 'I have good reason to pursue exclusively my own interests, and everyone else has equally good reason to pursue their own interests', thus satisfying the requirement of the impersonality of reasons but rejecting any commitment to take impartial account of other people's interests. The move from the example of the debtors to the example of the trumpet player is therefore illegitimate.

Even if we allow Hare this move, however, the route to utilitarianism requires a further step. It involves saying not only that everyone's interests should be taken into account, but that all these interests should be somehow *amalgamated*, added together, so as to lead to a judgement about what will produce the *greatest* satisfaction of people's interests. Again I do not think that this follows from the requirement of impartiality. We can see this if we compare the example of the debtors with the other two examples, of the trumpeter and of the judge. In the debtors example, universalizability merely requires B to say, 'If it is not right for C to put me in prison, then it is not right for me to put A in prison.' This is quite different from saying that B must somehow add together the interests of himself, of A, and of C, and arrive at a judgement about what will maximize their interests overall. That, however, is what Hare claims must be done by the trumpeter and by the judge. It is not at all clear why this should be so. If the trumpeter reasons as B is supposed to reason in the debtors example, he will have to say, 'I cannot accept that I ought to play jazz on the trumpet, since if I were in my neighbour's position with his likes and dislikes, I would not want this.' Hare's problem is that he thinks that the trumpeter will also have to say, 'I cannot accept that I ought *not* to play jazz on the trumpet, given my own likes and dislikes.' Universalizability thus seems to rule out both possible 'ought' judgements. It does not follow, however, that the trumpeter will then have to say, 'I ought to arrive at a compromise.' This judgement, too, is contrary to the trumpeter's interests and contrary to his neighbour's interests, and so if Hare were consistent he would surely say that this judgement too is ruled out. Perhaps the only conclusion we can reach is that there is *no* 'ought'-judgement which the trumpeter can universalize. It is an entirely arbitrary move on Hare's part to suggest, as he does, that 'the natural way for the argument then to run' (113) is for the trumpeter to arrive at a judgement which gives equal weight to his own and his neighbour's interests. In requiring the trumpeter and the judge to resort to a utilitarian weighing-up of interests, Hare is doing what he so often accuses his opponents of doing—smuggling in his own moral preferences under the disguise of the value-laden word 'natural'.

I conclude that Hare's attempt to derive a defence of utilitarianism from the idea of universalizability is as mistaken as was Kant's attempt to derive substantive moral conclusions from the same idea. The modern revival of interest in utilitarianism extends much more widely, however, than Hare's particular defence of it. It remains attractive in a more general way, for the sorts of reasons I have previously mentioned. There is an intuitive plausibility in the idea that what is of ultimate value is the welfare of human beings (or perhaps of sentient beings generally), and therefore that we ought to act in such a way as to maximize human well-being. This appears to accord also with the equally plausible idea that the essence of morality is a concern for other people's well-being and not just one's own. Utilitarianism therefore continues to prove attractive to many contemporary moral philosophers.

The revival of utilitarianism has brought with it also a renewal of traditional objections to utilitarianism. These have included the criticisms previously formulated by writers such as Ross that utilitarianism fails to correspond to our commonsense moral intuitions, particularly those of a deontological character. Utilitarian arguments could purport to justify actions which most people would think of as wrong, such as falsely convicting and executing an innocent person in order to prevent, say, a riot in which more people might be killed. Defences of utilitarianism against such criticisms have, in part, taken the form of trying to show that in practice it would not lead to such unacceptable conclusions. Some modern utilitarians have deployed the idea, which we encountered in Mill, that utilitarianism can account for our commonsense moral intuitions by recognizing the place of *rules* in moral thinking, and the debate has continued as to whether the appropriate theory to do this is an act-utilitarianism which incorporates 'rules of thumb', or a radically distinct 'rule-utilitarian' theory.[3]

Utilitarians can also, however, take a tougher line with counter-examples appealing to our moral intuitions. They can say that our commonsense moral views are sometimes confused and misguided, and that the advantage of utilitarianism is that, as a systematic rational theory, it can correct prevailing moral confusions. If our intuitions are in conflict with utilitarianism, then so much the worse for our intuitions. Criticisms of utilitarianism must therefore be more thoroughgoing if they are to be decisive. Its critics must argue not just that there are *ad hoc* discrepancies between it and our moral intuitions, but that these discrepancies point to deep structural features of utilitarianism which are incompatible with some essential characteristic of morality itself. To do this, the critics must present their own alternative moral theory in order to identify those essential features of morality which utilitarianism fails to accommodate. The most important non-utilitarian ethical theories which have emerged in the last forty years or so can usefully be seen as reactions to the perceived deficiencies of utilitarianism. In the rest of this chapter I shall sketch four main rival theories: rights-based ethics, contractarian ethics, agent-centred ethics, and virtue ethics.

Rights-Based Ethics

One of the most deep-seated features of utilitarianism is that it is an *aggregative* theory. In order to arrive at the right action, the interests of different individuals have to be *added together*, with the aim of producing the *greatest amount* of happiness or satisfaction overall. Utilitarians themselves have sometimes pointed to this as one of the merits of the theory—that it employs a simple model of practical rationality, one which we naturally accept at the individual level and can therefore properly transfer to the social level. Within our own individual lives we often forego short-term advantages, or accept short-term hardships, for the sake of greater long-term benefits. We save money now in order to be able to spend it later on something which we really need; we accept the short-term pain of treatment by the dentist in order to avoid the long-term pain of toothache; we resist the temptation of an extra drink in order to avoid a hangover the next morning. Such decisions are often thought to be the essence of a rational ordering of one's own individual life. What utilitarianism does is to employ the same model at the social level; the limited interests of some people have to be sacrificed for the sake of the greater happiness overall.

But, say the critics, this analogy is fallacious. As Robert Nozick puts it, 'there is no *social entity* . . . that undergoes some sacrifice for its own good. There are only individual people, different individual people, with their own individual lives.'[4] If an individual decides to sacrifice some of his own interests, he does so because it is he who benefits from it, and that is what makes the sacrifice a rational one. If one person's interests are overridden in a utilitarian calculation, however, that person is simply sacrificed. 'Humanity' or 'society' is not a single agent which makes such decisions. It is *other individuals* who benefit. 'Talk of an overall social good covers this up. . . . To use a person in this way does not sufficiently respect and take account of the fact that he is a separate person, and that his is the only life he has' (33).

Critics of utilitarianism have therefore looked for a theory which more adequately embodies the idea that individuals may not be sacrificed for the good of others. One such attempt consists in emphasizing the idea of *moral rights*. Individuals have rights, it is said, which may not be violated. This does not, of course, rule out actions to promote the interests of oneself or other people; but all such pursuit of goals must take place within the limits set by the rights of individuals. Those rights might typically be taken to include a right to life, and a right to liberty or perhaps to certain specific liberties such as freedom of speech and conscience, freedom to own and control one's own body, or the freedom to dispose of one's own property.

The idea of rights has been developed most fully by recent political philosophers, such as Nozick, and by the legal philosopher Ronald Dworkin.[5] Nozick emphasizes the contrast between utilitarianism and a 'rights' approach, distinguishing between the way in which moral *goals* or *ends* serve to guide actions and the way in which rights function as *side constraints* on action. Rights do not tell you what to aim for; they set limits to what you can do to other people in pursuit of your aims. Nozick rejects what he calls a 'utilitarianism of rights'—the idea of aiming to minimize the total extent of violation of rights, even if this means violating some people's rights in order to achieve it (for example by setting up a coercive state apparatus to keep the peace)—because this locates the function of rights in the wrong place. It turns them back into goals rather than side-constraints.

Nozick's primary interest is in working out the implications of rights for political philosophy, and he does not have a fully developed moral theory which would establish what rights people have, and why they have them. The basic right seem to be a right not to be the victim of physical *aggression*—not to have physical force used against you. This does not rule out a moral entitlement to use force in self-defence against those who are a threat to you and would otherwise violate your rights. It does however rule out most forms of coercion by the state, and in this respect Nozick's theory of rights has radical political implications. He argues that only the minimal state, whose role is limited to protecting people's rights, can be justified. Any more extensive state would itself violate people's rights. This means in particular that the state cannot justifiably use coercion to pursue the utiltitarian goal of the general welfare, or the goal of redistributive justice or greater social equality. Forcing some people to part with what they are entitled to, for example by paying taxes, in order to improve the position of the less well-off would be a violation of rights. This means that, according to Nozick, a society in which some people are immensely rich and others are dying of poverty and starvation is entirely just, provided that these inequalities have come about as a result of the voluntary and uncoerced activities and transactions of individuals. The only acceptable notion of justice, for Nozick, is what he calls the *entitlement* conception: justice consists in respecting people's rights and not coercively depriving them of what they are entitled to as a result of their own non-coercive transactions. Note that for Nozick rights are essentially *negative*. We do not have positive rights that others should provide us with certain goods—for example, a right to a job, or a right to health care, or a right to education. Note also that in practice rights not to be coerced will, in a political context, largely amount to *property rights*.

Although Nozick does not have a worked-out theory of the moral foundations of rights, he briefly sketches a Kantian approach. 'Side constraints upon action reflect the underlying Kantian principle that individuals are ends and not merely means; they may not be sacrificed or used for the achieving of other ends without their consent' (31). He also suggests that the status of human beings as 'ends and not merely means' rests on their capacity to shape their own lives in accordance with some overall plan, and thereby give a meaning to their lives. We have previously seen, in Chapter 6, that Kant's idea of 'respect for persons' does indeed seem to offer a promising foundation for rights. What those rights are, however, how large a place they should occupy within our moral thinking, and whether they are inviolable or can sometimes be overridden by other considerations, are questions which require further argument.

Ronald Dworkin's theory of rights is another account which starts out from the limitations of utilitarianism. Working with a preference-utilitarian version of utilitarianism, Dworkin distinguishes between two kinds of preference. There are *personal preferences*—desires for goods and opportunities for oneself. There are also *external preferences*—desires that particular other people should get goods and opportunities. A utilitarianism which aims at maximizing the satisfaction of preferences, without distinguishing between personal and external preferences, will have to take into account not only people's desires for themselves but also, for example, some people's racist preferences that whites should do better than blacks, or some people's preferences that other people's sexual preferences, say for pornography or for homosexual relationships, should be discounted. Including these external preferences in the utilitarian calculation, according to Dworkin, distorts the underlying moral basis of utilitarianism, that everyone should be given equal concern and respect. External preferences lead to a kind of double-weighting or under-weighting of certain people's personal preferences. And, roughly speaking, the role of rights is to counteract the distorting effect of external preferences on utilitarianism.

But why not simply discount external preferences? The problem is to identify the political institutions which will do so. Dworkin thinks that representative democracy is the best bet for identifying and implementing utilitarian policies. It enables everybody's preferences to be taken into account and acted on. But it is incapable of distinguishing between personal and external preferences. They are all lumped in together. This is why political rights are needed, to protect, say, minority sexual preferences which might otherwise be the object of prejudice, or to protect the preferences of particular racial groups from the effects of racial discrimination. In this way rights counteract the implications of a utilitarianism which runs together the two kinds of preferences. As Dworkin puts it, rights are 'trumps'; they carry a special weight which overrides ordinary utilitarian calculations. And particular political rights reflect the fundamental right to equal concern and respect which is the moral impetus behind utilitarianism itself.

Unlike Nozick, then, Dworkin does not think that there is a general right to liberty, a right not to be coerced. There are particular rights to particular liberties, such as a right to free speech or to the practice of one's religion, but what underpins these is not a right to liberty in general but a right to equality, to equal concern and respect. What Dworkin shares with Nozick is the strategy of arriving at an account of rights by starting from the problems of utilitarianism. And, as with Nozick, I am not convinced that this is going to provide an adequate way of determining what rights people have. The argument from external preferences looks altogether too *ad hoc*. If rights are identified by their role in counteracting external preferences, then what rights people have will depend on what external preferences happen to be prevalent in this or that particular society. If in a particular society there is widespread prejudice against gays, which is liable to prevent democratic institutions from giving the preferences of gays equal weight with other people's preferences, then there will be a right to practice homosexuality. If on the other hand there is no such problem, and there are no such widespread external preferences, then there will be no such right. What we then seem to lack is any conception of particular rights as rooted in deep features of human life.

The accounts of rights offered by Nozick and Dworkin both seem to me to point to the fundamental problem for any theory of rights. How are we to know *what* rights human beings have? Traditionally this question has been answered by saying that it is 'self-evident' that human beings are 'endowed by their Creator with certain unalienable rights' (as in the American Declaration of Independence), or that they possessed certain 'natural rights' in a pre-social 'state of nature'. These answers depend on untenable fictions, and in the absence of any alternative answer, claims to rights become apparently arbitrary. It is a feature of moral and political debates in the modern world that rights are invoked on all sides. In the abortion debate, the 'right to life' is countered with 'a woman's right to choose'. In the debate on pornography, rights to 'free expression' are sometimes countered with the idea of women's rights not to be degraded or treated as sexual objects. In debates about social welfare, property rights and rights to individual freedom are invoked as arguments against the higher taxes which would be needed to support other people's right to education or health care. Which of these, if any, are genuine rights, and why?

Utilitarianism and other goal-based theories are less vulnerable in this respect. We have at least some idea of how to establish what people's desires and interests are. However, classical utilitarianism, at least in its Benthamite version, and modern preference-utilitarianism are both too undiscriminating in their treatment of desires and preferences. We require some more positive account of what constitutes a good human life and therefore what desires are worth satisfying. I have suggested that such an account might be based on the idea of human needs, and that this idea is acceptable from the point of view of moral epistemology; there are rational and objective ways of determining what people's needs are. I would likewise suggest that an account of rights requires a similar foundation. The concept of 'rights' is a derivative rather than a foundational one, and in order to determine what rights people have, we have to refer to some more basic account of what needs and interests human beings have. We would then require some further argument as to why certain needs and interests should have the special status of 'rights'. And in order to supply this, we need to explore further the Kantian notion of 'respect' which Nozick rightly sees as helping to underpin a morality of rights.

Contractarian Ethics

We saw that a typical starting-point for rights-based theories is the rejection of the aggregative character of utilitarianism. Individuals, it is said, may not be sacrificed for the sake of a spurious 'social good'. The same impetus lies behind another type of theory, that of contractarian ethics. The basic idea here is that rationally acceptable moral principles are those which everyone could agree to as principles to govern their dealings with one another, and that if everyone could agree to them, then no-one's interests are being sacrificed. Unlike theories of rights, contractarian ethics aims to correct the deficiencies of utilitarianism at the level not of the *content* but of the *structure* of ethical theory. It offers an alternative account of how we are to arrive at correct moral principles. This approach is recognizably a descendant of the one sketched by Glaucon in Plato's *Republic*. We have considered some of the problems of that early version, and we must now consider whether its much more sophisticated modern successors can fare any better. As we shall see, a major problem for them is how to fill out the notion of what people *could* agree to. Moral principles do not rest on any *actual* agreement. At no time have the members of any society come together and asked, 'What moral principles shall we agree on as ones which we can all accept?' The 'contract' of contractarian ethics is a *hypothetical* contract; the relevant notion is that of what people *could* agree to. However, people could agree to anything if they were desperate enough. What it is in their interests to agree to depends on the *initial position* from which they enter into the agreement. We shall see that the problem of defining this initial position has been one of the preoccupations of modern contractarian ethics.

Like the idea of 'rights', the idea of a contract has played an especially important role in recent political philosophy. The major figure here is the American philosopher John Rawls, whose contractarian theory of justice is widely agreed to have been the most important contribution to political philosophy in the twentieth century.[6] He explicitly presents the theory as an alternative to utilitarianism and to its aggregative character, which 'does not take seriously the distinction between persons' (27). In contrast to this he thinks that we need a theory of justice which takes seriously the question of how rights and duties, benefits and burdens are to be fairly distributed between the members of a society. This is the question to which his contractarian theory of justice is addressed. We should note that he offers it only as a theory of justice, not as a complete theory of ethics, though he does suggest that 'the contractarian idea can be extended to the choice of more or less an entire ethical system' (17).

The question of the initial position from which individuals are to be imagined as agreeing on principles of justice occupies a central place in Rawls' theory. His 'original position' is one in which individuals are rational and mutually disinterested; they aim to maximize the satisfaction of their individual interests, and they do not take an interest in one another's interests. This is characteristic of contract theories; but the distinctive and striking feature of Rawls' version is that he imagines individuals making their choice of principles from behind a 'veil of ignorance'. We are to suppose that they do not know what position they will each occupy in society. They do not know what their particular talents and abilities will be. They do not know what their particular conception of the good life will be. The effect of these stipulations is to generate a pressure towards the choice of broadly egalitarian principles of justice. Individuals in the original position would avoid principles which allowed huge inequalities between rich and poor, since for all they knew they might end up at the bottom of that scale. They would tend to avoid principles which gave large rewards to the intelligent or the strong or the ambitious, since they might turn out to be lacking in those qualities. They would tend to avoid principles which especially favoured those interested in accumulating personal material wealth, since they might turn out to be devotees of the simple life. Rawls suggests that they would choose two basic principles:

1. Each person is to have an equal right to the most extensive basic liberty compatible with a similar liberty for others.

2. Social and economic inequalities are to be arranged so that they are both (a) to the greatest benefit of the least advantaged and (b) attached to offices and positions open to all under conditions of fair equality of opportunity. (60 and 83)

The first principle is elaborated in terms of specific basic liberties such as rights to freedom of thought and conscience, freedom of speech and assembly, and the right to vote and to stand for office, and thus gives a prominent place to the idea of rights. The second principle acknowledges the broadly utilitarian idea of maximizing people's well-being, but does so in non-utilitarian terms, as the idea not that the *sum-total* of well-being should be as great as possible, but that *everyone* should be as well off as possible. The test of this is whether inequalities are to the advantage of the least well-off. Arrangements which make some people better off than others can be justified only if they make even the least advantaged better off than they would otherwise have been. Only then can it be said that this is a state of affairs which everyone could agree to, and which does not sacrifice anyone's interests for the benefit of others.

The detailed elaboration of these principles and their implications for social institutions occupies Rawls' major work *A Theory of Justice*. Consideration of this would take us into the details of political philosophy, with which I am not concerned here. I want to assess the contractarian theory simply as a general approach to ethics. I have said that any such theory has to work with the idea of a *hypothetical* contract. This appears to be especially true of Rawls. He requires us to imagine an agreement under highly artificial conditions—his 'veil of ignorance'. The question which his account raises for us is: why should we accept certain principles simply because they are ones which would be chosen by everyone in these totally improbable circumstances? Why should this entirely hypothetical contract apply to us in the real world?

I have suggested that we can imagine people agreeing to any number of different moral principles, depending on where they start from, and everything therefore depends on what we take their initial position to be. Why does Rawls choose this particular set of initial conditions? The inescapable answer appears to be: because they are the conditions which will generate the principles of justice at which he wants to arrive. Rawls more or less acknowledges this, and has increasingly presented his contractarian approach as an *expository* strategy rather than a *justificatory* one. It does not provide an independent argument for why we should adopt that conception of justice, but merely helps to bring out the nature of that conception. Rawls is, in effect, saying, 'If you think of these as the conditions in which people could agree to such principles, you can see the sense in which they can be described as "fair" principles.' This is all very well, but it leaves us without any independent justification for the theory, any reason why we should adopt and abide by these 'fair' principles. In his more recent work Rawls has modified his position to suggest that his principles of justice are simply the principles appropriate to modern liberal democratic societies. In saying this, he abandons any strong ethical claim to be made on their behalf.

I turn at this point to another recent version of contract theory, which retains the original ambitions of that approach as a foundation for ethics. This is the version put forward by David Gauthier in his 1986 book, *Morals by Agreement*.[7] Unlike Rawls, he defends contractarianism as a general theory of ethics, not merely a theory of justice.[8] The moral practices which he thinks it can justify will not be identical with, but will have much in common with, what is thought of as commonsense morality such as honesty and fairness, assisting one's fellows, and keeping one's promises. As with any version of contract theory, the agreement on which he thinks morality is based is a hypothetical contract, but it is not hypothetical in the extreme manner of Rawls' version. He thinks that it would be in the interests of existing individuals to agree to accept the constraints of morality—in the interests of real human beings such as ourselves, not the imaginary human beings of Rawls' original position. Gauthier's contracting individuals are utility-maximizers (and as with Rawls, this does not mean that they are self-interested or egoistic in the normal sense, but simply that it is rational for them to aim at maximizing the satisfaction of their interests, whatever those interests may happen to be). They are, however, to be imagined as choosing principles not from behind a veil of ignorance, but with a full knowledge of their real interests and of the actual consequences of their accepting the constraints of morality.

Gauthier distinguishes between a 'straightforward maximizer' and a 'constrained maximizer'. Unlike the straightforward maximizer, the constrained maximizer will accept the constraints which morality imposes on her pursuit of her own interests, in order to reap the benefits of a system of mutual co-operation. She will therefore forgo the advantages which the straightforward maximizer would gain from being prepared to cheat or steal or break promises when it suits him to do so, but she will do so because it is in her interests to participate in the practice of morality and accept its constraints, provided others do likewise.

For Rawls the important theoretical work is done by the device of the 'veil of ignorance'. It is this that makes it advantageous to hypothetical contractors to accept the principles of justice. But why should it be to the advantage of Gauthier's real-world contractors to accept the constraints of morality? Gauthier has to deal with the problem faced by all who, from Glaucon onwards, attempt to base morality on self-interest. Of course we can see why it would be in one's interests to gain the advantages of other people's compliance with the constraints of morality, and therefore why it would be in one's interests to enter into the agreement in the first place. But why is it not also in one's interests sometimes to break the agreement, and to ignore the constraints of morality, if one can get away with it? An important part of Gauthier's theory is therefore taken up with the problem of *compliance*.

His answer to the problem is that the rationality of constrained maximization can be demonstrated by assessing it not as a *policy* but as a *disposition*. We have to ask not just what choices it is rational for a utility-maximizer to make in particular cases, but also what kinds of dispositions it is rational to cultivate—that is, what kind of person it is in one's interests to be. The answer, according to Gauthier, is that it is in one's interests to be a constrained maximizer, not a straightforward maximizer.

> Constrained maximizers are able to make beneficial agreements with their fellows that the straightforward cannot. . . . The latter . . . would not be admitted as parties to agreement given their disposition to violation. Straightforward maximizers are disposed to take advantage of their fellows should the opportunity arise; knowing this, their fellows would prevent such opportunity arising. (173)

Thus, if you have the disposition of a constrained maximizer, you will reap the benefits of co-operation. If you are a straightforward maximizer you will not obtain those benefits, because people will not trust you.

The response of sceptics from Thrasymachus onwards has been: why not pretend? Can we not conceal our real intentions, obtain all the advantages of having a reputation for being a fair and honest co-operator, and combine these with the advantages of deception when it will succeed? Gauthier deals with this response by introducing another important concept, that of 'translu-cency'. Human beings are not necessarily *transparent*. They can sometimes get away with wrongdoing and not be found out. They are nevertheless *translucent*—'their disposition to co-operate or not may be ascertained by others, not with certainty, but as more than mere guesswork' (174). You may be able to cheat on others and escape detection on particular occasions, but oth-ers will have a pretty good idea of the kind of person you are, they will know that you are in general disposed to do such things, and so they will not admit you to co-operative arrangements and agreements. You will be the loser.

This argument remains open to the same objection as all previous attempts, from Glaucon to Philippa Foot, to derive morality from self-interest. It over-simplifies the empirical facts. There are ways in which people can take advan-tage of others, where the consequent risk of being excluded from mutually beneficial co-operative arrangements is negligible. To take just one simple and obvious example, people cheat on their income tax and, especially if they can afford to pay a good accountant, they can be virtually assured of getting away with it. Most people's dispositions are neither uniformly co-operative nor uniformly non-cooperative. They are, at a general level, liable to feel genu-inely constrained by at least some of the requirements of co-operation, but also liable to yield to at least some kinds of temptations to cheat. I do not see how one can give them reasons for doing otherwise, so long as the appeal to rationality is equated with the appeal to individual utility-maximization.

That conception of practical rationality is built into all versions of contrac-tarian ethics, whether Rawls' or Gauthier's or anyone else's. They all start with the pre-moral and pre-social individual, and attempt to build an account of morality from there. We cannot, however, understand the nature of moral values and why they matter to us unless, with the Hegelians and others, we start from the fact that human beings are embedded in social relations, in rela-tions of family and friendship, of work and culture and political life, and therefore in ties and loyalties which shape our identity and which transcend the purely individual self. As one of Rawls' critics, Michael Sandel, puts it, con-tractarian theory works with the fiction of 'the unencumbered self'.[9]

It is significant that at the end of his book Gauthier appears to recognize the inadequacy of this individualistic picture. He seems to acknowledge that 'our social capacity to find value in participating is one of the main sources of enrichment in human life, making possible as it does the complementary real-ization of our varied human powers and capacities' (337). He acknowledges that those who initially accept the constraints of morality as a means to indi-vidual utility-maximization may 'then come to value participation in co-operative and shared activities', and the morality that goes with this social co-operation, as values in their own right, not just as unwelcome constraints (338). In this way, morality may come to engage people's affections and not just their reason. But he still thinks that we first have to show why morality is rational, by appealing to individual utility-maximization, before we can show how our affections build on this rational foundation. This seems to me to get things the wrong way round. The conception of rationality with which Gau-thier begins is question-begging, and is called into question by the facts of human sociality which he half-acknowledges.

Agent-Centred Ethics

The criticism of utilitarianism that it can justify sacrificing some individuals for the good of others is part of a wider criticism, that it can justify doing ter-rible things for the sake of a greater good. Alternative moral theories which aim to avoid this criticism have focused not only on the moral status of the recipient of an action (as 'rights' theories do), but also on the moral character of the agent. The two kinds of ethical theory which I shall consider in the remainder of this chapter are both of this kind. A good example of what has been called 'agent-centred ethics' is the work of Bernard Williams, and it is explicitly presented as a critique of utilitarianism in his contribution to a book, written with J. J. C. Smart, called *Utilitarianism: For and Against*.[10] The heart of his discussion is introduced by two examples.

1. George is an unemployed young scientist. He is offered a job in a labora-tory doing research into chemical and biological warfare. He is strongly opposed to the development of chemical and biological weapons, but he knows that if he does not accept the job it will be very difficult for him to find another one, and that this job will then be taken by another scientist who has no scruples about chemical and biological weapons. It can there-fore be argued that if he refuses the job, not only will he and his family suf-fer, but the development of chemical and biological weapons will go ahead in a much more uninhibited manner.

2. Jim is on a botanical expedition in South America. On entering a small town he finds that twenty Indians are about to be executed by a group of soldiers. The captain welcomes Jim as an honoured visitor and suggests

that, to mark the occasion, Jim himself should shoot one of the Indians, and the other nineteen will then be set free. If Jim refuses, all twenty Indians will be shot.

In these examples, George and Jim are invited to perform actions which they regard with abhorrence, but if they refuse to perform them the consequences will be even worse. A utilitarian would have to say that they should perform the actions. Williams suggests that a distinctive feature of both examples is that if George or Jim refuses to perform the action, the bad consequences will follow because of what *someone else* does (the other scientist, and the captain). Utilitarianism can make no fundamental distinction in principle between these and other kinds of consequences. Therefore, Williams suggests, it can give no satisfactory account of the idea that a person is specially responsible for what *he* does, rather than for what other people do. The choice for George is that if he makes one decision, *he* will promote the development of chemical and biological weapons, and if he makes the other decision, *someone else* will promote the development of chemical and biological weapons more energetically. The choice for Jim is that if he makes one decision, *he* will kill one Indian, and that if he makes the other decision, *someone else* will kill twenty Indians. Utilitarianism can give no special weight to this distinction.

In order to bring out its importance, Williams introduces the concepts of 'projects' and 'commitments'. The concept of 'projects' is the more general one, encompassing people's pursuit of all sorts of things for themselves and for their families and friends and other people. If the only project which people were engaged in was the utilitarian one of promoting the general happiness, then there would be nothing for utilitarianism to get to work on. It is only because people find happiness in all these multifarious particular activities that the general project of utilitarianism makes sense.

Among these various particular projects which people pursue, however, are some which have a special character and which Williams calls 'commitments'.[11] These may include a person's devotion to intellectual or cultural or creative activities, or to some moral or political cause (such as the abolition of chemical and biological weapons), or to some more general moral perspective (such as a hatred of injustice, cruelty, or killing). What is distinctive of these 'commitments' is that they are the sorts of project around which people build their lives, and which give them their moral identity. They are what makes sense of a person's life, and what makes him or her the sort of moral agent that he or she is.

Now the problem is that the only status which utilitarianism can give to these commitments is that they are, like any other projects, possible sources of satisfaction and dissatisfaction, of happiness and unhappiness. If, in order to avoid worse consequences, George were to take the job and help to develop chemical and biological weapons, contrary to his own moral commitment, then the guilt which he would feel would be, from a utilitarian point of view, just one particular piece of unhappiness, to be weighed along with all the other consequences. Jim's feeling that, if he were to shoot the Indian, he could not live with himself is likewise just one more potential source of unhappiness, against which is to be weighed all the suffering which will follow if Jim refuses and the captain orders all twenty Indians to be shot. For George and for Jim, however, these commitments are not just potential sources of happiness or unhappiness. They have, as Williams says, a much deeper place in their lives. We have seen that what Williams also emphasizes is that, from a utilitarian point of view, George and Jim will have to compromise their own deep moral commitments because of what *someone else* will do if they refuse. Utilitarianism therefore alienates a person from his or her own moral identity. To act as a utilitarian, in such a situation, would be to destroy one's moral integrity.

This talk of the importance of one's own moral integrity has appeared suspect to some philosophers, and not just to utilitarians. The moral perspective which Williams is presenting may look like an attitude of 'keeping one's hands clean'. It may seem to be a kind of 'moral egoism'—attaching more importance to one's own integrity than to other people's suffering. Williams would say, I think, that this wrongly locates the significance of 'integrity'. Integrity, fidelity to one's commitments, is not itself a value, to be weighed against other values in making a moral decision. Rather, having such commitments is a necessary condition of being a moral agent at all. Utilitarianism, Williams suggests, cannot itself give a satisfactory account of moral agency. It is not self-evident why the promotion of the greatest happiness should *matter* to a moral agent. It is difficult for utilitarianism to answer the question of why anything should matter, for the ideal that utilitarianism sets up is a purely impersonal one, a concern for consequences which stand in no significant relation to oneself. Williams would not deny that impartial principles have a place in moral thinking, but to suppose that moral agency could take the form simply of being guided by an impartial principle would be too impoverished a conception. 'Life has to have substance if anything is to have sense, including adherence to the impartial system; but if it has substance, then it cannot grant supreme importance to the impartial system, and that system's hold on it will be, at the limit, insecure.'[12]

The ideas of 'commitments' and 'integrity', then, challenge utilitarianism not by themselves being other values to take into account in making moral decisions, besides consequences such as happiness and suffering. Rather, they challenge the utilitarian account of moral agency. What is lacking in the utilitarian view of George's and Jim's dilemmas is the provision of a satisfactory reason why 'the greatest happiness' should matter to them, and matter in a way which could override their own deepest commitments. There remains, for philosophers such as Williams, the question of how extensive a role personal commitments should be seen as having in our moral lives; and if these, and related ideas of 'integrity', are thought to have a central place, then the problem of 'moral egoism' is not yet banished.

Virtue Ethics

One other moral concept which focuses attention on the agent is that of 'the virtues'. I have already referred to Foot's revival of this concept in the context of the fact/value debate, and I want now to return briefly to the idea of putting 'the virtues' at the centre of moral theory. We saw that Foot tried to ground the virtues in the idea of those qualities which any human being needs, but then abandoned this position, conceding that it is not always to every person's advantage to be virtuous. I suggested that the project of grounding the virtues in the agent's own needs and happiness might still be viable if we worked with a richer notion of needs and of a worthwhile and fulfilling human life. Some modern advocates of virtue ethics remain committed to this essentially Platonic and Aristotelian project. I want to consider briefly, however, two other accounts which reverse that relation between the virtues on the one hand and the agent's needs and interests on the other. Instead of treating the virtues as qualities which we need for the sake of our own interests, they treat needs and interests as, in a sense to be explained, *internal* to the virtues.

The first of these accounts is one to which I cannot possibly do justice in the space available to me. This is the work of Alasdair MacIntyre, especially in his book *After Virtue*.[13] His account of the place of the virtues in moral thought is embedded within an ambitious historical thesis about the contrast between the modern and the pre-modern world. In modern pluralistic cultures and societies, he claims, moral thinking has disintegrated and become fragmented. Moral disagreements—for example, about war, or about abortion, or about social justice—have become interminable and irresolvable. This is because, in such disputes, the different positions appeal to different and incommensurable values, and there is no way of weighing these different values against one another. In the modern world we lack a shared moral vocabulary, and above all we lack a shared and agreed conception of the good human life within which our arguments and disagreements could be located. Utilitarian theory attempts to impose a unity on the diversity of our moral vocabulary, by testing different values against the criterion of happiness. The unity, however, is a spurious unity, for happiness is itself not a unitary concept. There is not one thing, happiness; there is a multiplicity of different conceptions of happiness, and utilitarianism cannot tell us which one to choose because it too lacks any objective vision of the good life.

MacIntyre contrasts our modern moral predicament with ancient Greek moral thought, and above all with Aristotle's ethics and with the continuation of the Aristotelian tradition in medieval Christian moral thought. For Aristotle and the Aristotelian tradition, the various virtues go to make up an overall picture of a human life as a *unity*. In order to see a person's life as a unity, we need to be able to tell an intelligible *narrative* about that life, to tell the story of someone's life in a way which makes sense of it, from birth to death—as the life of a heroic warrior, for instance, such as might be narrated in the Homeric epic poems, or as the life of an active citizen in a Greek polis. The virtues can then be seen as the appropriate qualities to be possessed by someone living a certain kind of life, whose story can be narrated in recognizable terms. In order to be able to tell any such story, however, we have to draw on the literary and cultural resources of a shared *tradition*, the tradition of a community. It is because we lack any such shared tradition that, in the modern world, our moral thinking flounders.

Note that MacIntyre shares with Williams the idea that moral considerations are somehow linked with the ways in which we make sense of our lives and see them as having a meaning. Further consideration of MacIntyre's ethical theory would require us to look at the details of his historical claims about the changes in moral discourse which have accompanied the transition from the pre-modern to the modern world, and I cannot do that here. What I want to take from him, however, is the idea that aims and interests are internal to rather than external to the life of the virtues. It is not that the virtues serve some external purpose, but rather that they make up a conception of the good human life, *from within which* it can be seen as rational to pursue certain aims and values.

A similar idea is to be found in Philippa Foot's more recent writing on the virtues. A paper called 'Utilitarianism and the Virtues' marks a further stage in the modification of her earlier position.[14] The paper begins by questioning, in a radical way, the idea of an ultimate goal which the virtues, and actions generally, are supposed to serve. That goal, the general happiness, is presented by utilitarianism as being the proper goal of our actions because it is 'the best state of affairs'. Foot questions whether the idea of 'a good state of affairs' is really a meaningful use of the word 'good'. Certainly we do often talk about a particular outcome as being 'a good thing', but it is not clear that the word 'good' here means what utilitarians take it to mean. Something can be good *for someone*, or good *from a certain point of view*. If I am backing a horse in a race I will say it is 'good' that my horse has won, but this outcome is 'a good thing' from the particular point of view of the interest I take in the race; it will be 'a bad thing' from the point of view of someone who backed a different horse. This is what Foot calls a 'speaker-relative' use of the word 'good', and she argues that descriptions of an outcome as 'a good thing' will typically be speaker-relative. It would be absurd to ask whether it is, in the abstract, 'a good thing' that my horse won the race. Utilitarianism, however, supposes that an outcome can be 'the best state of affairs' from an entirely *impersonal point of view*, and Foot suggests that utilitarians can give no clear account of what this is supposed to be.

What might now be said is that a state of affairs can be seen as good or bad *from a moral point of view.* Is this the meaning of 'good state of affairs' which utilitarianism needs? Foot suggests that the only sense we can make of this is that an outcome may be seen as a good thing from the point of view of a moral person. In particular, someone who has the moral virtue of *benevolence* will see it as 'a good thing' that people are happy and 'a bad thing' that people are suffering. But this is a point of view constituted very specifically by the virtue of benevolence, and it is from this point of view that the desired outcome is apprehended. 'It is very important,' comments Foot, 'that we have found this end *within* morality, and forming part of it, not standing outside it as the "good state of affairs" by which moral action in general is to be judged' (235). In other words, we already need the idea of morality as constituted by the virtues *before* we can make sense of the idea of a certain end as 'a good state of affairs' from a moral point of view.

Foot is now in a position to comment on familiar objections to utilitarianism—that it would justify sacrificing some people, or doing other terrible things, for the sake of the general happiness. She has acknowledged that other people's happiness, or the relief of suffering, can be seen as a desirable end from the standpoint of benevolence. But benevolence is only one of the virtues. There are others. In particular, the virtuous person must have not only the virtue of benevolence but also the virtue of *justice*. From the point of view of justice it is not acceptable to promote happiness by, for example, increasing the wealth of rich people at the cost of misery to the poor, or by acting dishonestly, or by killing innocent people. Benevolence would cease to be a virtue if it involved acting unjustly, so benevolence cannot require us to do such things. Therefore they cannot be justified as being necessary for the promotion of happiness, since, as Foot has argued, the promotion of happiness is a desirable end only from the standpoint of benevolence as a virtue.

Foot's paper, then, puts the virtues at the centre of morality by turning the tables on utilitarianism. The utilitarian theory subordinates all action to an ultimate end which is the promotion of happiness and diminution of suffering. Foot, in contrast, is suggesting that any such end as the betterment of human life is an intelligible aim only from *within* a morality of the virtues. For her, therefore, the central notion of morality is not a certain end of human action, but a certain conception of the moral agent. In this general respect her position is akin to Williams' agent-centred account. Like the latter it may, therefore, seem open to criticism on the grounds that it invites a kind of moral egoism. It may seem to imply that any concern one might have for others should be derivative from one's concern to make oneself a morally good person. Altruistic action thus becomes a means to the promotion of one's own moral virtue. This, we saw, was a problem for Platonic and Aristotelian virtue ethics. Whether this is a legitimate criticism of Foot is a matter for argument, but I am inclined to think that, just as it is a defect in utilitarianism that it subordinates everything else to the promotion of an ultimate end, so also it is a defect in virtue-theory if it treats the rest of morality as derivative from the virtues.

Moral Pluralism

I have reviewed, all too briefly, a range of ethical theories which all have their contemporary advocates. They continue various themes of the historical tradition—the virtue theory of Plato and Aristotle, the utilitarianism of Mill, and a conception of rights which can be traced back to Kant's ethics. My criticisms have suggested that none of these contemporary endeavours can succeed as an all-embracing ethical theory. We might plausibly conjecture at this point that what they can do is contribute between them the necessary components of an adequate comprehensive theory. This would be in keeping with the Hegelian methodology which I espoused in my opening chapter, that of identifying, through a critique of past theories, the valid elements to be retained from them and giving each component its appropriate place in a total picture. The resulting overall theory will be one of moral pluralism. It will have a place for ideas both of utility and of rights, as representing two kinds of impartial concern for the needs of others. It will have a place also for the more personal, agent-centred concerns represented by one's personal commitments and by the idea of the virtues. My criticism of contractarian ethics has been more thoroughgoing, and I do not think that it can furnish a satisfactory approach. We may nevertheless retain a Rawlsian conception of egalitarian justice and its contrast with utilitarianism, if we regard it as grounded not in a hypothetical contract but in the concrete social relations of a real community. The notion of 'contract' could then serve as a limited but useful metaphor for the social relations of reciprocity which must underpin egalitarian justice.

Thomas Nagel, in an essay entitled 'The Fragmentation of Value' and elsewhere, has put the case for moral pluralism.[15] He identifies five fundamental types of value:

1. *Specific obligations* to other people or institutions, arising out of deliberate undertakings or special relations.
2. Constraints on action arising from *general rights*.
3. *Utility*, that is, consideration of the effects of one's actions on everyone's welfare.
4. *Perfectionist ends or values*, that is, the instrinsic value of certain achievements or creations, such as scientific discovery or artistic creation, distinct from their value to the individuals who experience and enjoy them.
5. *Commitment to one's own projects or undertakings*.

His list does not coincide with, but is recognizably close to, the one which emerges from my own discussion in this chapter. He argues that these are all independent kinds of value, none of which is reducible to any of the others, and which cannot be ranked or weighed against one another on a single scale. They are incommensurable values. Their irreducibility reflects, in particular, a fundamental division between two perspectives which we have on the world—the *personal*, or agent-centred, and the *impersonal*, or detached—and in his subsequent work he has explored the importance of this basic division in other areas of philosophy as well as ethics.[16] Agent-centred values include those of special obligations and personal commitments, and the constraints imposed by individual rights are also, in a rather different sense, agent-centred (a suggestion which I find unhelpful), whereas utility and perfectionist ends are impersonal values. It is neither possible nor desirable to abandon either of these points of view, or the values that go with it.

> The capacity to view the world simultaneously from the point of view of one's relations to others, from the point of view of one's life extended through time, from the point of view of everyone at once, and finally from the detached viewpoint often described as the view *sub specie aeternitatis* is one of the marks of humanity. This complex capacity is an obstacle to simplification. (134)

This accommodating pluralism is all very well; but the problem is that, as Nagel recognizes, it seems to imply that some moral conflicts, those between incommensurable values, are bound to be irresolvable. What if the attempt to act charitably or benevolently seems to require the violation of some people's rights or the breaking of a trust? What if the utilitarian pursuit of others' happiness seems to require the sacrifice of a friendship, or of some deep personal commitment? If we were to take one particular perspective, such as that of utilitarianism or or virtue ethics, as more fundamental than the rest, it might provide us with a crierion for resolving such conflicts; but if these competing values are irreducible and incommensurable, there would seem to be no rational way of resolving them. And if that is the predicament which we are in, then, at least at this level, moral scepticism seems to be back on the agenda.

Nagel suggests that, faced with such conflicts, we can still exercise what he calls 'judgement', in the Aristotelian sense—the use of 'phronesis' or 'practical wisdom, which reveals itself over time in individual decisions rather than in the enunciation of general principles' (135). I have discussed this idea sympathetically in the chapter on Aristotle, and I think Nagel may be right that *in particular situations* a decision to resolve a conflict of values in one way rather than another may be of this kind—a decision for which one cannot give further reason or justification, but which is nevertheless not just an irrational arbitrary choice. What I wonder is whether there is anything more which can be said at the general level about the relations between these different kinds of value, and therefore about the kind of weight each might carry in cases of conflict. Can we, whilst not trying to reduce them all to a single kind of value, at any rate attempt some account of a framework within which the various kinds of value can be located? Can we say something about the respective places which they occupy in our moral lives, and thus about the relative importance which each has? I shall return to this task in the final chapter.

Notes

1. J. J. C. Smart and Bernard Williams, *Utilitarianism: For and Against* (Cambridge, 1973), 7.
2. R. M. Hare, *Freedom and Reason* (Oxford, 1963), chs. 6–7.
3. Contributions to the debate around act-utilitarianism and rule-utilitarianism can be found collected in Philippa Foot (ed.), *Theories of Ethics* (Oxford, 1967); in M. D. Bayles (ed.), *Contemporary Utilitarianism* (New York, 1968); in Thomas K. Hearn (ed.), *Studies in Utilitarianism* (New York, 1971); and in Jonathan Glover (ed.), *Utilitarianism and its Critics* (New York, 1990). The distinction is discussed in R. B. Brandt, *Ethical Theory* (Englewood Cliffs, NJ, 1959), and at length in David Lyons, *Forms and Limits of Utilitarianism* (Oxford, 1965). Hare, especially in his book *Moral Thinking* (Oxford, 1981), defends a two-level utilitarianism which distinguishes between the *intuitive* and the *critical* level of moral thinking. He sees this as a form of act-utilitarianism, but one which incorporates the advantages of rule-utilitarianism.
4. Robert Nozick, *Anarchy, State, and Utopia* (New York, 1974), 32–3.
5. Nozick, *Anarchy, State, and Utopia*; Ronald Dworkin, *Taking Rights Seriously* (London, 1977). Neither Nozick nor Dworkin puts forward a theory of rights as a comprehensive ethical theory. That more ambitious project is defended in Alan Gewirth, *Reason and Morality* (Chicago, 1978) and *Human Rights: Essays on Justification and Applications* (Chicago, 1982); and in J. L. Mackie, 'Can There be a Right-based Moral Theory?', in Jeremy Waldron, *Theories of Rights* (Oxford, 1984).
6. John Rawls, *A Theory of Justice* (Oxford, 1971).
7. David Gauthier, *Morals by Agreement* (Oxford, 1986).
8. General contractarian theories of morality have also been put forward in G. R. Grice, *The Grounds of Moral Judgement* (Cambridge, 1967) and in David A. J. Richards, *A Theory of Reasons for Action* (Oxford, 1971).
9. Michael Sandel, *Liberalism and the Limits of Justice* (Cambridge, 1982). See also his 'The Procedural Republic and the Unencumbered Self', in Shlomo Avineri and Avner de-Shalit (eds.), *Communitarianism and Individualism* (Oxford, 1992).
10. Bernard Williams, 'A Critique of Utilitarianism', in Smart and Williams, *Utilitarianism*.
11. Elsewhere, Williams refers to these as 'ground projects'; see 'Persons, Character and Morality', 12 ff., in his *Moral Luck* (Cambridge, 1981). The essay 'Utilitarianism and Moral Self-Indulgence' in the same volume is also relevant.
12. 'Persons, Character and Morality', *Moral Luck*, 18.
13. Alasdair MacIntyre, *After Virtue* (London, 1981).
14. Philippa Foot, 'Utilitarianism and the Virtues', in *Mind*, 84 (1985); reprinted in Samuel Scheffler (ed.), *Consequentialism and its Critics* (Oxford, 1988). References will be given to the version in Scheffler.
15. Thomas Nagel, 'The Fragmentation of Value', in *Mortal Questions* (Cambridge, 1979).
16. Thomas Nagel, *The View from Nowhere* (Oxford, 1986). In that work (ch. 9) he employs the terminology of a distinction between 'agent-relative' and 'agent-neutral' values.

12
The Ethical World

Reading: Relevant reading to accompany this chapter can be found in James Rachels (ed.), *Ethical Theory 1: The Question of Objectivity* (Oxford, 1998). David McNaughton's book *Moral Vision* (Oxford, 1988), which is discussed in this chapter, can also be recommended as excellent further reading on many of the issues.

In the previous two chapters I have looked at twentieth-century developments first in meta-ethics and then in normative ethics. In this final chapter I return to meta-ethics. I shall briefly review the most recent work in this area, and then, in the light of the history I have traced in this book, I shall attempt a concluding response to the question raised originally by the Sophists and still at the centre of debate: can there be objective moral truths, or are the moral positions which we adopt ultimately matters of individual preference and social convention?

Realism and Anti-Realism

What is striking about recent discussions of this topic is the revival of a metaphysical or ontological mode of putting the questions. By this I mean an approach which takes the important questions to be questions about *what kinds of entities* are the subject-matter of moral discourse, and whether such entities really exist. The dominant current debate is formulated as one about 'moral realism'. That label implies that the questions to be debated are those such as 'Is there a moral reality which our moral beliefs describe?' and 'Are there real moral properties?', and the 'realist' is presumably someone who answers 'yes' to such questions.

I call such formulations 'striking' in view of what I said in Chapter 11 about the Wittgensteinian revolution in the philosophy of language and its impact on ethics. We saw the difficulties which Moore got into by assuming that 'good' is the name of a property and then trying to say what kind of property it is. The Wittgensteinian approach seemed to offer a way out of the blind alley into which Moore was led. Although it was used to defend positions of a non-cognitivist kind, it need not point in that direction. What the Wittgensteinian approach does is to change the question. Instead of asking 'What kinds of properties, if any, do moral words stand for?' we ask 'How do we use moral utterances? What do we do with them, what functions do they serve, and what kind of support can we give for them?' Those formulations leave it an open question whether there can be objective and rational grounds for accepting moral beliefs, but they guide us away from the attempt to answer this by trying to identify 'real moral properties' to which our moral beliefs might correspond.

The revival of the vocabulary of 'realism' and 'anti-realism' is in part to be explained as an extension of similar debates going on in other areas of philosophy—debates about whether what determines the truth of our beliefs, or the meaning of our language, is or is not in some sense 'mind-independent'. Some recent defences of moral realism can also be seen as responses to a challenge which was itself posed in ontological terms. This challenge was the advocacy of a version of moral scepticism or moral subjectivism by J. L. Mackie in his book appropriately titled *Ethics: Inventing Right and Wrong* (1977). Mackie's position has some affinities with those of the emotivists and of writers such as Hare. Like them (and like Nietzsche), he rejects the idea that there are moral facts. He does not, however, think that such a position can be arrived at simply by analysing moral language, for moral language itself embodies pervasive metaphysical illusions about its subject-matter. Our moral language encourages us to think that when we discuss questions such as 'Is this action right?' or 'Is this a good state of affairs?' we are investigating an objectively existing world of values. In thinking this, we are mistaken; but the mistake, according to Mackie, is built into our language. Mackie's theory is what he calls an 'error theory'. Our language of 'right' and 'good' implies that these words are the names of properties; but in fact there are no such properties, and what we are really doing in moral discourse is, as his title implies, *inventing* values, not discovering them.

For Mackie, then, the important question is not linguistic, but ontological, 'Are there real objective moral properties?', and his answer is 'No.' His principal argument to this effect is what he calls 'the argument from queerness'. Objective values, if they existed, would have to be 'entities or qualities or relations of a very strange sort, utterly different from anything else in the universe'.[1] They would have to possess the paradoxical characteristic of 'objective prescriptivity', combining real objective existence with some peculiar kind of magnetism, a power of motivating us to act in certain kinds of ways. Mackie thus shares Hare's idea that moral language is essentially action-guiding, and he asks how objective properties could possibly be action-guiding in this way. They would have to be something like Plato's Forms, with a quite mysterious metaphysical status, and the kind of knowledge we would have to have of them would likewise have to be mysterious and quite unlike the kind of knowledge we have of other things in the world—something like Moore's or Ross's 'intuitions', with all the difficulties which that notion involves.

That is Mackie's anti-realism. Formulated in ontological terms, it has evoked responses in the same terms. What would 'moral realists' have to maintain in reply? As the term 'moral realism' has gained in currency, it has acquired a variety of nuances, and a range of positions now go under that label. At the very least, however, moral realists would have to reject non-cognitivism. They would have to say that there can be genuine moral *knowledge*. And since to know something is to know it as *true*, realists must maintain that moral utterances convey statements which can be true or false. Moreover, this would have to be 'truth' in something more than a trivial sense. Even extreme emotivists could give a trivial sense to the idea that moral utterances can be true; they could say that someone who says 'It is true that abortion is wrong' is simply emphasizing his or her commitment to the emotional attitude which he or she is expressing. Moral utterances to which the speaker is committed are 'true' for the speaker. Realists clearly require a stronger notion of 'truth' than this. They must maintain that true moral beliefs are true in virtue of something which is independent of the beliefs themselves. This requirement of 'independence' has to be carefully formulated. We cannot require that moral facts or moral properties must be 'mind-independent' or independent of human beings and human mental states in a quite general way, for of course it is quite legitimate for the moral realist to say that moral facts include facts about human desires and emotions. What the realist must maintain is that a moral utterance is made true by something independent of the particular mental state which consists in the speaker's being committed to that utterance. To put it simply, for the realist, moral beliefs cannot be true just because we think they are; there must be something which *makes* them true. This way of putting it brings out the point of the vocabulary of 'realism'. Nevertheless, I should want to suggest that we should not be too preoccupied with the ontological formulation. The important questions are the epistemological ones, for it is these that importantly affect how we view our engagement in moral deliberation and debate. Can we have rational and objective grounds for moral beliefs? Can they be objectively true?

Realist responses to Mackie typically start from a point conceded by him. Common sense favours the realist. When we engage in moral deliberation and debate, we normally think we are trying to arrive at the truth. We do not normally suppose that we are making it up as we go along. We assume that there are right answers to be discovered, and that it is important that we should arrive at the right answers rather than wrong ones. The onus is therefore on the anti-realist to show that these commonsense assumptions are mistaken. Mackie has made a case for this; the commonsense assumptions are mistaken because they involve extravagant and implausible metaphysical commitments. If the realist can undermine that case, then the commonsense plausibility of realism can be reinstated.

Internalism and Externalism

I want to look at two versions of realism, which typify two kinds of response to Mackie's case. I shall refer to two books which I recommend partly for their accessibility—they provide admirably clear introductions to the realism debate—but also because they represent the two contrasting approaches: *externalism* and *internalism*. The internalist realist retains the idea that there is some kind of internal connection between moral beliefs and action—that moral beliefs are intrinsically action-guiding—and therefore still has to meet Mackie's 'argument from queerness' and show how moral facts can have objective prescriptivity. The externalist realist drops the idea of an internal connection between moral beliefs and action, accepts that it is an open question whether we have good reason to act in accordance with moral beliefs, and is thereby able to meet Mackie's challenge.

I take as an example of externalist realism David Brink's book *Moral Realism and the Foundations of Ethics* (1989). Brink distinguishes between two versions of internalism, both of which he rejects.[2] One version is formulated in terms of *motives*: that moral considerations necessarily motivate agents to act in accordance with them. The other version is formulated in terms of *reasons*: that moral considerations necessarily provide reasons for acting in accordance with them. Brink agrees that there are important connections between morality and both motives and reasons for actions, but he thinks that externalism gives a more satisfactory account of these connections. For the externalist, the fact that people are motivated by moral considerations is an important but contingent psychological fact, to be explained, for example, by the widely shared feeling of 'sympathy' in the Humean sense (49).

Brink argues that neither version of internalism can account for the *amoralist*, whom he defines as 'someone who recognizes the existence of moral considerations and remains unmoved' (46). There surely are such people, but motive-internalism would make the amoralist conceptually impossible. Reason-internalism can accept the existence of the amoralist, but must regard as incoherent the amoralist's challenge '*Why* should I care about moral demands?' (59). Brink thinks that even if the challenge can be met, the amoralist's question is a perfectly intelligible one, and what is wrong with internalism is its inability to recognize this.

Brink's argument here seems to depend too heavily on the particular connotations of the term 'morality'. We have seen, for example, that Nietzsche is in one typical sense an amoralist; he questions those values which are standardly thought of as distinctively 'moral'. Does Nietzsche nevertheless have something which could be called, in a wider sense, his own 'morality'? A morality in this wider sense would be a set of values by which one lives one's life, or a set of beliefs about how one ought to live. I have suggested in Chapter 1 that we should not be too diverted by the purely linguistic question of what we mean by the term 'morality'. We can at any rate allow that this wider notion is one possible meaning of 'morality'. But now it is surely to this wider notion of 'morality' (or whatever else we call it) that the thesis of moral realism is most importantly applied. What we want to know is not whether there is a 'moral reality' in the narrow sense of 'moral', but whether there are objective answers to the question of how we ought to live, and whether these answers are grounded in facts about the world. For this wider notion of morality, however, internalism is surely the correct account. It is necessarily, indeed trivially, the case that beliefs about how we ought to live provide us with reasons for acting accordingly. That is true simply in virtue of the meaning of the word 'ought'. And if directed at 'morality' in the wider sense, the amoralist's question is indeed incoherent. He or she is asking, 'Why should I do what I ought to do?' If this means anything, I suppose it means, 'Why should I do anything at all?' But that is still an incoherent question.

Brink's externalism, then, makes for a disappointingly weak version of moral realism. The weakness of its claims is exacerbated by another feature of Brink's position, his *coherentist* moral epistemology. He distinguishes between 'coherentism' and 'foundationalism' as alternative accounts both of knowledge in general and moral knowledge in particular (100). For a foundationalist epistemology, all justified beliefs must either be foundational beliefs or inferences from foundational beliefs. An example of a general foundationalist epistemology would be traditional empiricism, which claims that our foundational beliefs must be direct reports of sense experiences, and that all other justified beliefs must be inferences from these. An example of a specifically moral foundationalism would be moral intuitionism such as Moore's or Ross's, which claims that there are basic moral truths which are self-evident, and that all our other justified moral beliefs must be derived from these. The appeal of foundationalism is that it appears to provide a guarantee that our beliefs are grounded in reality. Our foundational beliefs provide a basis, a hook-up with reality, and without this all our beliefs will be 'free-floating' (106). It looks, therefore, as though moral realism and any other form of realism ought to be allied to a foundationalist epistemology.

Brink, however, thinks that, on general grounds, foundationalism is unacceptable. It cannot deliver what it promises. No version of foundationalism can provide the guarantee of truth which it purports to offer. Even if there were infallible foundational beliefs, the rest of our beliefs, including our commonsense beliefs about the world, would not follow deductively from such foundations; they could be derived from such foundations only by a weaker form of inference, which would make them merely probable (115). But in any case there can be no self-justifying foundational beliefs. A belief is justified only if there is some reason for holding it. So for any belief which we accept, we must be able to refer to some other belief to say why we accept it (116 f.). In that case, the search for 'foundations' for our knowledge is illusory.

Coherentism, it seems, is all that we are left with; but according to Brink it is all that we need. Coherentism is the view that the justification for any belief consists in its being shown to be coherent with all our other beliefs. On the face of it, this looks insufficient. A set of beliefs consistent with one another may nevertheless be false. A train of justifications which is circular must surely be invalid. 'How do you know there's a God?'—'Because it says so in the Bible.'—'How do you know the Bible is true?'—'Because it's the word of God.'—such an argument is patently unsatisfactory. Brink suggests, nevertheless, that though a particular limited argument or inference will be invalid if it is circular, when it comes to a total system of beliefs the justification for those beliefs consists in their overall coherence. The appropriate method of justification in ethics is therefore, roughly speaking, what Rawls has called the method of 'reflective equilibrium'.[3] We start with our existing, particular moral beliefs. These are unlikely to be consistent with one another. We look for a set of underlying general principles which will best explain as many of our particular beliefs as possible, especially those of which we are most confident. In the light of these general principles we go back to our particular beliefs, and change those which are most obviously incompatible with the principles. Through this process of mutual adjustment between particular beliefs and general principles, we aim to arrive at a coherent system. Brink adds that we have to seek also coherence of our moral beliefs with non-moral beliefs, with meta-ethical beliefs, and with second-order beliefs about the conditions under which our beliefs are most likely to be reliable.

It is the combination of externalism and coherentism that seems to me to make Brink's realism excessively modest in its claims. We have seen that his externalism apparently requires that his version of moral realism be applied to 'morality' in a narrow sense. It now looks as though the realist credentials of that morality depend only on its internal coherence. By that reckoning one could be a realist about just about anything. One could be a realist about the rules of football. Provided the rules are consistent with one another, with our purposes in playing football, and with any other beliefs which might be relevant, this system of 'oughts' would meet the requirement of coherence. It would, however, admit of a 'realist' reading only in a very weak sense, first, because we lack any notion of an independent reality which the rules are *about* and which they have to match. The rules of a game are paradigmatically things which we invent rather than discover. Moreover, the rules of football are action-guiding only in a weak sense: whether our actions are guided by the rules depends entirely on whether or not we happen to be interested in playing football. In the case of the rules of a game, externalism is the correct construal of their action-guiding force. But if morality is not action-guiding in any stronger sense than this, and if the 'oughts' of morality have no more objective justification than the 'oughts' of the rules of football, then moral realism does not amount to very much.

This comparison is, admittedly, unfair to Brink. The coherence which he requires for morality is wider than the coherence of the rules of football. I have noted that it involves, for instance, coherence between our moral and nonmoral beliefs. Nevertheless, I suggest that coherence is not enough. Brink's contrast between coherentism and what he understands by 'foundationalism' is a false dichotomy. I agree that 'foundations', in the sense in which he characterizes them, are unattainable. There are no self-justifying beliefs which provide a guarantee of truth. Nevertheless, the important point which at least traditional empiricist versions of foundationalism have imperfectly recognized is that, in the process of justifying our beliefs, an essential role is played by the *appeal to experience*. It is this that underpins the idea that our beliefs are true *of* something, and are not just a free-floating, internally coherent system. Any form of realism needs to hang on to this idea of the appeal to experience in some interpretation or other, without thereby being committed to any claim that this experience, whether perceptual experience or moral experience or whatever, provides us with self-evident and indubitable foundational truths. Brink's coherentism does admittedly leave room for this. He includes observational beliefs among those with which our moral beliefs must be coherent (136–8). What is needed, however, for anything other than a very weak moral realism, is some more positive account of the role that our experience of the world might play in the justification of our moral beliefs.

Vision and Meaning

I have not done anything like justice to Brink's powerful and impressive defence of externalist realism. Other philosophers, too, have ably defended such a position.[4] Nevertheless, I believe that this version of the moral realist project is the wrong one. I turn now to internalist realism. I shall take as an example of such a position David McNaughton's book, *Moral Vision* (1988). The book is intended as an introduction to current debates in ethical theory, and can be strongly recommended as such, but McNaughton also takes a position in those debates. He draws on the work of John McDowell to defend a form of moral realism which avoids the two weaknesses I criticized in Brink's position, its commitments to externalism and to coherentism.[5]

McNaughton suggests that the externalist position clashes with our experience of the nature of moral thinking. 'We do,' he says, 'find something very odd in the suggestion that someone might conclude that an action was morally required of him but maintain that he had no reason to do it.'[6] He maintains that moral beliefs (perhaps in conjunction with other beliefs) are sufficient to provide someone with a reason to act in a certain way. In maintaining this, he rejects the assumption, common to externalist realism and to non-cognitivism, that there is a fundamental division within our psychological states between *beliefs*, which are essentially passive, and *desires*, which are active. The non-cognitivist maintains that, since moral language is action-guiding, the meaning of such language must consist in its primarily express-ing desires (or 'feelings', or 'inclinations', or 'prescriptions') rather than beliefs, since beliefs are insufficient to motivate actions. The externalist realist main-tains that moral language does express moral beliefs, but agrees that beliefs are insufficient to provide us with reasons for actions or to motivate us to actions, and therefore thinks that some additional desire is needed for action. McNaughton criticizes their shared assumption, the belief–desire theory, arguing that it runs counter to what we know about the motivating force of moral requirements. Morality makes *demands* on us, and these 'appear to be independent of our desires—they may even conflict with what we want' (48).

The fact that McNaughton's version of moral realism is an *internalist* one seems to me to be a merit of his position. Its other advantage, in contrast to Brink, is that it offers an account of the role which the *appeal to experience* plays in moral understanding. That account employs the notion of 'moral vision' referred to in the title of his book. This may now suggest that, whereas Brink's version of realism is over-modest, McNaughton's is in danger of being over-ambitious. As he acknowledges, 'it is frequently claimed that the realist must construe moral observation as requiring the use of some mysterious and suspicious faculty of moral intuition—a faculty for whose existence we have, and could have, no conceivable evidence' (56). It conjures up suggestions of a Moorean ontology of unanalysable non-natural properties which we just 'see' and about which there can be no argument. McNaughton wants to distance his own notion of moral observation from that of some special kind of moral intuition. The notion of observation which he employs is, he says, of a quite ordinary kind. I want now to look at his account of it, and to explore a little further the idea of moral vision, as a way of trying to formulate a viable ver-sion of realism.

Here are two examples with which McNaughton illustrates the idea of moral observation:

> If I see several children throwing stones at an injured animal I may claim that I can just see that what they are doing is cruel. Similarly, the insolence of a drunken guest's behaviour seems no less observable than the cut of his suit. (56)

These examples and the subsequent discussion imply that McNaughton regards moral observation here as 'seeing' in a quite literal sense—compara-ble, he says, to seeing that a cliff is dangerous, or that someone is worried, or that one thing is further away than another. What, however, of cases where others might see the situation differently, and where it is therefore a matter for dispute what is there to be seen? McNaughton says:

What the realist needs is an account which makes it plausible to suppose that, in moral experience, we can be genuinely sensitive to what is there independently of us, but which also explains how moral disagreement is possible. To accommodate this last point the realist needs an account which allows for misperception and even for a complete failure to see what is there. (58)

He suggests that what is involved here is the experience of coming to see a situation in a new light. This may come about as a result of noticing particular features of the situation, or having these brought to one's attention by someone else, thereby 'revealing an overall shape or pattern' (59). McNaughton illustrates this with another example, the Old Testament story of King David, who arranges for Uriah the Hittite to be killed in battle so that he can take for himself Uriah's wife Bathsheba, and who is then visited by the prophet Nathan. Nathan tells David a story, a moral fable the point of which is 'to get David to see his own behaviour for what it really is—not a smart piece of one-upmanship, but an act of mean injustice by a powerful and wealthy man against someone powerless to defend himself against royal authority'. This is an example of coming to see a situation in a certain light; the recognition of his behaviour as 'mean injustice' is the achievement of greater moral awareness.

Now it seems to me that this kind of 'moral vision' is rather different from that in the two previous examples. Seeing as pattern-recognition, as perceiving the salient features of a situation, is not now literal vision. 'Moral vision' has become a metaphor for the kind of awareness that is involved. It is not like the case of cruelty, where the literal 'seeing the boys throwing stones at the animal' is at one and the same time 'seeing the cruelty'. Seeing his behaviour as mean injustice is something which a blind King David could have been brought to 'see'. In saying that the term 'vision' has now come to refer to a non-literal kind of seeing, I am not suggesting that we revert to the idea of some special power of moral intuition. The information which we draw on in such cases is of a perfectly ordinary kind, obtained from perceptual experience; but what we do is to order it and arrange it in such a way as to bring out the appropriateness of a certain characterization of the situation. The fact that 'vision' has now become a metaphor for this kind of awareness leaves room for the possibility, to which I shall revert, that other metaphors may also be applicable.

Such examples also bring out another aspect of McNaughton's own position. This is what he calls *moral particularism*.[7] King David's recognition is a matter of coming to see the character of this particular action; it is not a matter of applying a general principle to the particular case. It is not that he accepts a principle such as 'Do not act unjustly' or 'Do not use your power for the selfish exploitation of others' and reads off from the principle the conclusion that his action was wrong. As McNaughton puts it:

The only method of arriving at correct moral conclusions in new cases will be to develop a sensitivity in moral matters which enables one to see each particular case aright. Moral principles appear to drop out as, at best, redundant and, at worst, as a hindrance to moral vision. (62)

This notion of moral awareness as a sensitivity to the particular case, a capacity to recognize the salient feature of the particular situation and thereby to realize what is to be done here and now, is reminiscent of Aristotle's conception of moral judgement (a conception which, as we saw in the previous chapter, Nagel also makes use of).

This particularistic account of moral vision is, I think, correct and important as far as it goes; but I also believe that a *purely* particularistic account is inadequate. There is, first, the obvious point that we can recognize an action as cruel or generous, as a case of loyalty or betrayal, of justice or injustice, only if we possess and understand the appropriate universal concepts. This is a matter not just of understanding the meaning of the relevant words. It *is* that, but knowing what cruelty or loyalty or injustice is involves recognizing the place of these concepts and values in human life, and understanding their importance. I agree that the model of applying general principles to the particular case is the wrong model; but seeing the particular case in the right way does require the application of a wider and more general understanding. Conversely, coming to see the particular case in a new way may also involve a change to one's wider vision of life. Consider another example, Tolstoy's famous story 'The Death of Ivan Ilyich'. Ivan Ilyich's life has been governed by mundane social ambitions of an entirely conventional sort—sowing his wild oats, marrying well, climbing to the top of his profession, mixing in the right social circles and furnishing his house in the best possible taste. He falls ill; the best doctors are called but are unable to do anything for him; and the final sections of the story describe the last weeks of his painful illness. Confronted for the first time by the inevitability of his own death, he is led to review his past life and to ask himself what it has amounted to. He realizes that the values and ambitions for which he has lived have been hollow. What he thought of as success and enjoyment turns out, on reflection, to have been a false happiness. His earliest memories of childhood recall genuine pleasures, but 'the farther he departed from childhood and the nearer he came to the present, the more worthless and doubtful were the joys'.[8] They have been an evasion of the consciousness of his own mortality. He struggles against the thought that he has not lived his life aright, but after a night of physical and mental agony he recognizes that this is the truth. The insincerity of his family and attendants when they visit him in the morning is a mirror in which he sees the falsity of his own life. 'In them he saw himself—all that he had lived for—and saw plainly that it was all wrong, a horrible, monstrous lie concealing both life and death' (157—note the conjunction of literal and metaphorical 'seeing' in this sentence). In his last days he wrestles with the question of how he ought to have lived, and the answer is revealed in the uncomplaining patience and simple genuine concern of his servant Gerassim, and finally in the tears of his young son:

it was revealed to him that his life had not been what it ought to have been but that it was still possible to put it right. He asked himself: 'But what *is* the right thing?' and grew still, listening. Then he felt that someone was kissing his hand. He opened his eyes and looked at his son. He felt sorry for him. His wife came up to him. He looked at her. She was gazing at him with open mouth, the tears wet on her nose and cheeks, and an expression of despair on her face. He felt sorry for her. . . . And all at once it became clear to him that what had been oppressing him and would not go away was suddenly dropping away. . . . He felt full of pity for them, he must do something to make it less painful for them: release them and release himself from this suffering. 'How right and how simple,' he thought. . . . He searched for his former habitual fear of death, and did not find it. . . . In place of death there was light. 'So that's what it is!' he suddenly exclaimed aloud. 'What joy!' To him all this happened in a single instant, and the meaning of that instant suffered no change thereafter. (160–1)

What is revealed to Ivan Ilyich is the importance of sincere emotions and of authentic sympathy and pity. He *sees* this, and Tolstoy's language is, in part, the language of vision. He sees this, first, as the truth of what he must do here and now, in his last moments. He sees it also as a truth about his life as a whole. But it is not only a truth about his own life; it is at the same time a recognition of what is important generally in human life and a realization of the real nature of happiness. The understanding is both particular and universal, and the universal is recognized *in* the particular. What Ivan Ilyich finally understands would, if expressed as general principles, be utterly banal—'Be sincere in your emotions', 'Feel genuine sympathy for others'. Ivan Ilyich has to come to see this, and to see it by seeing what was lacking in his own life. The general values are given substance only through an understanding of what they mean in the particular life. This is why the creative fiction of writers such as Tolstoy plays an important role in the achievement of moral understanding: in presenting us with the imagined individual life, they enable us to understand our own lives, to see a shape and a pattern in them, and to recognize what is important in them.

With this example, then, I am agreeing that the model of moral awareness as the deriving of practical conclusions from general principles is the wrong model. I am also suggesting, however, that a purely particularistic model is inadequate. A moral understanding of the particular situation and the particular life encapsulates and is informed by an understanding of human life in general.

It is clear that, at this level, talk of such understanding as 'moral vision' is a metaphor. It is a useful metaphor, as a corrective to the 'general principles' model, and it helps to bring out the relevance of notions of drawing attention to particular features, recognizing a pattern, and shaping our experiences into a total picture. But if it is only a metaphor, this leaves room for the possibility that other metaphors may also be illuminating. I want to suggest that, in addition to the metaphor of vision, another metaphor can also helpfully characterize the kind of understanding we are dealing with here, and that is the metaphor of *meaning*. Coming to see our experience in a certain way is also, we may say, a matter of *making sense* of our experience, find a *meaning* in it. Indeed, the very idea of 'understanding' is inseparable from those of 'sense' and 'meaning'. What Ivan Ilyich achieves, in Tolstoy's story, could be appropriately described as achieving an understanding of the meaning of life and of his own life.[9] The process of finding a sense and a meaning in our experience is also closely tied up with coming to understand literal meaning, the meaning of language. I have said that seeing the morally salient features of a situation is impossible without an understanding of the relevant terms such as 'cruelty' or 'loyalty' or 'respect' or 'trust' or 'injustice'. In turn, learning the meaning of these words is inseparable from coming to understanding their significance as features of our experience. Imagine teaching a child the meaning of the word 'loyalty'. The child cannot come to understand what the word means except by coming to understand the importance which certain relationships and social groups such as family or friendship have in his or her life and experiencing what it is, for instance, to be 'loyal' or 'disloyal' to one's friends.

At this point I want to return to the question of internalism, in order to suggest that the metaphor of 'meaning' can help with this. Robert Nozick has suggested that the notion of meaningfulness 'has the right "feel" as something that might help us to bridge an "is-ought" gap.'[10] By the same token, I think it is the right kind of concept for making the connection between cognition and action. Making sense of our experience is a cognitive task. It involves becoming aware of how things are, recognizing patterns and relationships, and directing attention to (or drawing other people's attention to) pertinent features. But, at the same time, to find a meaning in our experience is to orientate ourselves practically in the world. To recognize that we live within a network of ties and loyalties is to recognize what those relationships require of us. To recognize, as Ivan Ilyich does, the emptiness and pointlessness of a life dominated by social ambition and the pursuit of money is to recognize that we have good reason to live differently. To recognize, as he does, that what give a point and a meaning to our lives are simple and spontaneous feelings of human warmth and sympathy is to recognize our reasons for living accordingly. Considerations which make our lives meaningful are necessarily reason-giving. If we can give no meaning to our lives, we have no reason for doing anything. But if we do find a sense and a meaning in our experience, we thereby identify what matters to us, and this is inseparably both a cognitive and an affective awareness of our world and our place in it.

For Ivan Ilyich, the recognition of the meaning which his life could have had, and which it still can have in the brief time left to him, is an immediate and intuitive recognition. One's conception of the meaning of one's life can also, however, have a more theoretical dimension. When fully and explicitly articulated, it provides an account of what I shall call a 'world-view'.[11] This has something in common with what MacIntyre refers to as a 'narrative', the story which one can tell about one's life, a unifying pattern into which the particular elements of one's life can be fitted in order to make sense of it as a whole. But, as I have suggested previously, MacIntyre's way of putting it focuses too exclusively on the self, whereas what I am looking for is the idea also of a conception of one's world and one's place in it. It will be the unifying framework which, I suggested in my discussion of Nagel, we need in order to place the various kinds of value in relation to one another. A 'world-view' in this sense is implicit in each person's pattern of actions and choices, though it may in practice be muddled, incoherent, and even contradictory. In its most fully explicit and articulated form it may consist in some version of one of the classic belief systems such as those provided by the world's religions. A fundamental classification of world-views, indeed, is the division between those which are *religious* and those which are *humanistic*. For a religious world-view, belief in a divine creator or a plurality of divine beings to whom we owe reverence and obedience will be the overarching conception into which the other elements are fitted. Such a world-view may have much common ground with a humanistic world-view. They may share conceptions of what makes for a worthwhile and happy human life, and of our responsibilities for the well-being of others; but within the religious world-view these will be seen at the same time as conceptions of how, in living a fulfilling life and relating appropriately to others, we should be fulfilling the purposes set for us by a god or gods.

I do not intend to argue here for a religious or a humanistic world-view, or for any particular variant of these. The important point is that we *can* do so. We engage in rational debate and deploy rational arguments for and against the existence of a god or gods, about the relations in which any such divine being might stand to human beings, and about the implications which this must have for how we should live. What I want to focus on here, however, are two other dimensions of rational argument about our moral view of the world. Such a view will be shaped by one's personal experience, as it is for Ivan Ilyich; but, though personal in this sense, it is not purely private and subjective. It is an attempt to make sense of the world *as it is*, in terms which can be endorsed by others and supported by our shared experience. I want to suggest that there are two sets of considerations which must inform any rational argument about our moral vision of the world, and they are considerations which emerge from a review of the moral philosophies discussed in this book. Any moral view of the world which is to do justice to the facts of our experience must have a place for:

(a) a conception of what makes for a worthwhile and fulfilling human life, and in particular some conception of what can give meaning to a human life in view of the finite character of that life and the inevitability of death; and

(b) a conception of one's relations to other human beings—both special relations to particular others and to particular social groups and communities, and relations to other human beings in general, including past and future generations.

These, I suggest, are necessary components of any rationally defensible world-view. There are facts about human needs and the conditions of human flourishing, and about our social relations, and these facts, as I suggested in Chapter 10, have an inescapable moral import. They set constraints on what can count as a rationally defensible moral perspective. More positively, they provide us with a shared moral vocabulary in which we can rationally debate our moral beliefs. I want now, in the light of the preceding chapters, to look at these two sets of considerations and at the place which they should have in our moral thinking.

Components of a Naturalistic Ethics

Under the heading of 'a conception of one's relations to other human beings' I want to recall my emphasis in previous chapters on the ethical significance of social relations. One's understanding of the world is an understanding of a social world, one's identity is a social identity, and the network of social relations which makes up one's life necessarily carries with it ethical commitments and loyalties. These social relations, I have said, include small-scale, intimate relationships of family and friendship and sexual relationships; relations of agreement and trust and contract voluntarily entered into; relations of co-operation with colleagues and fellow-workers, and with fellow-members of political, religious, or other voluntary groups of various kinds; and membership of local, national, and perhaps trans-national communities. None of these kinds of social relationship is intelligible without a recognition of the ethical responsibilities and obligations which it carries with it, and, as Hegel and Bradley and others recognize, much of our moral life is made up of these loyalties and commitments.

One's relations to other human beings include not only these various kinds of special relations, but also *universalistic* attitudes to others. The loyalties involved in family ties or friendships or community membership are commitments to some people rather than others, and when I discussed these in connection with Bradley and Hegel I raised the question, at the end of Chapter 8, of where this leaves the idea of a generalized humanitarianism, a concern for the needs of all other human beings. The two fundamental universalistic attitudes which we have considered previously are Humean *sympathy* and Kantian *respect*, and I need now to say something about the comparison of these two attitudes with one another, the comparison between both of them on the one hand and special relations on the other, and hence about their place within an overall world-view. I want first to focus on the contrast between sympathy and respect. I take the former to involve an identification with others' ends and purposes, leading to a sharing in those purposes and a concern to help in promoting others' well-being. Respect, in contrast, though it involves identifying with the other in the sense of recognizing him or her to be a human being like oneself, involves also a kind of distancing, a recognition that the other has his or her own life to lead and that it is not for me to try to live it on the other's behalf. Whereas sympathy is essentially an attitude towards the other as the recipient of one's own actions, respect is an attitude towards the other as an independent agent. These two attitudes correspond to two basic human needs, the need for help and assistance from others, and the need to be in control of one's own life and to have a sense of one's own agency. I take these two stances to be the bases of the moral values of *utility* and of *rights* respectively, and to confirm that any adequate ethical theory must have a place for both of them. I have said that the problem for a pluralistic ethics is how to deal with conflicts between radically different kinds of values, and the conflict between utility and rights is one which is liable to face us in practice. I cannot offer a formula for resolving such conflicts, because there is none; but I suggest that we can, at any rate, see how to think about such conflicts if we identify the underlying contrasts of attitudes and of needs in which they are rooted. This kind of practical dilemma is, for instance, familiar to any parent who wants his or her children to be happy, and wants to promote their happiness, but also recognizes that as they grow older they increasingly have to live their own lives and make their own mistakes, even at the cost of their own happiness. Recognizing this does not make the dilemma any easier to resolve, but at least we have a better idea of what is at stake than we would have if we saw it simply as an abstract moral conflict between utilitarian and rights-based arguments.

What now of the comparison between universalistic attitudes and special relations? I want to stress the interplay between them. The former are both a *precondition of*, and an *extension of*, the latter. If we were not, by nature, capable of responses of sympathetic identification with and respect for other human beings, we could not form specific relationships of friendship and love and co-operation. In that sense, the general capacity is the precondition for the specific relations. But the general capacity is initially realized not as a response to human beings in general, but as a response to specific others. It is in the context of interaction with parents and siblings and friends that the child learns to take others' needs and feelings into account and to put himself or herself into other people's position. It is a familiar fact that people may be loving parents, loyal friends, or devoted members of a community, and yet be insensitive to the needs of others outside their own circle of relationships.

Both historically and within individual lives, a generalized recognition of and concern for the needs of all human beings develops as an extension of specific relationships.

This has a bearing on the question discussed in previous chapters and raised initially in Chapter 4 as the problem of egoism and altruism. Altruistic concern for others is thought to be at the heart of modern conceptions of morality. But can we give anyone a reason why they ought to exhibit such concern for others? Can we, in that sense, give anyone a reason for being moral? The answer is that it depends where we start from. If we start from the notion of the purely egoistic individual, then we cannot give such reasons; we cannot conjure up altruistic concern out of nothing. But if we start, as we must, from the notion of the social individual, already embedded in significant relations with others, then what we can do is to give reasons for extending altruistic concern. To the loving parent who, perhaps in circumstances of war or civil strife, supports and relishes the infliction of suffering on the children of 'the enemy' it can be said, 'How can you love your own child and yet be indifferent to the suffering of other people's children?' That does not by itself point to a logically compelling reason for greater altruistic concern. We have seen that part of what is important in the parent's love for her child is the fact that it is *her* child, that she stands in a quite special relationship to this particular child and that this is why she feels a quite special kind of devotion and concern. But it also a feature of this concern that she is moved by the joys and sufferings of her child *as another human being*. When she is moved to action by the child's suffering, it is the fact of the suffering, as well as the special relationship, that weighs with her. Therefore she can be given a reason for extending her concern in the sense that she can be awakened to the reality of other children's suffering, to a recognition of what it is like for them and of the fact that they too are an appropriate object of concern. If she fails to respond she is not guilty of an error in logic; she is not being formally inconsistent. Nevertheless she is being given a reason for greater altruistic concern in some sense of that notion. I shall return shortly to the question of whether there are other sorts of reasons which might also be given.

I turn at this point to the other necessary component of our moral thinking—the conception of a worthwhile and fulfilling life. A central role will be played here by the concept of *needs*. I have suggested previously that this, like the concept of social relations, is an important bridge between fact and value. It is a fact about our nature that there are certain things which, as human beings, we all need, but that fact is one which also necessarily gives us a reason for acting to satisfy such needs. In Chapter 11 I indicated that twentieth-century defences of ethical naturalism have identified both needs and social relations as important concepts for a viable naturalism. I also argued that we need a richer account of human needs, drawing on the material which I considered in Chapters 8 and 10. Fundamental human needs include the need for a coherent identity, the need for recognition, the need for meaningful work, the need for autonomous agency, the need for emotional balance, and the need for mutually supportive relations with others. I have suggested that these are, at one level, needs whose satisfaction is necessary for effective functioning, but also, at a higher level, needs whose satisfaction makes for a fulfilling and happy life. It is a mistake to try to make the concept of happiness, in utilitarian fashion, do too much work here; but I have suggested that the status of these needs *as* needs has ultimately to be backed up by our *experience* of the rewarding and satisfying character of a life in which such needs are met.

It is important to recognize the distinct places occupied in our moral thinking *both* by the conception of our relations to others *and* by the conception of needs and a worthwhile life. Neither is reducible to the other. We should resist the temptation to assimilate, in Aristotelian fashion, the importance of relations with others to an aspect of eudaimonia, and to argue that we ought to carry out our obligations to others because this will make for a happy life. Relations with others are ethically significant in their own right. They make claims on us, whether or not such relations are conducive to our needs. Someone might, for example, be stuck in a joyless marriage and doubt whether the continuation of the relationship will do anything to meet her needs, but nevertheless recognize that this relationship is at the same time an ineradicable part of her life and her identity and that she has a loyalty to her partner. She may then face a conflict—but it is a conflict only because her own needs and her loyalty to the other person each make their own competing claims on her. The traditional distinction between 'teleological' and 'deontological' conceptions of ethics reflects the distinction between these two fundamental kinds of considerations, 'needs' and 'social relations'. Both are essential components of an adequate theory.

At the same time, there is also an interplay between them, and it goes in both directions. My commitments to others mean that I have reason to act to satisfy not only my own needs, but also those of others. This, I suppose, is obvious, and I have already elaborated a little on how the different categories of needs generate both reasons to promote the well-being or prevent the suffering of others, and reasons to respect the rights of others. I want to stress again that it is a mistake to assimilate all concern for the needs of others to a uniform utilitarian perspective. The *different* relations in which we stand to others generate *different* kinds of commitments to the satisfying of others' needs. My devotion to the needs of my friend is different from the obligations I may have to meet the needs of my fellow-citizens, and this in turn is different from my concern for the needs of those in other parts of the world who may be starving or destitute. All these have their claim on me, but it would be a distortion to derive them all from a single general obligation to promote the general happiness. If they cannot all be measured on a single scale, how then do we weigh these competing claims against one another? What we can do is attempt to make sense of the place which each of these various underlying relationships has in a human life.

That, then, is one aspect of the interplay between needs and social relations: one's relations with others underpin a concern for the needs of others as well as one's own needs. The interplay also goes in the other direction: certain kinds of relations with others contribute to the meeting of one's own needs. This is where we can give an appropriate place to points made in Chapter 4, and to the familiar and banal-sounding, but important facts of experience— that our lives are enriched by co-operation with others and the satisfaction of shared endeavour, by all the many forms of friendship and love, and by a devotion to the needs of others which transcends the narrow circle of one's own individual life. Note also that it is these kinds of connections with others that give a meaning to a life which is finite and mortal. Our identification with the aspirations of others who will live on when we are gone, our membership of communities which will continue into the future, rescues us from the apparent pointlessness of a life which will one day be no more.

Like the argument from specific social relations to a universalistic altruism, these considerations provide what we could call 'reasons for altruism'. But, like that previous argument, such reasons cannot conjure up an altruistic concern out of nothing. They are considerations which can appeal only to someone who already knows what it is to feel authentic and spontaneous concern for others. To the complete egoist, if there were such a person, the thought that one can be happier if one shares one's life positively with others could produce only an instrumental concern for others—and, if understood in those terms, would constitute a somewhat unconvincing case at that. But someone whose life is already embedded within a network of relations with others, and who is sensitive to the joys and sufferings of others, can come to see that his or her life is impoverished if these feelings and relationships are pushed to the margins of his or her life by ruthless personal ambition, or by attitudes of bitterness and resentment. It is because Ivan Ilyich still feels pity for his son and his wife that he can reflect on what he has been missing, and can recognize after all the importance of those simple and spontaneous feelings.

I discussed in Chapter 4 the problem of 'moral egoism'. The dilemma was this: that on the one hand it seems a simple and obvious truth that a life shared with and in harmony with others is thereby made more fulfilling; but, on the other hand, if this is one's reason for living such a life, it appears to subordinate altruistic concern to the promotion of one's own happiness. I hope that we are now in a position to see at least a possible way out of this dilemma. I have said that the categories of 'needs' and 'social relations' are not reducible to one another. Our commitments and loyalties to others, and our sensitivities to other people's well-being, are important in their own right, and provide us with a moral framework within which the rights and wrongs of altruistic and selfish actions have an independent place. But we can also step back from our lives and look at them as a whole, and we can then be guided, as appropriate, by the thought that we need to be more attentive to others and that doing so will enrich our own lives. The position I am sketching here employs the distinction between *two levels* of reason-giving which I originally introduced in Chapter 4. It has affinities with other versions of two-tier moral thinking—rule-utilitarianism, Hare's 'intuitive' and 'critical' levels of moral thinking, and so on. The content of my own version is different. It is also a version in which the two levels of moral thinking are genuinely distinct, and in which they each have an appropriate place so that the one does not collapse into the other. One's commitments to other people, both to particular others and to other human beings in general, have an independent moral status which does not derive merely from the contribution which they make to one's own happiness. But, as well as acting on these considerations, we can also step back from them and assess them and their place in our lives in the light of our own needs.

It is along these lines, then, that I suggest we can see our way to a moral perspective which gives a central place to altruistic concern, which does justice to the fact that such concern also meets one's own needs, but which avoids the pitfall of moral egoism. At the same time it is a perspective which also avoids the opposite pitfall, of a narrow moralism such as is attacked by Nietzsche and others. It is a morality of altruism, but not one in which altruism is equated with self-denial and self-sacrifice. It is not an alienated morality imposing an altruistic 'ought' on us from some supposedly external and extra-human standpoint. The morality of altruistic concern is here rooted in our own deepest feelings and our deepest needs.

I do not want to make this perspective sound over-cosy. Of course we are sometimes confronted with difficult dilemmas, and of course those dilemmas sometimes involve having to sacrifice our own interests for the sake of others. I may have to sacrifice my career in order to stay at home to look after a sick child. I may recognize that my affluent lifestyle is unjustifiable when other human beings are starving, and that I ought to do without things which I enjoy in order to give more to others. But these decisions need not be the product of an alien 'ought', a 'categorical imperative' of a Kantian kind. These considerations may weigh with me because at a deeper level they stem from commitments and sensitivities which are an ineradicable part of my own identity.

As against a narrow moralism, such a perspective also has room for the recognition of the limits of individual responsibility. It has room for a Nietzschean recognition of the phenomenon of self-sacrifice rooted in resentment. If people's own needs are not met, they may to that extent be less able to respond genuinely to the needs of others. If I am immersed in the struggle for survival, then generosity may be a luxury which I cannot afford. If I am deeply frustrated, confined within a cramped existence which allows no room for my talents and my personality to flourish, my ostensibly selfless concern for others may be embittered and resentful. In such circumstances the possibility of a greater sympathy for others may depend not on the exercise of 'the moral will', but on changes to the social and psychological conditions which constrain one's sympathies.

The Question of Realism

Where does this leave the question of moral realism? If the choice is between realism and anti-realism, then the position which I have been defending is to be located on the realist side of that divide. At the same time I want to repeat my thought that the important questions here are not primarily ontological ones, and that to formulate them in ontological terms may not be terribly helpful. The position I have been presenting does not require us to posit any distinctive 'moral reality' which our moral beliefs reflect, and to talk in those terms may be misleading, suggesting a mysterious Platonic world of 'ideal forms' which is all too vulnerable to Mackie's objections. The only world presupposed by my account is the natural world, the world of everyday experience which we try to make sense of, a world in which people are born and die and strive to be happy, a social world in which people form friendships and sexual relationships, live in families and households, work with colleagues in various kinds of social and economic institutions, and so on.

We can, if we wish, talk about the reality of 'moral properties'. Our actions can be 'just' and 'unjust', 'honest' and 'dishonest', 'kind' and 'cruel', and so on. These are objective properties, and in virtue of them our actions may be, objectively, 'right' or 'wrong'. What is important here, however, is the epistemological claim rather than the ontological one. The version of moral realism which I have been presenting shows, if it succeeds, that there can be objective reasons for actions, objective reasons for living a certain kind of life. The practical choices which we make are not just a matter of subjective preference; one kind of life is objectively better than another.

What I have called a 'world-view' is both cognitive and action-guiding. It is, inseparably, both a conception of what the world is like and a framework of reasons to guide our actions. A world-view in this sense is not a definitive theory which uniquely determines what we ought to do. It is not a set of principles which we can apply to particular cases and from which we can then read off practical decisions. Rather, it is a framework in terms of which we can make sense of our experience. I have been identifying certain facts about what makes for a fulfilling life, and about our relations with one another, which I have suggested must find a place in any rationally defensible world-view. Different people, in the light of their experience, may argue for giving different degrees of importance to different elements. In the light, for instance, of the experience of the disasters of paternalistic intervention, some may argue for giving a primary importance to rights and autonomy. In the light of the facts of the increasing interdependence of all human beings within a global society, some may argue for giving greater importance to the needs of 'strangers' than we have done, and for widening the circle of concern. In all such cases, the important point is that we can rationally debate these claims on the basis of shared experience and a shared conceptual vocabulary.

Non-cognitivists are likely to reply that this idea of a synthesis of the cognitive and the action-guiding is illusory. They will argue that the two can be prised apart. Facts about the world are one thing, the practical stance which we adopt towards them is another, and though they may be run together in our thinking they are logically distinct. The non-cognitivist may, for instance, point to the prominent role which I have been giving to Humean sympathy, and may suggest that a Humean account of this is more appropriate. A world-view which embodies the response of sympathy is strictly speaking, it may be said, not an *understanding* of the world, but an expression of *sentiment*.

Hume himself, I suggest, offers a better account of the matter. Although his meta-ethical theory is predominantly a subjectivist one, we have also noted the important passage in which he talks about the importance of 'general standards'. Because our sentiments, he says, vary in strength with time and place and from one person to another, we require a 'general language' of moral appraisal which will 'render our sentiments more public and social'. According to Hume's more considered account, then, moral judgements are not the *direct expression* of sympathy. The relation between such judgements and our sentiments is mediated by a *public language*. Hume says, 'The intercourse of sentiments . . . , in society and conversation, makes us form some general unalterable standard by which we may approve or disapprove of characters and manners.'[12] As I noted in Chapter 5, this is not an entirely satisfactory way of putting it. It suggests that a public language encapsulating public standards of judgement is something which we deliberately and consciously adopt. Of course, that is not the case. Language is not something which we invent and decide to employ, it is a collective inheritance. As individuals we are born into it, and as we learn it, it shapes our thinking. To that extent Bradley's account of the matter is better than Hume's, but the important point which we can take from both Hume and Bradley is this: that as speakers of a public language we possess shared resources for understanding our moral experience and shared criteria for making moral evaluations and decisions. The fact that sympathy, and other fundamental human responses, are a deep feature of our nature makes possible our shared use of this language and these criteria. It is because, as human beings, we share the capacity to be moved by one another's joys and sufferings that we live in a world where actions can be cruel or kind, generous or mean, considerate or insensitive, and where such judgements have both objective status and practical import. Judgements of that kind are not themselves *expressions* of feelings and emotions, but our natural capacity for feelings such as sympathy is a *precondition* for our making such judgements and employing such criteria.

Some contemporary philosophers would say that this line of thought leads to a position, not of realism, but of 'quasi-realism'. Our language, they would say, induces us to talk *as though* we were describing objective features of the world, when what we are really doing is *projecting* our own feelings and attitudes onto it. Simon Blackburn, the most prominent advocate of this position, enlists Hume in support of it. He quotes Hume on the respective roles of reason and sentiment:

> The one discovers objects as they really stand in nature, without addition or diminution; the other has a productive faculty and, gilding or staining all natural objects with the colours borrowed from internal sentiment, raises in a manner a new creation.[13]

Blackburn agrees with Mackie that our moral language involves the projection of emotions, sentiments, and attitudes on to the world; but, unlike Mackie, he does not think that this need lead to the conclusion that our ordinary use of moral language involves an *error*. If it can be shown that our moral language provides a convenient way of talking about the world, and that there are advantages in describing the world as though it really did have the features which we project on to it and in treating such descriptions as statements which can be true or false, then no error need be involved. This is the force of labelling such a position 'quasi-realism', in contrast to anti-realism.

My doubts about such a position in part echo what I have said about Hume's talk of 'forming' a general language incorporating general standards in order to 'render our sentiments more public and social'. Both Blackburn and Hume talk about inventing a general language, and projecting attitudes on to the world through that language, as something which *we do*. But of course we do not literally do this. We do not decide to employ language for these purposes. It may be that Blackburn's position simply comes down to the claim that there are advantages in having a language with these features; but then it is not clear what the force of the metaphor of 'projection' amounts to.

The other problem with this idea of 'projection' is that of saying what it is exactly that our feelings and attitudes are projected on to. The idea presupposes a world which is describable quite independently of our human attitudes and interests, a world which can be characterized in entirely neutral terms which would be intelligible to any rational being with no particular biological or psychological nature.[14] There are huge issues here in epistemology and the philosophy of language, and I can only say dogmatically that I do not think that this notion of a world as it is 'in itself', stripped bare of any characterizations which reflect our distinctively human interests in it, is an intelligible one. Nietzsche's perspectivism seems to me to be a better account of the matter than Blackburn's projectivism. *All* knowledge of the world is *from a point of view*: it involves selecting and organizing experience from the stand-point of the particular interests which we have in understanding it. We can indeed achieve a kind of neutrality, we can abstract from specific interests, and can do so for specific purposes. For example, the kind of knowledge aimed at in the natural sciences involves varying degrees of abstraction. An action describable in everyday language—moral language—as an act of cruelty might be describable by the physiologist in terms of electrochemical processes in the nervous system and the movements of muscles and ligaments, or by the physicist in terms of the relations between sub-atomic particles. The language of the scientist is neutral in respect of moral characterizations, but it abstracts from these precisely in order to serve more effectively the interests in predic-tion and control which are the business of the scientist. The ethical world is no less real than the world of science. It is simply that the language which we use for the one kind of description reflects different interests from the language which we use for the other.

I have invoked Nietzsche's perspectivism, but he too is misleading. He is inclined to say that because our ways of describing and understanding the world, and the language in which we do it, reflect our point of view and our interests, they are 'illusions', 'falsifications', 'conventional fictions'.[15] To say this is to imply that there is a 'real world' which we falsify. It is again to set up a dis-tinction between 'the world as it is for human beings' and 'the world as it really is'—a distinction which Nietzsche himself has recognized as untenable. That we should describe the world in a language which reflects our human nature and human interest is not a falsification; that is what it *is* to experience and understand the world.

That, then, is what we are doing in our moral thinking, as much as in our scientific thinking or any other kind of thinking. We are trying to understand our own needs as human beings, our relations to one another, our commit-ments and obligations to one another, and our relations to the non-human world, and we are trying to understand how we should live in the light of all this. There are no simple answers, any more than there are in any other area of enquiry. Nevertheless, the attempt at achieving such understanding can be a rational and objective enquiry. I have tried to show, in this book, how the tra-dition of the great moral philosophers and their contemporary successors can provide us with the resources for such an enterprise.

Notes

1. J. L. Mackie, *Ethics: Inventing Right and Wrong* (Harmondsworth, 1977), 38.
2. David Brink, *Moral Realism and the Foundations of Ethics* (Cambridge, 1989), 39.
3. Ibid. 131; John Rawls, *A Theory of Justice* (Oxford, 1971), section 4, 19–20.
4. Another important defence of externalist realism is Peter Railton, 'Moral Realism', in *Philosophical Review*, 95 (1986). Railton's article links with two other

strands in contemporary moral realism which I do not have space to discuss: (a) the defence of realism which appeals to the role which moral properties play in *explanations* of human behaviour; on this see Nicholas Sturgeon, 'Moral Explanations', in James Rachels (ed.), *Ethical Theory 1: The Question of Objectivity* (Oxford, 1998); (b) the attempt to base moral realism on a 'dispositional theory of value', see e.g. Michael Smith, 'Moral Realism', in Peter Singer (ed.), *A Companion to Ethics* (Oxford, 1991), and his *The Moral Problem* (Oxford, 1994).

5. McDowell's work has appeared in the form of a number of articles. These, as McNaughton says, are difficult, but the best one to look at for a general picture of his position is John McDowell, 'Are Moral Requirements Hypothetical Imperatives?', in *Proceedings of the Aristotelian Society*, suppl. 52 (1978). Another influential theme in McDowell's work which I have to pass over is the comparison between awareness of moral properties and perception of secondary qualities such as colours. On this see John McDowell, 'Values and Secondary Qualities', in Ted Honderich (ed.), *Morality and Objectivity* (London, 1985). The comparison is criticized from a moral realist standpoint in Jonathan Dancy, 'Two Conceptions of Moral Realism', *Proceedings of the Aristotelian Society*, suppl. 60 (1986), and from a standpoint critical of moral realism in Simon Blackburn, 'Errors and the Phenomenology of Value', in Honderich, *Morality and Objectivity*.

6. David McNaughton, *Moral Vision* (Oxford, 1988), 47.

7. See also Lawrence A. Blum, *Moral Perception and Particularity* (Cambridge, 1994), especially the essay with the same title.

8. Leo Tolstoy, *The Death of Ivan Ilyich and Other Stories*, translated by Rosemary Edmonds (Harmondsworth, 1960), 153.

9. Cf. the discussion of Tolstoy's story in this connection in Ilham Dilman, 'Life and Meaning', in *Philosophy*, 40 (1965).

10. Robert Nozick, *Anarchy, State, and Utopia* (New York, 1974), 50.

11. I take this term (*Weltanschauung* in German) from the philosopher Wilhelm Dilthey (1833–1911), without thereby being committed to the account which he gives of world-views.

12. David Hume, *Enquiry Concerning the Principles of Morals*, Section V, para. 42.

13. Hume, *Enquiry*, App. I, final para. Quoted in Simon Blackburn, *Spreading the Word* (Oxford, 1984), 145. Chs. 5 and 6 of Blackburn's book set out the theory of quasi-realism.

14. Bernard Williams has called this the 'absolute conception' of the world. See e.g. *Ethics and the Limits of Philosophy* (London, 1985), 111, and cf. McNaughton, *Moral Vision*, ch. 4 section 2, and ch. 5.

15. See e.g. his essay 'On Truth and Lie in an Extra-Moral Sense', included in *The Portable Nietzsche*, ed and trans. by Walter Kaufmann (New York, 1954), 47 (quoted by Blackburn, 181); and *Beyond Good and Evil*, trans. R. J. Hollingdale (Harmondsworth, 1973), sections 4 and 21.

Index